Busy in the Cause

LOWELL J. SOIKE

Busy in the Cause

Iowa, the Free-State Struggle
in the West, and the Prelude
to the Civil War

University of Nebraska Press
Lincoln & London

Publication of this volume was assisted by the State Historical
Society of Iowa through a Federal Highway Administration
enhancement grant received from the Iowa Department of
Transportation.

Library of Congress Cataloging-in-Publication Data
Soike, Lowell J.
Busy in the cause: Iowa, the free-state struggle in the west, and
the prelude to the Civil War / Lowell J. Soike.
pages   cm
Includes bibliographical references and index.
ISBN 978-0-8032-7189-0 (pbk.: alk. paper) —
ISBN 978-0-8032-7385-6 (epub) — ISBN 978-0-8032-7386-3 (mobi)
— ISBN 978-0-8032-7384-9 (pdf) 1. Antislavery movements—
Iowa—History—19th century. 2. Abolitionists—Iowa—History—
19th century. 3. Iowa—Politics and government—19th century.
4. United States—History—Civil War, 1861-1865—Causes. I.
Title. II. Title: Iowa, the free-state struggle in the west, and the
prelude to the Civil War.
E445.I8S65 2014
973.7'11—dc23   2013045096

Set in Lyon Text by Renni Johnson.

For James Hill, with thanks

CONTENTS

ILLUSTRATIONS

Antislavery events west of the Mississippi River commonly get short shrift in histories, leaving the impression that almost everything consequential happened farther east. Bleeding Kansas and John Brown may receive nods as precursors to the Civil War but mainly as brief introductions to congressional developments associated with creating the Kansas-Nebraska Act or in connection with the Harpers Ferry raid and its consequences. I have embarked on this book with an eye to helping readers ponder certain western circumstances that have fallen into the cracks of history but have shaped antislavery life and political struggles in Iowa and Kansas.

Other states invariably are a part of the story. Missouri, the closest slave state that was most involved in deciding slavery's fate in Kansas, receives particular consideration. Others that were instrumental in sending Free-State settlers to Kansas, such as Ohio, the New England states, and, of course, the Nebraska Territory through which they traveled, enter the discussion as well. So while the theme of this book is the relationship of Iowa to the Kansas Territory, in a larger sense it covers Iowa's relationship to the western Midwest.

Iowa, as the closest Free State to the territorial struggle, became a refuge, a source of arms and supplies, and a northern land route for the Kansas Free-State settlers who helped check slavery's expansion. Moreover, Iowa developed into an escape route for persons fleeing Missouri enslavement through Kansas. I realize that this book, with its main focus on Iowa and Kansas, does some injustice to the full involvements of other states, but I do so in hopes that future studies will illuminate the territory's relationship to these states as well.

Passions ran deep among proslavery's friends and their antislavery opponents toward the issue of westward expansion. Shaping the rising fervor over slavery was the increasing influence of evangelical Protestant faiths in the North that intensified agitation and pressed a view of slavery not simply as mistaken but also as evil and an abhorrent sin. Evangelicals' moral disgust with slavery regularly inserted itself in politics, especially in the frontier West, aggravating and creating a more radicalized political mood without room for compromise.[1]

Lacking the restraints of a political past, new western territories allowed the increasingly radical views of antislavery evangelicals room to expand in the white heat of territorial politics. Members of Congregationalist, Quaker, Wesleyan Methodist, and Presbyterian faiths who settled the open West in these times often developed more antislavery sentiments than did kindred denomination members back east who held to traditional church practices and were led by ministers hesitant to test parishioners with advanced evangelical views on slavery.

One aspect of my research methods, the extensive use of newspapers as source material, deserves mention. First of all, in the frontier West of that time, surviving sources—letters, records of laws proposed and enacted, government reports, messages of elected officials, and newspapers—are less plentiful. Of them all, newspapers provide the window through which regular weekly local matters and broader public opinion are revealed.

Despite shortcomings of political bias and incomplete or inaccurate stories, newspapers supply historians with the daily stream of popular opinion and alignments over slavery, shedding light on what local opinion leaders thought about current discussions over the slavery issue, their political enemies, and efforts being made by parties, governments, courts, and law enforcement officials to shape and control events. The news report of a local proslavery or antislavery meeting—noting who officiated, who attended, and what resolutions were adopted—can reveal what led up to significant incidents, and newspaper sketches of leaders in the slavery issue can disclose who was admired or thought to be obstructive, unworthy, or dangerous. Together these newspaper reports open to view the political climate of the frontier areas by highlighting their squabbles, divisions, and concerns over the slavery issue. Accordingly, for this book, I examined slavery-related articles in all surviving Iowa newspapers from 1850 to 1861 along with several newspapers in Kansas Territory and a few for Missouri during the period 1855 to through 1859.

The Kansas turmoil has been told from many angles, with the earliest works displaying exaggerated partisanship and today's narratives being relatively free of such extreme sentiments. In recent decades, scholars have explored the complex people and series of events that shaped the Free-State movement's character. We have come to the time when the roles of states near the territories' ensuing Free-State story ought to be evaluated as well for the period's issues of slavery and antislavery in the West are bound up with the American story, and in them, Iowa played its part.

The work of examining this unfolding issue in the West and its related Underground Railroad activity has been made possible by the State Historical Society of Iowa's receipt of an enhancement grant under the Intermodal Surface Transportation Efficiency Act of 1991 (ISTEA; Public Law 102-240) from the Federal Highway Administration through the Iowa Department of Transportation.

ACKNOWLEDGMENTS

I became interested in antislavery and Underground Railroad activities several years ago when, working at the State Historical Society of Iowa, I prepared a proposal to draw more attention to the state's story of antislavery. For the next twelve years as time permitted in other duties, I directed the project through a federal grant. One of its results is *Busy in the Cause: Iowa, the Free-State Struggle in the West, and the Prelude to the Civil War.* I am grateful to the State Historical Society of Iowa, which received and managed the grant, for the generous facilities and help provided by administrator Gordon Hendrickson and staff members to employ personnel and contract for other work as needed.

In particular, I wish to thank staff archeologist Douglas Jones for his devoted interest in ferreting out many local connections to this history in his work with local researchers and in completing and overseeing related archeological fieldwork. My grateful thanks goes to Shari Stelling, Mary Bennett, Sharon Avery, and Becki Plunkett for their library assistance and professional guidance and to Berry Bennett, Don Hirt, and Charles Scott for their abundant technical help on photographic and graphics needs.

John Zeller, our lead researcher, gave incredibly generous support for the project. He uncovered difficult to find sources of information, talked to numerous local informants, provided keen insights into the way events happened, and mapped Underground

Railroad routes across counties and regions of the state. My colleague and friend carried out all of this work while delighting us with his many stories.

This book has benefited from several people for whose help, advice, and criticism I would like to express my gratitude. These go first to James Hill, then midwest regional coordinator of the National Underground Railroad Network to Freedom. He shared a wealth of information about persons and sites in adjacent states, and I received beneficial insights from our many discussions that improved this book. The intellectual generosity of G. Galin Berrier is greatly appreciated. The solid feedback he gave from reading versions of the manuscript saved me from embarrassing errors, and his welcome advice given during our visits on topics and themes of this book helpfully challenged my assumptions. My thanks and appreciation go to Kristin Zapalac, who with the Missouri State Historic Preservation Office answered my various questions and shared information she had gathered about the kidnapping of three Garner family members from Iowa and their rescue by Ira D. Blanchard in St. Louis.

I would also like to thank the library and manuscript staff of the Kansas State Historical Society for the assistance provided me in using their splendid collections. Also I want to express my appreciation for the helpful professional assistance given in accessing collections at the State Library and Archives of the State Historical Society of Missouri, the Spencer Research Library at the University of Kansas, and the Abraham Lincoln Presidential Library of the Illinois Historic Preservation Agency.

Finally, to Karen go my grateful thanks, which are beyond anything that could be said in these acknowledgments.

Busy in the Cause

Uncertainty Rising

I

Political compromise on the national level was becoming impossible by the late 1840s. Though holding onto its national power, the South felt its slavery system increasingly threatened by rising antislavery sentiments in the North. Conversely, the North saw the levers of national government firmly in the hands of the "slave power." While the American Antislavery Society under William Lloyd Garrison's leadership had poked and prodded slavery's protectors since 1830, challenging the "peculiar institution" by trying to change public sentiment, a broader force against slavery was emerging.

A series of religious revivals began in the early 1800s and reached its peak in the 1840s. They aimed to awaken spiritual life and promote conversion and individual rebirth, and they subsequently became known as the Second Great Awakening. The northern form of these revivals linked the personal religious conversion of participants to a spirit of applied Christianity for improving the health of society. Movements born of these religious beliefs fostered reforms to end unsanitary, abusive, and dehumanizing conditions in prisons, almshouses, and asylums and to reduce liquor use and its ills. But these efforts became politically overshadowed with the movement to abolish the greatest iniquity of all, slavery.

Gradually northern evangelicals shifted discussion of the slavery issue from political and economic arguments to a struggle against evil. Though many Lutheran, Catholic, and other churches shrank from abolitionists' condemnation of slaveholders as innate sinners and unworthy of church membership, evangelical Protestant churches—Congregational, antislavery Presbyterian, Wesleyan Methodist, Quakers, and others—did not. These groups and missionary organizations, such as the American Missionary Association (AMA) and the mainly Congregational American Missionary Association, pushed hard against what they saw as the moral bankruptcy of proslavery political power and against slavery's practitioners.[1]

Discomfited slavery defenders, seeing their lives and personal liberty challenged by such northern interference, denounced their attackers as religious fanatics and cried disunion. As each side incited the other, the political extremes of both gained power. Amicable conversation withered as fewer congressmen crossed the aisle in debates, deliberations, and votes, and the rising rancor over slavery poisoned their chances to resolve differences mutually. Howls of abolitionism, secession, and disunion and the northern states' nullification of fugitive slave law enforcement fueled political disputes. Naturally, any congressional discussions of westward expansion and opening new territories to settlement raised questions of what to do about slavery.

Debates over the annexation of Texas in 1844 and in 1848 had added fuel to the disagreement over the status of slavery. Also Congressman David Wilmot offered a controversial proviso to the 1846 appropriations bill that would have prevented slavery in any territory acquired in the Mexican-American War (1846–1848) or thereafter. The bill passed the House but failed in the Senate, which southerners dominated, exacerbating north-south relations. Slavery's protectors judged Wilmot's act as an insult while slavery's detractors saw the southerners' ability to block the bill as visible proof that the South controlled the nation's destiny. Feelings were running high when in 1850 a series of five measures moved through Congress to deal with slavery issues in the western territories.

Since the 1830s when the Democratic Party under Andrew Jackson and the Whig Party led by Henry Clay and others replaced the Federalist and Republican Parties dating from the nation's creation, a system of competitive parties had emerged in what had previously been one-party states. But now this system of national parties also was in trouble as the closely divided parties were unable to contain the debate over the slavery issue and the massive influx of Irish Catholic immigrants that proved frightening to Democratic and Whig Protestant voters. The various compromise measures debated in 1850 represented congressional efforts to resolve questions of slavery that were straining national party alignments and causing regional divisions to reassert themselves.[2]

The resulting Compromise of 1850, crafted by Kentucky senator Henry Clay (Whig) and largely brought to passage by Illinois Democratic senator Stephen Douglas, defused the worsening north-south strife over slavery in the territories.[3] The most controversial element of the compromise, one of particular concern to border slave states, was a new Fugitive Slave Act that exacerbated northern fears of slave power control.[4] The act strengthened the enforcement of fugitive slave laws by giving local authorities the power to enlist local citizens in capturing runaway slaves. It also circumvented local courts by giving a federally appointed commissioner control over the decision to turn over the captured person to a slaveholder claimant. This law effectively removed the accused runaway's rights to a writ of habeas corpus or to testify on his or her own behalf before a jury. For this service the commissioners received payment of $5.00 if they released an accused runaway and $10.00 for each person they extradited to slave territory.

At the time of the compromise, the state of Iowa was four years old and safely in Democratic hands. The state party tended to sympathize with southern rights, was unopposed to slavery in the South, and initiated laws against blacks' migration into Iowa, staving off antislavery initiatives and fostering national party unity. Indeed, being responsive to the proslavery wing of their party, Iowa's two Democratic senators, Augustus Caesar Dodge and George Wallace Jones, joined Senator Daniel Sturgeon of Pennsylvania in casting the only senatorial votes from non-slave states in support of the Fugitive Slave Act.[5]

The Democratic editor of the *Fort Madison Iowa Statesman* admitted the fugitive slave bill "may be too stringent in its measures" but cautioned the public "to give to the South their rights" until the bill was "amended or repealed," for it is "the duty of every man, who loves his country, and her institutions, to abide by the will of the majority."[6] Not all Iowa citizens were willing to wait patiently. The editor of the *Burlington Hawk-Eye* deplored the "clerical fanatics" who attempted "to induce men to break the law," noting that various Baptist, Congregational, and New School Presbyterian churches and organizations had condemned the compromise for making Free-State citizens into slave hunters for their southern neighbors without regard to "the 'higher laws' of God."[7] True enough, Iowa's Denmark Congregational Association wrote that "deep sympathy is felt for the oppressed in our land and a righteous indignation" against "free people of the North" being made "liable to be called on to assist in returning to bondage one who has escaped thence."[8] At a Free-Soil Party meeting at Yellow Springs in Des Moines County, attendees counseled resistance: "We believe the law is anti-republican and anti-christian, and without any binding moral power."[9]

Nevertheless, Iowans and most of their fellow Americans seemed relieved that the compromise had taken steam out of the controversy. As one Democratic editor noted about other Iowa newspapers, "With a solitary exception, her presses are in favor of lawful and law-abiding measures" regarding the Fugitive Slave Bill.[10] And for the most part, despite expressions of "sellout" by southern and northern extremists, agitation of the slavery issue temporarily receded.

As the Compromise of 1850 quieted arguments for the time being over slavery, however, it left unanswered the question of slavery in future unorganized territories.

II

By 1853 Iowa and Missouri were advocating for a bill to organize Nebraska lands into a new territory. Opening adjacent western lands would promote their states' growth by encouraging railroad development and boosting settlement of their own western counties. Though Nebraska bills introduced in previous sessions had never made it beyond committee, in December 1853 Iowa's Democratic senator Dodge introduced a bill to organize the Nebraska Territory west of the Missouri River. Like its predecessors, the bill contained no reference to slavery.[11]

Iowans had shown interest in the land to their west since 1850, at which time the Iowa legislature had passed a joint resolution urging Congress to organize the Nebraska Territory. In the fall of 1853 Nebraska promoters met at the county seats of Glenwood (Mills County) and Sidney (Fremont County) in southwestern Iowa and passed resolutions encouraging the territory's organization plus electing delegates to the upcoming January 8 convention in St. Joseph, Missouri. And at a November 1853 meeting in Council Bluffs in western Iowa, Senator Dodge and Col. Samuel R. Curtis—a U.S. commissioner of the Union Pacific Railroad (later an Iowa congressman and Union general)—advocated for both the organization of the Nebraska Territory and the construction of railways to the West.[12]

Dodge's 1853 bill drew quick attention from the Senate Committee on Territories, led by the foremost promoter of popular sovereignty, Illinois senator Stephen Douglas.[13] Douglas, in fact, had introduced bills in 1844 and 1848 to establish the territory of Nebraska, though he had not strongly pushed their advancement. This short, bright, energetic brick of a man, though indifferent to slavery, spoke for the westerners' readiness to move into unsettled lands and for expanding the railroads to the Pacific. But with southerners dominating the Senate, he knew the bill would go nowhere as it was.

Douglas's first report from the committee on January 4 left "all questions" about slavery in the territory to the settlers residing there through their representatives. The good news prompted Senator Dodge immediately to introduce a bill for laying out the town of Council Bluffs on Iowa's western border. But Douglas's "popular sovereignty" effort to hold together the Democratic Party's northern and southern wings was not enough for southern partisans. They wanted to end the hated Missouri Compromise, the provision in the 1820 act that had excluded slavery from territories north and west of Missouri's southern border.[14]

On January 23, 1854, to quench the fires, Douglas sent forth a second version of the Nebraska bill stating that the Compromise of 1850 "superseded" and made "inoperative" the 1820 compromise. Still unsatisfied, Douglas shifted ground again when on February 6 he found the 1820 compromise to be "inconsistent with" the 1850 Compromise "and is hereby declared inoperative," and then again the next morning he changed it to read "inoperative and void." Behind all this effort was Missouri senator David Rice Atchison's influence along with that of his supporters among powerful southern Democratic colleagues.[15]

The second version of the bill also divided Nebraska into two territories—Kansas, next to Missouri and Nebraska, and Nebraska, next to Iowa and Minnesota. Iowa's congressional delegation had been instrumental in the decision to divide the land into two territories, as the members hoped that a possible Platte Valley railroad route could compete with one promoted west of Missouri and up the Kaw Valley.[16]

The emerging Kansas-Nebraska bill that would end the Missouri Compromise angered the North. Horace Greeley hit the

Map showing Iowa's and Missouri's relationship to Kansas and Nebraska Territories. *Source*: Thomas Goodrich, *War to the Knife: Bleeding Kansas, 1854–1861* (Lincoln: University of Nebraska Press, 2004), 6.

roof in his *New York Tribune*, described by his traveling reporter as the newspaper that "comes next to the Bible all through the West." He blasted the bill's supporters for pretending that Kansas would not become a slave state: "The Kansas Territory . . . is bounded in its entire length by Missouri, with a whole tier of slave counties leaning against it. Won't be a slave State! What liars there are in the world!"[17] Though Greeley admitted that Kansas's climate was "not fit for growing cotton and sugar," allowing slavery in the territory still would make it but "a slave-breeding district" and an area "effectually yoked forever to the car of slaveholding dominion."[18]

Nevertheless, on March 4, 1854, the Senate, a bastion of southern strength, easily passed the measure 37–14. It took two months of arm-twisting in the northern-dominated House of Representatives, however, before the bill won a narrow victory of 113–100 on May 22.

Horace Greeley's *Daily Tribune* foresaw ominous times ahead. The bill, Greeley stated, "can then be regarded in no other light than a declaration of war by the slaveholders against the North."[19]

Meanwhile, seven days before the Senate approved the bill on March 4, Iowa senator Dodge made it apparent in a lengthy speech before his colleagues that he was fully ready and willing to eliminate the Missouri Compromise restriction on slavery's territorial advance. "The adoption of measures like the Missouri restriction of 1820, or the Wilmot proviso, are dangerous assumptions of power," he argued. Moreover, "want of confidence in the people" to decide the territory's free or slave status would have the effect of Congress withholding "from the West and the whole nation the immense benefits of territorial governments for Nebraska and Kansas solely that they may continue on the statute-book the Missouri restriction law; irritating to the men of the southern States, and of no practical advantage to those of the northern states."[20] Dodge seemed oblivious to the apprehensions that many in his own Democratic Party back home in Iowa were having about his position.

Over two weeks before Dodge's speech, the Democratic newspaper editor in Muscatine, Iowa, had printed that "this bill [is] a direct violation of the compact between the contending forces of the North and the South, made in 1820," and "is a needless and wanton renewal of the slavery agitation; and we fear, is the prelude, to a more desperate struggle than any our country has yet witnessed."[21] In addition, otherwise friendly Democratic papers in Iowa were now divided on the Douglas bill, but Dodge and his fellow Democratic senator George Wallace Jones chose to ignore the warnings.[22]

Whig newspapers could not help piling on. "At no period in the history of this nation has [sic] the propagandists of the slave power been in greater strength in Congress," wrote the Ottumwa editor of the *Desmoines Courier*, "and never have they with more audacity and pertinacity put forward their unholy claims to overrun and make slave States of country made free by solemn compact." The shaky Democratic press tried to ignore it, but a Keosauqua editor could not help sneering, "What the whigs may do is a matter of little concern to us; they are a used up party, and may as well tie to one ism or another and niggerism being about the strongest one afloat . . . they are doing very well in joining the 'mid night cry.'"[23]

How times had so quickly changed. Only a year ago in Iowa, railroad fever had absorbed nearly every village, town, crossroads, and city. Competition was furious, with residents championing their favorite railroad projects and the counties of Dubuque, Linn, Mahaska, Keokuk, Warren, Marion, and Muscatine supporting bond issues to aid railroad construction.[24] By February 1854, however, the Iowans' hopes for a transcontinental rail line across the state to the West were linked to promoting a bill to organize the Nebraska Territory, but it had taken an abrupt political turn when the U.S. Senate Committee on Territories coupled the bill's passage to ending the Missouri Compromise, which previously had prohibited slavery in the new territory.[25] Iowa politics erupted over the reintroduction of the slavery issue into public debate, which grew even more turbulent when an energetic Whig, a man who was willing to push the Kansas issue to the limit, entered the governor's race.

2

The Morning Star

The meaning of the new Kansas-Nebraska Act was not lost on James W. Grimes. The direct-talking Burlington, Iowa, lawyer and active Whig jumped into the 1854 race for governor and became the nominee for the joint Whig–Free-Soil coalition. Winning would not be easy because Iowa's Democratic Party, with its upholders of slaveholder rights in states where it existed, had controlled state politics since Iowa had achieved statehood and expected it to continue. But the new slavery debate caused by the soon-to-be-passed Kansas-Nebraska Act, which Iowa's two Democratic senators supported and voted for, gave Grimes and Iowa's divided Whigs, Free-Soilers, and antislavery partisans their chance. By the end of March opposition to the Democrats coalesced behind Grimes's candidacy.

To open his campaign Grimes issued a pamphlet on April 4 that included a pointed attack on the proposed repeal of the Missouri Compromise. Iowa "would to-day be a slave state," he declared, "but for the prohibitions of the Missouri Compromise act." If passed, he wrote, Iowa would face the risk of an antagonistic "slave State on our western border," and Grimes foresaw "nothing but trouble and darkness in the future. For bounded on two sides by slave States, we shall be intersected with underground railroads, and continually distracted by slave-hunts."[1]

Fig. 1. Governor James W. Grimes, antislavery leader and Free-State supporter. State Historical Society of Iowa, Iowa City.

Democrats tagged Grimes a foolish *ism* candidate infatuated by abolitionism and Prohibitionism who was doing his utmost "to bolster up and substantiate if he can, the batch of incongruities" separating his candidacy's Whig and Free-Soil coalition partners. In his stop at Des Moines on his stump speech tour, Grimes dwelled "longest and most earnestly" on the Kansas-Nebraska Act. Grimes also aimed his criticism at Iowa's Democratic Congressional delegation, applying "the words TRAITOR and TREASON with as much *sangfroid* as possible."[2]

In particular Grimes claimed the Kansas-Nebraska Act to be part and parcel of the growing nationalization of slavery, which Iowa would never consent to as "the only free child of the Missouri Compromise."[3] Grimes, along with his fellow coalition members, believed that slavery's expansion must be stopped. As a skilled and imposing figure on the stump, he energetically traveled the state in the ensuing months and denounced the "Nebraska infamy."[4]

The growing political energy over the Nebraska issue prompted many localities throughout the state to organize meetings for public discussion. All did not go smoothly, however. At Muscatine on the evening of March 21, townspeople gathered to "make known their views on the Nebraska question." Though ostensibly a general meeting, a few friends of the Nebraska bill arrived early, quickly organized, rapidly presented resolutions, and moved to a vote. After the vote showed three remained silent and nine in favor of the Kansas-Nebraska Act to allow potential slavery in Nebraska, one committee member rose and commenced a long-winded speech favoring the Nebraska bill. Soon, however, other attendees arrived, and the crowd expanded to some two hundred persons of mainly anti-Nebraska bill sentiment. Upon learning the "game" that "had been played upon them," they reacted in "wrath and confusion" toward the filibustering speaker. The meeting soon disintegrated and adjourned, after which each side met separately. In other Iowa towns, the gatherings—though spirited—passed strongly worded resolutions against repealing the Missouri Compromise in the Nebraska bill.[5]

Such meetings revealed anti-Nebraska voters to be excited, and the August election totals confirmed Grimes's campaign strategy. Grimes won a narrow victory, and in the legislature the Democrats lost their majority, which they would not regain for the next thirty-five years. This development ensured the loss of the Democrats' two candidates for the U.S. Senate when the legislature next met to select their successors, and the seats would be in Republican hands for seventy years to come.

Democrats lay part of the blame for their decisive losses at the doorstep of religious abolitionists. A Dubuque editor had decried the Congregational Association meeting of Iowa ministers at Davenport on July 7 as "strongly tinctured with politics" for renouncing "all communion with slave holders" and the "action of the national government in declaring the ancient prohibition of slavery in the great region west of us inoperative and void." Such actions, declared the editor, "seemed determined to bring about a state of public sentiment—to urge on a warfare between the North and the South—which, if not checked must inevitably result in civil anarchy and a dismemberment of the Union."[6] Abolitionists of religious stripe, wrote the Democratic editor in Keosauqua, "prostitute the pulpit, and debase even the [political] hustings by their insane declamations against slavery." Day in and day out "the clank of chains is the only sound they hear, black the only color they see" as they devote sole compassion to the slave.[7]

Astonished at his success in the election, Grimes confidently wrote to Senator Salmon P. Chase, the antislavery champion from Ohio, that "the Whigs are just now learning that it does not hurt them to be called 'abolitionists, woolly-heads,' etc., and, when the great contest of 1856 comes on, they will be prepared for and callous to all such epithets."[8] In reply, Chase credited Grimes with "fighting the best battle for freedom yet fought." And two years later, with the creation of the Republican Party, Chase recognized that Grimes's 1854 victory "was the morning star. The sun has risen now."[9]

II

In Missouri, the leading defender of the Kansas-Nebraska Act and its proslavery possibilities for Kansas Territory was Senator David Atchison, whose main strength lay in Missouri's western slave counties nearest Kansas. Though not an orator or a clever man, the bachelor had a clear and logical mind, which combined with hard work and a gift for skillful intrigue and manipulation, made him an able lawyer and politician. More important was his personal likability both among Senate colleagues and his constituents. When at home, he could often be found trading stories with his friends while lounging about Elisha Green's hotel in Platte City or eight miles northwest at the St. George Hotel in Weston.[10]

Closely allied with the southern faction of the Democratic Party, Atchison had enough clout to push a repeal of the Missouri Compromise. He now needed to take the reins and make the Kansas Territory a slave state in order to prevent his exposed border state of Missouri from being surrounded on three sides by Free States. As the final bill divided Nebraska into the separate Kansas and Nebraska Territories, proslavery men foresaw, and expected "abolitionists" to be satisfied with, Kansas as a slave state and Nebraska a Free State.

Democrats, however, recognized this outcome was no sure thing. Atchison's fellow Democratic senator from Iowa, Augustus Dodge, who introduced the Nebraska bill and was accepting of slavery's extension westward, doubted many slaveholders would move to the new territory. During debate on the bill, Dodge had told Atchison what he predicted in practice would happen under the bill: "You rarely find a man, the owner of slaves, ready to dash in among a new community like that which will people Kansas and Nebraska. There will be quite an emigration from Missouri and Arkansas to these territories, but in the main it will be of that class of citizens who are in needy circumstances and own no slaves."[11]

Nonetheless, David Atchison, working together with his chief aide, Benjamin Franklin Stringfellow, set out to stoke public excitement for a proslavery Kansas and oppose any who thought otherwise.[12] Stringfellow had been Missouri State's attorney general from 1845 to 1849. In 1853, he moved with his brother Dr. John H.

Stringfellow to Weston, in Platte County, across the river from Kansas in northwestern Missouri. The town bustled as a steamboat port for westbound settlers and a center for the hemp and tobacco trade. In 1854, the thirty-eight-year-old radical joined Atchison's Kansas cause. Described by a local minister as five foot six, with a "florid complexion, yellow hair, [and] indisposed to exertion," Stringfellow took up organizing proslavery's friends.[13] Together Atchison and the Stringfellow brothers became the public image of proslavery opposition to Free-State settlement.

Atchison and Benjamin Stringfellow also needed a proslavery Kansas to ensure their political futures. Atchison had failed to muster a majority of votes for another U.S. Senate term from a newly elected Missouri General Assembly, over which his eastern Missouri rivals had gained greater control. Political pundits predicted that "Atchison will claim a [Kansas] senatorship in lieu of the one he lost in Missouri, and Stringfellow, no doubt, will . . . demand the other."[14] The admission of Kansas into the Union with a proslavery constitution could make that happen for Atchison and Benjamin Stringfellow who now staked their political futures on bringing off a proslavery win.

III

Events moved quickly, surprisingly so for proslavery Missourians.[15] Scarcely had President Franklin Pierce signed the Kansas-Nebraska Act into law on May 30, 1854, when New Englanders began forming emigration societies to advance Free-State settlement. By July agents of the Massachusetts Emigrant Aid Company (later renamed the New England Emigrant Aid Company) had determined to settle in Kansas and had selected a townsite forty miles inland from Kansas City, Missouri, in Douglas County. They named the town Lawrence for a major benefactor, the Ipswich textile miller Amos Adams Lawrence. Its first group of twenty-nine settlers left Boston in mid-July, and a second party of sixty-seven was slated to leave at the end of August. These small advance contingents of New Englanders ultimately would be far outnumbered by Midwestern Free-State settlers, with Iowa contributing nearly the same number as all of New England.[16]

New England Free-State emigrants especially angered proslavery Missourians, for they judged New Englanders to be at the heart of antislavery radicalism. Feeding proslavery anger were rumors that the Massachusetts Emigrant Aid Company was a corporation with several millions of dollars, that it boasted high numbers of settlers would be sent west, and that it aimed to be a profitable enterprise that would found towns and build saw and grist mills to attract other pioneers. Proslavery leaders depicted such eastern capitalists as bringing west their vagabonds and tramps, or the dregs of eastern states, and as exploiting the white working people of the West. The western Missourian and the New Englander definitely were not at home in each other's worlds.[17]

Rankled, the proslavery Missourians viewed these easterners as interlopers, extremist invaders into lands they considered theirs. Kansas, the western Missourians believed, had "fitness" for "slave labor," and "they themselves should have the right to occupy the land in their neighborhood." Particularly galling to them, antislavery New England states were home to offensive, "preachy," moralizing outsiders who were indifferent or condescending to down-to-earth Westerners like themselves, the common men.[18]

It was not long before western Missouri slaveholders, many of them small farm operators, saw steamboats landing to unload Free-State easterners at Kansas City and passed them traveling on roads and standing about at ferry crossings. And noting their peculiarities of speech and manner, wary Missourians might have thought they overheard loose talk about the Aid Company's having the men and the money to make Kansas a Free State.[19]

The unnerved proslavery men listened closely to the warnings of their leaders—Senator David Atchison and brothers Benjamin Stringfellow and John Stringfellow. "Another crew of Abolitionists landed at Kansas," they cried and claimed the eastern fanatics were aiming to "abolitionize" Kansas. Atchison and the Stringfellows portrayed the Emigrant Aid Company as a hated group—"*the scum and filth of the Northern cities*; sent here as hired servants, to do the will of others; not to give their own free suffrage"—just the spur they needed to organize their supporters in Missouri border counties.[20]

During the late summer and fall of 1854 and into 1855, the Stringfellows and Atchison stumped Missouri border towns and sympathetic Kansas towns, especially Leavenworth and Atchison. They organized secret societies called Blue Lodges or Sons of the South to push proslavery settlement and thwart those who would "abolitionize" Kansas. The secret lodges pledged their readiness to carry the fight into the territory.[21]

Benjamin Stringfellow called one such meeting on July 29 in Weston. At the gathering he rallied people against the invading abolition fanatics who would tempt the enslaved to run away (four had escaped two weeks previously). The meeting established the Platte County Self-Defensive Association, which aimed to remove Kansas settlers brought in "under the auspices of Northern Emigrant Aid Societies."[22]

But it was an uphill climb for the fire-eaters. Stringfellow's Self-Defensive Association would provoke local opposition for its excessive zeal. Further, fiery proslavery resolutions and vigilantism shortly antagonized an important share of Weston's community, especially merchants irate over the association's resolution to trade only with proslavery advocates.[23]

Atchison and Stringfellow, however, were not defeated. Knowing they would need support from the South, they also wrote and traveled to southern states and made their appeals for planters and supporters to move to Kansas to help defeat antislavery designs.

Initially, incoming settlers were of mixed opinions about the slavery question. "Notwithstanding the threats and brow-beatings of the Missourians," wrote one Free-State settler emigrating from back east, "the greatest proportion of the settlers here are Northern people" with the balance being "honest Southerners, who are coming, as they say, to get rid of slavery."[24]

But predictions for creating a Free State without conflict soon evaporated. On one side, the proslavery editor of the *St. Joseph (MO) Gazette* rejoiced in predicting that "emigrants are pouring into Kansas," with hundreds "going in from Arkansas and Tennessee," and that most of those "from the western free States, such as Indiana and Illinois, are in favour of making Kansas a slave State."[25] Conversely, a Massachusetts emigrant saw the arriving throngs pointing in the opposite directions: "The hotels and stables at Kansas are always full, and will be for some time. The roads are lined with teams from the border states. In about every fifth or eighth wagon you will see a sprinkling of negro slaves." The emigrant foresaw "a terrible struggle before us at the very first election" because slaveholders know they must "have a law recognizing Slavery at the first meeting of the Legislature. If they do not get it then they never will."[26]

Atchison knew that prevailing in territorial elections meant holding them early while his group had a numerical advantage. The first election was held in late November 1854 to elect a territorial representative to Congress. Atchison and his followers and friends hoped the proslavery candidate would trounce the Free-State nominee from Iowa, John A. Wakefield. The election of territorial legislators would be held the following spring.

Taking no chances in both the November 1854 and March 1855 elections, Atchison and his friends led fellow Missourians over the border en masse to augment the votes of those who had staked claims. In Boonville, Missouri, Kansas-bound Free-State man Samuel Walker saw handbills "posted all over town offering 'three dollars per day, and grub and whisky for recruits'" willing to cross the border to vote. "The next morning," Walker reported, "150 of these men started for Kansas, well armed and with flags flying."[27]

The editor of a newspaper in nearby Liberty, Missouri, made sure they knew the score: "Emigrant Aid Societies are shipping Abolitionists to Kansas by every steamboat, and the roads are crowded with them. Citizens of Missouri, you must act; talking won't do. You must go to Kansas. . . . [If] the blow is not struck now . . . it will take the hardest kind of blows hereafter to regain what we may lose."[28] Atchison, urging his fellow Missourians to join his upcoming incursion to Kansas for the territory's legislative elections on March 30, based his appeal partly on rumors that Free Staters were poised to enter from Iowa and influence the election's outcome.[29]

To kindle further proslavery support, Dr. Stringfellow joined with a Missouri hothead editor, Robert S. Kelley, to found the *Squatter Sovereign* newspaper during February 1855 at Atchison, Kansas Territory. In the hands of the two fire-eaters, this most provocative of proslavery newspapers fueled base partisan emotion for their cause, with "murder and hanging mingled in every editorial."[30]

Five days before the March 1855 election and in advance of other Missouri bands arriving in Kansas to vote, Atchison crossed into Kansas with eighty men and twenty-four wagons of supplies to oversee the proslavery vote and to ensure the result went their way. Atchison and his allies succeeded, gaining control over the thirty-nine-member territorial legislature. The resulting easy victory came at considerable cost, however. A preelection census showed only 2,905 voters in the territory, yet 6,307 votes were cast. When 4,909 were later judged illegal, Free-State forces responded.

Free Staters refused to recognize the newly elected proslavery legislature, run by its fervent Speaker of the House, Dr. John

Stringfellow of the *Squatter Sovereign*, and angrily labeled it as the "bogus" legislature. They also shunned subsequent territorial elections. By the fall of 1855 they had organized their own extralegal and parallel "Topeka" government to seek admission as a new state.

Proslavery disciples denounced the Topeka action as a treasonous subversion of popular sovereignty and responded by forming the Law and Order Party. Meanwhile the proslavery legislature passed and acting governor Daniel Woodson signed into law an extreme slave code aiming to repress antislavery activity and frighten abolitionists. This "Act to punish offences against Slave Property" mandated the death penalty for any person who "shall aid or assist in enticing, decoying or persuading or carrying out of any State or Territory, any slave belonging to another, with intent to effect or procure the freedom of such slave."[31] Doubtless many Free-State settlers judged the law as did U.S. senator Charles Sumner, who in his famed "Crime against Kansas" speech before his colleagues on May 19, 1856, spoke of the act as "wickedness, without a parallel."[32] However, Benjamin Stringfellow lauded their slave codes, which had been drawn largely from Missouri enactments, as "laws more efficient to protect slave property than any State in the Union" had.[33] Largely unenforced, as soon as Free-State forces gained control of the territorial legislature, they would effectively annul the law in early 1857 by simply "repealing slavery."[34]

V

By the end of 1855, despite their pleas to the southern sympathizers for settlers, Atchison and his western Missouri partisans were seeing the trend of slavery sentiment in Kansas changing. As early as the previous spring, the editor of the *St. Louis Evening News* sought to distance at least his part of the state from depredations arising from intimidation and voting fraud. He claimed, "Missouri is no more responsible for the exploits of Atchison and

Stringfellow than Christianity is for the treachery of Judas."[35] But the *Daily Gate City*'s editor in Keokuk, Iowa, did not buy the argument: "We think Missouri is, as a community, to a great extent responsible for the acts of Atchison and Stringfellow, and their ruffian tools," for the state's "leading and active journals either openly defend it, or refrain from stigmatizing it." What is more, complained an editor in Davenport, Iowa, the widely circulated *St. Louis Missouri Republican* "boldly affirms that the charge of wrong-doing attributed to these men is grossly unjust, while the wrong itself is merely imaginary. Did crime so deep and unmitigated ever find so bold and reckless a defender?"[36]

By the fall of 1855, some open hostility in eastern Missouri to Atchison's actions was evident. "Emigrants from the Northern or Free States have ceased to go to Kansas," wrote the editor of the *St. Louis Intelligencer*, "because they can find as good lands elsewhere, not cursed by mob law, nor ruled by non-resident bullies."[37] Consequently, judged a Chicago editor, "Western Missouri stands infected by the horrible contagion of outlawry," and its towns' economies dwindle as merchants find fewer settlers to buy their outfits, equipment, horses, mules, and livestock. The blame, at bottom, rested with Atchison and Stringfellow, who with their Missouri followers, "overwhelmed the settlers in Kansas, brow-beat and bullied them, and took the government from their hands."[38]

VI

Especially galling to proslavery Missourians had been New Englanders' immigration to Kansas with their reputed extreme antislavery sentiments. Both sides issued enough propaganda to make it appear that Kansas was home to people mainly from those two areas.

True enough, in New England states numerous residents were moving away, having exceeded resources to make a living. As one editor put it, "We stand in each other's way. All the existing employments, agriculture, commerce, and the learned professions are overflowing. Our young men are placed in that peculiar condition when emigration to a country or vicinity less occupied is imperative."[39]

But Kansas, not easily accessible and more dangerous from the political turmoil, was less attractive to New Englanders than were the vacant lands and opportunities in Iowa, Minnesota, Illinois, and Missouri. In fact, more New Englanders settled in Missouri than in Kansas from 1850 to 1860 (4,793 and 4,208, respectively). And Iowa attracted nearly five times as many New England-born settlers than Kansas did (20,306 compared to 4,208). In fact Iowa was sending to Kansas nearly as many of its own settlers as did the combined New England states (4,008 compared to 4,208).[40]

As for Missouri, one would have expected its citizens to move in and overwhelm all others by virtue of its proximity to Kansas and their wishes to thwart antislavery plans. But in fact the flow of Missourians into the territory soon failed to keep up with the others. During 1854 and into 1855 Missourians' settlement in Kansas gave hope to Atchison and Stringfellow that they could outpace the rest. In fact during midyear even Iowans worried about how "now, that the South consider[s] the question of Slavery in Kansas settled, and her destiny fixed, they are beginning to turn their attention to the southern portion of Nebraska."[41]

By 1860, however, the 11,356 Missouri-born settlers in Kansas had been exceeded by Ohio's emigrants. The decline owed much to Missourians deciding to occupy the state's own thinly settled areas and pursuing opportunities from economic expansion that the state enjoyed during the 1850s. Additionally the state's varied mix of incoming northern and foreign populations was making it less united on the slavery question, despite strong proslavery interest in Missouri's western counties.[42]

The major contributors to the Kansas Territory's population were today's midwestern states, then the country's western frontier. Kansas residents could see it as they watched the surge of settlers during 1855. "The tide of emigration continues to flow into the Territory," wrote the editor of the *Lawrence Kansas Free State*. "A great portion of that which is permanent is from the western States. They come with good teams and wagons, seeds and agricultural implements all ready to go to work, being principally from the States of Ohio, Indiana, Illinois, Wisconsin, Iowa and Missouri."[43] And whereas many "disheartened" easterners return home, "our western people," wrote another Kansan," understand pioneer life, and know how to prepare for it. They come to remain, and are rarely seen beating an inglorious retreat."[44] Undeniably, "the daily arrivals overland of large covered wagons from Iowa, Wisconsin, Indiana, Illinois, etc.," have "packed all the paraphernalia of the farm and fireside, ready for distribution in their proper places as soon as a claim is selected."[45]

Southerners, meanwhile, seemed to resist the appeals of fellow agitators in Kansas. Many southerners thought Kansas to be worthy of well-organized propaganda, for "it is impossible to exaggerate the importance of Kansas to the South," wrote one South Carolina editor. "If we lose Kansas we lose Missouri, bring free soil to the borders of Arkansas and Tennessee, and will have to struggle for the Indian Territory behind Arkansas."[46]

But vital as it might be to border state interests, states in the Deep South that saw their population was already bleeding away to western slave states agreed that taking slave property to Kansas was a gamble.[47] So the partisans in the lower south instead left it to those in the upper south to ensure Kansas became a slave state.[48]

An editor of the *St. Louis Intelligencer* clearly summarized the situation in late 1855:

Emigrants from Southern States do not go to Kansas, because they will not put their slave property in peril by taking it into a Territory where there is a strong Free Soil element threatening the security of slaves. . . . Alabama and Georgia may hold public meetings, and resolve to sustain the slaveholders in Missouri in making Kansas a slave State. But their resolutions comprise all their aid, which is not material enough for the crisis. When slaveholders of Alabama and Georgia emigrate, they go to Louisiana, Arkansas, and Texas.[49]

VII

Proslavery men thus feared that 1856 would bring a new flood of incoming Free-State settlers to Kansas and lead to their eventual defeat unless the South delivered massive support. Senator Atchison, Benjamin F. Stringfellow, and others had toured the South in late 1854 and then repeatedly corresponded with newspapers there, pleading for southerners to come to Kansas. "The cause of Kansas," wrote Stringfellow to a southern friend, "is the cause of the South," which needs to "put forth her energies and exert her strength to save our neighboring Territory from the leprous touch of abolition fanaticism. If Kansas slavery fails, other border states will follow," Stringfellow believed, for "when the hoop breaks, the cask falls to pieces." Missourians, he maintained, should not have to defend southern rights in Kansas alone.[50]

Atchison in early 1855 penned a lengthy letter to a proslavery editor in Georgia and implored the state's young men to reach Kansas speedily: "Let them come well armed, with money enough to support them for twelve months, and determined to see it out! One hundred true men will be an acquisition. The more the better. I do not see how we are to avoid civil war—civil war of the fiercest kind—will be upon us. We are arming and preparing for it. Indeed, we of the border counties are prepared. We must have the support of the South. We are fighting the battles of the South."[51]

The Republican editor of the *Burlington Weekly Hawk-Eye and Telegraph* reprinted Atchison's letter. As the editor saw it, the letter amounted to a criminal and damnable movement by a "treasonable and bloody-minded villain" acting in concert with Stephen Douglas and President Pierce to undo the Missouri Compromise.

Iowa could not ignore the challenge, the editor judged. "How can, or will the citizens of Iowa, acquit themselves to the world if lieing [*sic*] so close to the scene of intended rapine and murder, they shall fold their arms, and look on the bloody tragedy with indifference?" Iowa, he declared, must "be prepared if necessary to risk our persons in behalf of our friends in Kansas."[52]

3

Prairie, Dust, and Wind

I

If proslavery leaders worried about controlling Kansas in the early months of 1856, Free-State settlers constantly worried that border raiders might appear any day. Moreover, until their numbers grew, Free-State leaders counseled that they keep a defensive posture and avoid any aggressive contact with U.S. troops that would give President Franklin Pierce's slavery-friendly national government an excuse to send troops against them. After all, on January 24 the president's special message to Congress on the Kansas Territory's troubles had warned that "organized resistance by force" to federal law and general government authority would be considered "treasonable insurrection," and it would be his "duty to exert the whole power of the Federal Executive to support public order in the Territory."[1]

The Free Staters seemed no better off than described in an eastern newspaper the previous November: "Thus far, the warfare has been pretty much all on one side, the settlers from the North adopting a passive course, except when they were forced in defense of their individual lives to depart from it. The active, belligerent movements have been carried on exclusively by the pro-slavery party . . . to enforce the rule of a set of sanguinary invaders and ruffians from a border State, by virtue of the revolver and the Bowie knife."[2]

The deep snows and bone-chilling winter of 1855–56, coupled with rumors and reports of border intimidation, violence, and election fraud, encouraged sympathetic coverage from Iowa newspapers. Because Iowa was the closest Free State to the Nebraska and Kansas Territories, the state grew increasingly alarmed about the Free-State situation. Several Iowa towns, including Keokuk, Muscatine, Burlington, and Davenport, held meetings to learn the state of affairs that Kansas settlers faced, both the hardships of emigration and political troubles. Speakers included Mr. Mallory, the territory's quarter master general of the Free State Army of Kansas, and James S. Emery, a thirty-year-old lawyer from New York who in 1854 had come to Lawrence with the second group of Free-State emigrants and, with recognized public speaking skills, was on a tour of Free States to gather resolutions of aid.[3]

Proslavery intimidation doubtless discouraged some from going to Kansas, frightened others into heading back home, and forced others to find ways besides the river route to reach Kansas unmolested. Already in mid-April 1856 the Iowa editor of the *Clinton Mirror*, wrote of how the "border ruffian" outrages in Missouri were "having the effect to turn all the northern travel from that route through Iowa" for "although the distance is somewhat longer, the great security afforded more than compensates for it."[4]

Persons going overland across Iowa in 1855 had found it a rough and unpleasant way to avoid the hostility lurking along the Missouri River's muddy banks and shoreline cottonwoods. The land, replete with unfamiliar and unmarked trails, greatly slowed their progress. As one traveler described his journey to the Kansas Territory, when he pulled his team onto a new wagon track, "at length, all traces of a road vanished except stakes stuck up in the naked unbroken prairie. On we went, through sloughs, round ridges and over millions of gopher hills, and in the afternoon through a wood, and toward nightfall with jaded horses and almost broken bones, we reached the old road."[5]

Such pitiable and hardly inviting overland conditions made many emigrants willing to risk the river route until proslavery Missourians made river travel impossible, leaving Free-State emigrants no choice but the Iowa route. As late as early May 1856, Kansan men were still trying to negotiate safer and better steamboat travel arrangements with people in Alton, Illinois. The town was only three miles from the mouth of the Missouri River compared to St. Louis, which was twenty miles downriver and served as the terminus of two railroads from the East. Kansans still thought an overland emigration route through Iowa to be "wholly impracticable for the vast amount of emigration now setting Kansasward," at least until Chicago interests built their railroad lines farther through the state.[6]

II

Most Iowa residents who moved to the Nebraska and Kansas Territories had lived in the populated eastern counties of the state.[7] Those folks with Free-State sympathies who packed their belongings and hitched up teams bound for the territories were genuine settlers, but some rode there to take advantage of the turbulence.

One such Iowan was a man identified only as Roberts, who came from Dubuque to Topeka leading a bunch of rough men. They had come to Kansas, Roberts said, to help make the territory free and to fight border ruffians. Suspicions arose about these intentions, according to John Armstrong, an antislavery Kansan, when Roberts and his band disappeared for a week and reappeared with a dozen horses weighed down with plunder. Carrying "all kinds of household goods and merchandise seemingly taken from stores and dwellings," they said they had taken the goods and horses from an attack on a proslavery settlement on the Neosho River and hauled the loot to their camp down in thick brush by the river. When word leaked that Roberts and his gang had been raiding settlers regardless of their slavery affiliation, Armstrong and others went to the camp and gave the men twenty-four hours to leave. The group complied. Armstrong later learned that the men had returned to Iowa, crossing via the Missouri River ferry at Nebraska City.[8]

Most Free-State settlers from Iowa, however, were not of Roberts's stripe. The stories of three Iowa men who went to Kansas during the active period of troubles between Free-State and proslavery partisans suggest the demands that the new settlers faced. These three Iowans—John A. Wakefield, Charles E. Lenhart, and Pardee Butler—became important to the antislavery story of 1855 and 1856 in the Kansas Territory.

III

John A. Wakefield, at age fifty-seven, was getting up in years for a Kansas-bound settler. Within a week of President Pierce's signing the Kansas-Nebraska Act, he and his large family moved six miles west of what would become Lawrence, Kansas Territory. They had arrived from their Allamakee County, Iowa, farm in two wagons plus a red carriage and buggy carrying John; his wife, Eliza; three sons; a daughter; and a niece.[9]

Wakefield, a lawyer, built a reputation based on his military background as a scout in the Black Hawk War of 1832 and a writer of its history. Since 1851 he had been living in northeastern Iowa on land he had received from a military grant for his service in the Illinois volunteers during the War of 1812. Building a large house on a ridge eight miles west of the Mississippi River town of Lansing, Wakefield was the first settler to build a water ram down by a creek that forced water up to his dwelling, a luxury that was the envy of his arriving neighbors. He went by the title of colonel or major, which fit his ambition for office and prominence. Eager to share deeds of valor from his youthful days as a military scout, the talkative, outgoing Wakefield quickly won the local postmaster appointment and the presidency of the Allamakee County Agricultural and Mechanical Society. South Carolina born, he had lived in the Minnesota Territory and earlier had spent years in Illinois, where he had helped to defeat a pro-slavery measure and gained two terms as a Whig in the Illinois State legislature.[10] By the time he and his family hitched up their wagons for migration to Kansas in mid-1854, he was a Free-Soil Party man.[11]

At their new farm site, the Wakefields unloaded their belongings next to the California Road in the yet largely vacant southern Kanwaka Township of Douglas County. Wakefield and his boys set about building a large six-room, one-and-a-half-story log house and some outbuildings while getting to know their neighbors. Within two months at a public meeting of claims setters in the vicinity, the assembled body selected Wakefield to act as a judge in matters of claims disputes. The position evolved into serving as a judge for the Mutual Settlers' Association of Kansas Territory.[12]

Such responsibilities were no surprise for, unlike most of his young fellow settlers, Wakefield was an experienced and mature professional with some accumulated wealth. The portly man also presented an impressive figure as he rode about in his red carriage driven by one of his workers. As Free-State politics organized in response to forceful proslavery activity, Wakefield soon plunged into the territorial fray.[13]

The Iowa transplant came to occupy numerous leadership positions at the various Free-State meetings, and when in November 1854 the first election was held for a delegate to Congress, he became the Free-State candidate. Of the three candidates—Gen. John W. Whitfield, a proslavery man; Judge Robert P. Flenniken, a Pennsylvania administration Democrat with Free-State leanings who had been brought in for the election; and John A. Wakefield, who was proclaimed as the only bona fide resident, solid Free-State man, and pioneer westerner—Wakefield faced the toughest challenge. Though he gained the largest percentage of votes at Lawrence, the new Free-State town and center of the growing political storm, they were about the only ones he received. Whitfield won with a large majority, though more than half of the votes came from companies of proslavery men who had crossed the Missouri River at ferry points on horseback and in wagons filled with their supplies and tents.[14]

Wakefield's appeal to Free-State settlers was based, in large degree, on his down-home personality. One who knew him saw in his portly figure "a plain, honest man, a hearty free-soiler, and a unique character," as well as his being "enthusiastic, earnest and honest, and in speech was most amusing when most serious." To listeners of this western Free-Soiler, they heard "something delicious" in his speeches that departed from "the dull monotony of egotism and politics." Quite a talker, his public speeches and conversation, though sounding provincial, showed a man "sound and shrewd in his opinions, and honest to the core."[15]

The man's bravery was apparent in the March 1855 election for the territorial legislature. Several hundred Missourians arrived early in the morning at Wakefield's Bloomington polling station to vote while "armed with double-barreled guns, rifles, bowie-knives, and pistols, and had flags hoisted." Their leader, arch proslavery radical Claiborne F. Jackson, told them "they had a right to vote if they had been there but five minutes, and he was not willing to go home without voting." The crowd cheered, and each man tied a white tape or ribbon to his buttonhole to show he was not an abolitionist. The men then pressed forward to the voting window, demanding to vote on grounds that they were in the territory on Election Day and that residency was not required. When two of the three judges refused, the Missourians broke through the window, destroyed the polling box, and with guns pointed at the judges, demanded their resignation.[16]

At that point one of the judges slipped the poll books into his coat pocket, walked out through the crowd, and then handed them off to another man. The Missourians, however, caught on and chased the man down to retrieve the books. They next turned on the "old soldier," John A. Wakefield, who described what happened next: "I ran into the house and told Mr. Ramsay to give me his double-barreled shot-gun. The mob rode up, and I should think a dozen or more presented their pistols at me. I drew up the gun at [proslavery sheriff] Jones, the leader. We stood that way for perhaps a minute." After some tense exchange, Wakefield agreed to return to the polling place, whereupon he climbed onto a wagon and spoke briefly. "I told them I was an old soldier, and had fought through two wars for the rights of my country, and I thought I had a privilege there that day. I said they were in the wrong,—that we were not the Abolitionists they represented us to be, but were Free-State men; that they were abusing us unjustly, and that their acts were contrary to organic law and the Constitution of the United States." One yelled out, "Shoot him! He's too saucy!" Wakefield, though, made it through his speech. Then he left the Missourians to select their own poll judges.[17]

The Wakefields' situation only worsened in 1856 as the conflict intensified. In early May when proslavery chief justice Samuel D. Lecompte of the U.S. District Court instructed a grand jury at Lecompton to examine witnesses leading to indictments of Free-State leaders for high treason, one grand jury member went during the night to warn Judge Wakefield and other Free-State leaders as well. Some fled the territory, including Judge Wakefield, who, hearing of a writ issued for his arrest, headed for Illinois to wait for the storm to blow over. At Leavenworth, Missouri, however, some South Carolina men of Maj. Jefferson Buford's regiment arrested him and took him back to Lecompton. Brought before U.S. Territory chief justice Lecompte, Wakefield demanded to be read the writ of arrest. When neither Lecompte nor his clerks could find a record of issuing a writ, instead of discharging the case, Judge Lecompte delayed proceedings by telling Wakefield to "take out a writ of habeas corpus!" Once the delay of this procedural impediment was overcome and the review completed, the chief justice approved Wakefield's release to return home.[18]

Wakefield's troubles did not end there. In mid-July a Kansas neighbor, writing to relatives back in Iowa, reported a disturbing event involving Judge Wakefield and his family. A mob had entered and searched his house and fired a pistol, "the ball of which passed within two feet of a bed where three children were lying."[19] Worse for the family came September 1, shortly after the proslavery burning of Osawatomie, when a marshal with a handful of writs to arrest Free-State leaders rode out from Lecompton with deputies and bands of proslavery militia into Wakefield's vicinity. An Ohio resident, writing to his brother the next day, described how he expected his house to be burned next because that night he could see some five other houses afire, all occurring within sight of several hundred troops nearby. The Ohioan's daughter, writing her aunt the next day, also told how "on Sunday morning Judge Wakefield got word that his house would be burnt in 48 hours, so the judge moved his family to Lawrence." They escaped just in time, for by nightfall his house was in flames and the house of Wakefield's son-in-law was in ashes. Also burned was the neighboring house of Free-State militia leader Capt. Samuel Walker, whose unit sixteen days earlier had captured Fort Titus two miles away. The fire destroyed Wakefield's library, a seven-hundred-page manuscript ready for publication, furnishings, and a barn filled with grain.[20] The proslavery militias then retreated to Lecompton with confiscated goods.

IV

But times were changing for proslavery roughnecks. Up to mid-1856 marauding proslavery groups operating as a posse had made life miserable and uncertain for Free-State settlers at will. They regularly pillaged Free Staters' houses or burned them, stopped and searched wagons, and stole cattle and horses, all with the unspoken acquiescence of the territory's officials. As summer approached, however, Free-State segments started forming their own guerrilla bands to fight back. Soon roving proslavery groups found their own horses stolen, their wagons attacked and anti-slavery captives freed, and their houses and stores robbed in reprisal. These actions forced proslavery partisans to stay closer to their protected enclaves.

Of the Free-State guerrilla leaders who emerged, the earliest and most aggressive was a lean young man from Iowa named Charles E. (Charley) Lenhart. He had been working as a printer in Davenport, where his widowed mother lived, when he departed for Kansas Territory in the spring of 1855. The nineteen-year-old Charley, described as "a tall, black-eyed, lithe specimen of the Western American youth," found work as a typesetter with George W. Brown, editor of the *Herald of Freedom* (organ of the New England Emigrant Aid Company) in Lawrence.[21] Lenhart worked at the Free-State paper, which held moderate antislavery views and promoted emigration and economic development, through the fall of 1855. During this time he initially slept with his blanket on the prairie and later on made his evening bed on the floor of the newspaper office.

November and December 1855 had been a time of high excitement in Lawrence, beginning with collisions between proslavery and Free-State individuals that led Territorial Governor Wilson Shannon to call out the militia. Within days the order had brought some fifteen hundred western Missourians into the territory, and they lay siege to Lawrence. Ultimately, the threatened disorder ended with a negotiated agreement between contending forces. It all left a large impression on Charley Lenhart. From that time on, recalled his boss at the newspaper, "I could not count on him with certainty, [for] if there was any wild adventure on foot he was the leader and away!" After the "destruction of the *Herald of Freedom* office in '56, Lenhart seemed to have adopted a guerilla [sic] life, and I only heard of him through others thereafter."[22]

What the cautious newspaperman heard was unsettling. To his way of thinking, as well as that of the local defensive-minded leader and agent of the Emigrant Aid Company, Charles Robinson, the young guerrilla leader—though "fearless and brave"—was becoming an unmanageable radical. Lenhart was leading young men "of the dare-devil stripe" fully in support of Free-State men with fight in them. Typifying the more unruly wing were James Lane, the shabby former military man and politician of gripping impulsive passion, and John Brown, the old unrelenting warrior standing against Free-State enemies.[23]

New York Tribune reporter William Addison Phillips admitted that Lenhart led "some twenty of the wildest and most daring young free-state guerillas [*sic*]." This reckless risk-taking bunch—"a harum-scarum set," Williams described them—was "as brave as steel, mostly mere boys" who had few compunctions about running off with a proslavery man's horse. "At various times," he wrote, "they have made more disturbance than all other free-state men together." Lenhart's young men loved the excitement and were dead-set on doing to proslavery men what had been inflicted upon their Free-State friends. Throughout the county on their own initiative, they would ambush and skirmish with proslavery men wherever and whenever they could and acted as cavalry scouts with larger militia actions when the opportunity arose.[24]

Looking upon the slender, young guerrilla combatant, one man could not easily reconcile Lenhart's "reputation as a daring reckless, Fighting man" with his appearing to have a laid-back "indolent, inoffensive manner."[25] But despite his unassuming appearance, Lenhart's vigorous guerrilla operations worried the cautious defensive-minded leadership of the Free-State cause. The leaders denounced the guerrilla tactics, fearing they would become a pretext for the U.S. military to intervene against them all on grounds of keeping order and peace.

Dismayed, *New York Tribune* newspaper correspondent Phillips wrote how "these boys have been most bitterly maligned" and did not deserve the resolutions "passed by the sensitively moral [conservative] free-state people, or the *sensitively timid*, declaring that these daring young guerillas were a nuisance" and they ought not to "be held responsible for them." But "to all this moralizing," continued Phillips, "these young braves turned up their noses," seeing such complainers as too cowardly to fight a war already begun.[26]

Armed marauding bands on both sides now ranged about the country, stealing cattle and horses and carrying out their own brands of intimidation and harassment. Those who had tried to stay out of the mess and mind their own business now felt obliged to join one side or the other.[27] As events drove Free-State action forward during 1856, Lenhart was in the thick of it.

When, for instance, some armed Missourians shot an unarmed man south of Lawrence on May 19, 1856, Charley Lenhart was the first to act.[28] Lenhart gathered together two friends—a young clerk and medical student named Stewart and John E. Cook. (Trained in law and an excellent shot, Cook was a brave, impulsive fellow who later joined John Brown's raid at Harpers Ferry.) With Sharps rifles in hand and Cook carrying at least one revolver, they rode toward the site of the shooting. When they were a mile and a half away, they saw two armed men.[29] Stewart confronted them and asked what they knew of the shooting. With rifles raised the two Missourians fired first. One shot struck Stewart in the head, sending him reeling to the ground. Lenhart and Cook attempted to shoot, but their pieces failed to fire (a common problem then with otherwise highly accurate Sharps rifles). The Missourians galloped off on their mules as Cook ran after them while discharging his revolver. He wounded one assailant in the arm. Lenhart and Cook then carried their dead friend back to Lawrence.

Ten days later Lenhart's guerrillas fought again, this time ambushing a party of southern marauders menacing settlers along the Santa Fe Road of the Neosho Valley to force them out of the territory. A correspondent for the *Chicago Tribune* reported what happened: "A company of seventy men—Missourian [*sic*], South Carolinians and Alabamians—after scouring round the country all day driving off and plundering the Northern emigrants, were surprised and attacked by a party of [twenty-one] Free State boys, commanded by a young printer formerly from Iowa, who fired upon them as they were passing a wood, and killed six, and mortally wounded one of them. As soon as their companions fell, the invaders fled in great disorder. Only one volley was fired." Another report reduced the numbers of men involved but agreed that the proslavery men lost horses, mules, provisions, and arms to Lenhart's Free-State guerrilla party.[30]

Constant but futile efforts to capture Lenhart and his twenty-some cavalry scouts added risk to the group's forays; perhaps that danger is what sent Lenhart riding north during the end of July. Upon crossing into Iowa he met Col. James Lane, the restless and energetic Free-State militia leader encamped near Sidney with his emigrant company about to enter Nebraska. Lenhart continued on his way overland and reached Davenport ten days later. After he stopped at his former newspaper office for a visit, the paper printed his mention of Lane's whereabouts and noted that Lenhart "has been in Kansas for a year past, and has seen considerable service. He is a printer, a gallant fellow, and graduated at this office."[31]

The young raider soon returned to Kansas. On September 13 he and his "cavalry scouts" were with James Lane's Free-State militia at the Battle of Hickory Point (on the north side of the Ft. Leavenworth–Ft. Riley territorial road in Jefferson County) and acted as a rear guard to the militia.[32]

Thereafter, little is known of him until 1858. In early February of that year, while working as a printer on the Free-State *Crusader* newspaper at Doliphan, Kansas, Lenhart exchanged public threats with a notorious proslavery store owner. During quiet inactive times Lenhart, in his boredom, would turn to whiskey, and six weeks later he was shot by a barkeeper in a drunken dispute while attending a ball at Geary, just north of Doliphan.[33] Within a few months of recovering Lenhart headed east after the failed Harpers Ferry raid. There, posing as a proslavery man, he became one of the militia guards at the jail in nearby Charles Town and attempted without success to aid his friend John Cook escape from imprisonment.[34] Four years later Charles Lenhart was dead, claimed by sickness while serving as a first lieutenant in northwest Arkansas with Col. John Ritchie's Second Indian Home Guard Regiment.[35]

V

Border quarrels commonly occurred at steamboat stops of western Missouri River towns. Frustrated Missouri partisans, lounging about the wharves and landings, pestered and intimidated the Free-State arrivals. A widely reported instance of these encounters in the small proslavery river town of Atchison, Kansas Territory, concerned the brutal treatment of Rev. Pardee Butler and his resulting heroic Free-State reputation.

Butler, known as a "quiet and unassuming minister of the gospel," had lived with his family near Poston's Grove in eastern Cedar County, Iowa, for five years. In May 1855, the family agreed that the thirty-nine-year-old Pardee should search out cheaper lands to farm in northeastern Kansas. He located 160 acres on the banks of Stranger Creek, where lived fellow Campbellites, a frontier faith today known as Disciples of Christ. There, about twelve miles away from a proslavery town named Atchison and close to the Missouri River, he completed a cabin by mid-August. With that work done, he headed to Atchison. At that time Butler described the small village as "built among the cottonwood trees on the banks of the Missouri River, about twenty miles below St. Joseph." Butler intended to travel downriver from there by steamboat and bring back his family.[36]

Finding the steamboat delayed until the next day, he took a hotel room. Then, wanting to take back something so friends in Illinois could learn of the strong proslavery attitudes and behavior in the area, he walked over to the printing office of Atchison's

Fig. 2. Rev. Pardee Butler, an Iowa Campbellite minister who twice withstood the abuse of a proslavery mob for his Free-State views. Kansas State Historical Society.

Squatter Sovereign paper. Stepping inside, he asked to buy some extra copies from Robert S. Kelley, the coeditor, who waited on him. Butler described him as "a handsome, broad-shouldered, muscular, blue eyed man," the kind of a natural "born leader among such a population as at that time filled Western Missouri." As he paid for the papers, Butler happened to mention he would have become a subscriber, but "I do not like the spirit of violence that characterizes it." To this observation Kelley replied, "I consider all free-soilers rogues, and they are to be treated as such." When Butler retorted, "Well, sir, I am a free-soiler; and I intend to vote for Kansas to be a free state," Kelley growled, "You will not be allowed to vote."[37]

Butler then walked outside, where an accompanying friend grabbed him and nervously told him that saying such things could get him killed, but the preacher—a man of strict probity—took little heed of the danger. Instead the strong-willed Reverend Butler freely expressed his disgust with the recent beating of a Free-State man in Atchison and of local attempts "to cow free-soilers into silence." Butler went on about how the Kansas-Nebraska bill gave Free-State men as much right as others to come to Kansas and as much right to speak their sentiments.[38]

The next morning, Kelley and six others found Butler writing letters at the head of the stairs in the boarding house. "Bristling with revolvers and bowie-knives," recalled Butler, they "came up stairs and into my room," where Kelley handed him a list of resolutions. They had been cut out of the *Squatter Sovereign* and pasted on a sheet of paper, and one forbade the presence of "agents of the underground railroad, for the express purpose of abducting our slaves." The group demanded he read and sign the list. To calm himself Butler looked it over for some time and then refused to sign. He then began reading the resolutions aloud until the mob interrupted, at which point Butler arose, went down the stairs, and walked into the street.[39]

Fig. 3. Proslavery flag that was fixed to the log raft that carried Rev. Pardee Butler downriver. Kansas State Historical Society.

There, Butler recalled, "they seized me and dragged me to the river, cursing me for a damned abolitionist, and saying they were going to drown me." At the riverbank Kelley painted an *R* (for rogue) on his forehead, and for the next two hours Butler "was a sort of target at which were hurled imprecations, curses, arguments, entreaties, accusations and interrogatories" as they fashioned a small raft of two cottonwood logs.[40]

Though they did not accuse him of tampering with slaves, said Butler, Kelley's group alleged that "I had spoken among my neighbors favorable to making Kansas a free state, and had said in the office of the *Squatter Sovereign*, 'I am a free-soiler and intend to vote in favor of making Kansas a free State.'" While they admitted he was no abolitionist, but a Free-Soiler, they would stand for neither. They sat him on the cottonwood raft, which they towed with a canoe out into the middle of the Missouri River; stuck onto it a flagstaff with a derogatory banner; and threatened to shoot him if he tore it down.

Six miles downriver, Butler used a penknife to tear down the branch with its banner reading, "Greeley [of the *New York Tribune*] to the rescue: I have a nigger. Rev. Mr. Butler, agent for the underground Railroad." Using the branch as a paddle, he gradually reached the shore. The news of what had happened to Butler traveled like wildfire, he remembered, and made many previously intimidated Free-State men ready to fight.[41]

In November the gutsy preacher was back in Kansas, evidently unmoved when Kelley's group threatened to hang him if he returned to Atchison. Butler passed unmolested through town with his family and reached the cabin of his wife's brother. There his wife and children stayed through the winter while he returned to Illinois for preaching work. Five months later, on April 30, 1856, Butler returned to rejoin his family, crossing the Missouri River to Atchison. After briefly speaking to two merchants about his accounts with them, he walked toward his buggy when, as he described it, "I was assaulted by Kelley, co-editor of the *Squatter Sovereign*, and others."[42]

Butler continued, "I was dragged into a grocery, and there surrounded by a company of South Carolinians." The Carolina group had been reportedly sent by a southern Emigrant Aid Society (part of Major Buford's estimated 350 soldiers quartered in Atchison and other Missouri river towns). Of the others, he recognized only two from the previous year's mob. With few of them being Atchison shopkeepers or residents, Butler was up against a more dangerous situation. Now he faced unruly South Carolina adventurers loafing about in the pent-up heat of proslavery feeling, which would lead them to participate in sacking Lawrence three weeks later.[43]

One of them walked up to Butler and demanded, "'Have you got a revolver?' I replied, 'No.' He handed me a pistol saying, 'There, take that, and stand off ten steps, and d——n you, I will blow you through in an instant.' I replied, 'I have no use for your weapon.'" Furious though the fellow was, Butler recalled, his companions "dissuaded him from shooting me, saying they were going to hang me." Then, yelling, "'Hang him! Hang him! Hang the d——d abolitionist!'" the mob "pinioned my arms behind me [and] obtained a rope."[44]

At that point a Missouri slave-owning lawyer interrupted. He wanted Kansas made a slave state but said that Butler was peaceably passing through town and urged the others, "'for the sake of the pro-slavery cause, do not act in this way.'" The plea caused the men's plans to shift. Pardee Butler remembered: "They dragged me into another grocery, and appointed a moderator. Kelley told his story." But when Butler rose to give his side of the matter as had been civilly allowed him the previous time, the South Carolina men "savagely gagged me in silence, by rapping my face, choking me, pulling my beard, jerking me violently to my seat, and calling out, 'd——n you, hold your tongue.'" The Missouri lawyer, as well as an Atchison lawyer and a merchant, then stepped in to urge Butler's release. Then Robert Kelley—evidently fearing he could be held responsible for the violent treatment that seemed to be leading to the preacher's killing—intruded, saying he did not intend that Butler be hanged but given the tar and feather treatment.[45]

Disappointed, the leader of the South Carolinians sneered he had not come all the way to Kansas to do things in a timid "milk and water style." Several of his group pressed to add thirty-nine lashes to Butler's punishment. In the end they did not inflict lashes; instead, in Butler's words, they "stripped me naked to the waist, covered my body with tar, and then for the want of feathers, applied cotton wool."[46]

Warning him to never return to Atchison, mob members tossed Butler's clothing in the buggy, took him to the edge of town, and left him with a few parting screeches and yells. Alone upon the prairie, Reverend Butler recalled, "I adjusted my attire about me, as best I could, and hastened to rejoin my wife and two little ones. . . . It was rather a sorrowful meeting after so long a parting, still we were very thankful . . . it had fared no worse with us all." Three months later Pardee Butler was sufficiently recovered to be in charge of transporting to Topeka a second group of muskets removed from the Iowa Arsenal. His unswerving courage earned Reverend Butler high regard among Free-State Kansans, and his ordeals were widely covered in the press. As for Robert S. Kelley, the bully ringleader and the *Squatter Sovereign* coeditor, within eleven months he and his partner, John Stringfellow, had sold their newspaper; his house had burned down in Doliphan; and he had left the county.[47]

4

"Do Come and Help Us. Come On through Iowa"

I

The growing dread among proslavery Missourians that northern arrivals might soon outnumber southern emigrants in the Kansas Territory reached a tipping point in the spring of 1856. Facing these doubts about the months ahead, the moment—for slavery's sake—seemed to call for greater force. Proslavery leaders grimly turned the screws tighter.

The arrival of southern help had buoyed their spirits. To the joy of the *Atchison Squatter Sovereign* and *Leavenworth Kansas Weekly Herald*, southern recruits began arriving in the Kansas Territory during 1856.[1] A *New York Tribune* correspondent in Tennessee wrote, "There is not a train of cars that passes between Nashville and Augusta, Georgia, that does not have quite a number of men outward bound for Kansas; and they are forming companies all through South Carolina, Georgia and Tennessee." The men were reportedly well armed and traveling without having to pay fares on the southern railroads.[2]

Proslavery's most celebrated arrival was the expedition estimated to number three hundred to four hundred men recruited and provisioned by Maj. Jefferson Buford and financed partly by his sale of several slaves. The forty-eight-year-old lawyer and plantation slave owner on Alabama's Chatahoochee River had earned the rank of major during the Creek Indian War of 1836 and now enlisted men from Alabama, South Carolina, and Georgia to help Kansas become a slave state. He offered recruits free transportation and a guaranteed one year of support. Buford's expedition arrived by steamboat on May 2, 1856. Dubbed "Buford's regiment" by the northern press, his command was decried as being not bona fide settlers but adventurers interested only in making Kansas a slave state and then returning home. The Iowa editor of the *Keokuk Daily Gate City* pointed to the two boatloads coming with "each man having a rifle, and a belt stuck with revolvers and knives. Arms were stacked about the decks, and sentinels were on duty, day and night, in military style." After the arrival of these southern reinforcements, Buford's men were quartered in Missouri at various places close to the territory. The men lived on the largesse of proslavery townsfolk supplemented by foraging in the surrounding countryside, but before long their welcome degenerated into public dislike of their presence. "Some of the men brought out by Buford are acting rascally," wrote a proslavery visitor from South Carolina to his sister. "They are robbing and plundering and don't always confine themselves to Abolitionists. They came for nothing else."[3]

Since March Free-State forebodings of bad times ahead were alive, fed by rumors of border men gathering military stores and organizing into companies to launch a spring assault. Proslavery adherents hoped for but thus far had failed to incite a clash that would prompt a U.S. military intervention against Free Staters. Their opportunity for such a collision came after the first week in May.

Chief Justice Samuel Lecompte of the U.S. District Court, a proslavery sympathizer, had formed a grand jury at Lecompton to ferret out those who were resisting the territorial legislature's proslavery legitimacy and charge them with high treason. On May 5, the grand jury issued its report recommending that the Free-State Lawrence newspapers, *Herald of Freedom* and *Kansas Free State*, be shut down and removed as nuisances, as well as the

Free State Hotel—charged with being built as a military stronghold to resist laws—and that some forty Lawrence men involved in organizing a separate Free-State government be indicted for high treason. Judge Lecompte issued the warrants on May 6, and via Territorial Governor Wilson Shannon's request, a few troops were assigned to aid the Douglas County sheriff and a U.S. marshal in executing the warrants.[4]

Enforcement actions were delayed, however, until an adequate posse of Missourians and Major Buford's forces could be placed around Lawrence, in fulfillment of U.S. Marshal I. B. Donaldson's orders in a "Proclamation to the People of Kansas Territory" issued on May 11. His proclamation called upon law-abiding citizens of the territory to gather at Lecompton "in numbers sufficient for the execution of the law," by which he meant the sheriff's posse and Atchison's Missourians. Copies of the proclamation went out to proslavery parts of the territory and to Missourians, but it did not go to anyone in Lawrence.

Among the men charged was the Lawrence Free-State leader, Charles Robinson, whom the Topeka Free-State convention had elected as the governor. When he refused to appear and orders went out compelling his obedience, Robinson and his wife escaped eastward. They were recognized at Lexington, Missouri, and removed from the steamboat. Within a week Robinson was extradited by Governor Shannon's request on indictment for treason, and afterward Robinson was imprisoned at Lecompton.

Responding to Marshal Donaldson's proclamation, numerous bands of proslavery men in mid-May were proceeding toward Lawrence. Approaching from the north was ex-senator David Atchison's Platte County Rifles with two artillery pieces, and arriving from Atchison were Benjamin Stringfellow, John Stringfellow, and John's partner, Robert Kelley of the *Squatter Sovereign* newspaper, accompanying armed bodies of Missourians from Westport, Liberty, and Independence. Reinforcing them were loosely organized collections of men such as the Leavenworth detachment, which was formed from assorted volunteer recruits organized for the occasion. Finally Major Buford's forces were encamped with others southeast of Lawrence. All told, by May 20 the total assembled force numbered between five hundred and eight hundred men. While waiting for action, armed men of the various bands stopped wagons, and the undisciplined among them robbed the travelers and rummaged through their boxes of goods in the wagons, taking what they thought to be worth seizing. Cattle and horses in the area gradually disappeared into their camps.[5]

Lawrence citizens appealed for protection first to Governor Shannon, who replied that the only legal force available was the posse of the U.S. marshal and the county sheriff seeking to enforce arrest warrants (the very force Lawrence wanted protection from), and then to U.S. Marshal Donaldson, who refused to provide assistance. With proslavery forces acting under government sanction, Lawrence leaders were intimidated by the weight of federal authority and decided against defensive measures. The town's Committee of Safety instead adopted a policy of nonresistance and sent word to various Free-State militias preparing to march to their rescue that they should return home.[6]

On the morning of May 21, Lawrence residents' eyes were fixed on the high point overlooking the town. There they saw arrayed along the crest two hundred horsemen. Behind them men on foot shortly appeared and planted both a red flag emblazoned with the words "Southern Rights" and beside it a U.S. flag. From there Marshal Donaldson's deputy U.S. marshal and ten men rode into town unarmed and arrested two men. After staying to eat dinner, they returned to the hill assemblage, where the deputy announced that Sheriff Samuel Jones would be entering town with some processes to serve. Jones, an intense partisan, entered town in mid-afternoon with ten armed men and demanded that the townsfolk hand over all arms or his group would shell Lawrence. Townsmen complied on the artillery side by bringing before them a twelve-pound brass howitzer and three small brass cannon. Concerning other arms, the sheriff accepted the residents' explanation that Sharps rifles were the private property of each man and the Safety Committee could not force the men to give up their guns. While this process was under way, proslavery forces descended from the hill with their cannon, and at the south end of town, David Atchison gave a boastful speech. Before its completion, Sheriff Jones returned and, to enthusiastic cheers, told the gathering that he carried with him U.S. District Court orders to tear down the Free State Hotel and demolish the two Free-State newspaper offices.[7]

The invading force formed a line, marched into town, and descended on the *Kansas Free State*'s printing office, breaking up the press and throwing it into the river while scattering other materials into the street. The Carolinians followed and attacked the *Herald of Freedom* with the same energy and results. Next they turned on the stone Free State Hotel. After several failed attempts to demolish the sturdy building with fifty rounds fired from their cannon, men set the hotel's interior on fire. Before long only a solitary wall remained standing as other walls collapsed to yells and cheers of the proslavery fighters. The men also entered various stores, ostensibly to ferret out arms, but they mainly plundered the establishments. Finally, before returning to their surrounding encampments, some set fire to the house of Free-State leader Governor Charles Robinson.[8]

Though flush with success after their sacking of Lawrence on May 21, proslavery men soon were aware of their provoking more backlash than fear through the North.[9] Magnifying these emotions nationally was news that Senator Charles Sumner's May 19 "Crime against Kansas" speech had prompted South Carolina congressman Preston Brooks to beat him senseless with a cane in the Senate chamber. Iowa's Democratic senator George Jones regretted Brooks had not "killed the d——d scoundrel."[10]

One man had his own answer to the dangerous Free-State situation. John Brown, who had joined his Ohio sons in settling the territory in 1855, saw angrily that the Free-State settlers endured much without retaliating. For Brown, the time for patience in the face of wrongs inflicted was over; a resort to violence was necessary.

Three days after the destruction in Lawrence, several men under the resolute John Brown retaliated. They descended on proslavery homes in the Pottawatomie Creek vicinity of Franklin County and massacred five proslavery men with broadswords. Twelve days later on June 2, a band of Brown's men combined with that of Samuel T. Shore (for twenty-nine men total) attacked a proslavery company led by Henry C. Pate that was hunting for Brown. A five-hour fight ensued at Black Jack on the Santa Fe Trail (today about three miles east of Baldwin City in Douglas County). The clash then swung in Brown's direction, and the force captured Pate and twenty-two of his men. This first armed skirmish between proslavery and antislavery forces, in addition to Brown's executions at Pottawattamie Creek, set off panic in proslavery communities while giving a sense of relief and payback to beleaguered Free-State residents.[11]

II

All the same, Free-State forces were in desperate straits after the sacking of Lawrence. "At that time," recalled one militia leader, "the prospects for the free state party looked worse than ever before or since. Our leaders were either prisoners in the hands of the United States troops, or were away, back East, looking for aid and succor there. Our forces did not amount, all together, to more than 400."[12]

Northern calls for militant action came from a great mass meeting at the courthouse square in Chicago and other meetings elsewhere. "For the first time in the history of the nation," wrote an incensed editor upon learning the fate of Lawrence, "the Federal authority [is] allying itself with lawless marauders to make war upon a community of quiet and defenseless people."[13] Emi-

FREEMEN ATTEND

CIVIL WAR IN KANSAS!

LAWRENCE IN ASHES!

By late reliable accounts from KANSAS, we learn that the FREE STATE MEN have been attacked by

BORDER RUFFIANS!

from Missouri, under Gen. WHITFIELD, and that Gov. SHANNON supplied the invaders with U. S. Muskets and Ammunition, with which unarmed men have been shot down in the streets of Lawrence, and innocent women and children driven from the town; their husbands and parents murdered and their houses destroyed. The U. S. Troops not permitted by the authorities to interfere.

While these outrageous tragedies are being perpetrated in Kansas, by authority of the U. S., a UNITED STATES SENATOR is brutally attacked and beaten till almost dead by a

Slave Bully of South Carolina,

in the United States Senate. Such outrages unparalleled in the history of our Government, call upon all who love their country better than the chains of bondage, to speak in tones of thunder, that shall cause the SLAVE OLIGARCHY to tremble. The North should arouse! The cause is ours! Shall the bloody tyrant " subdue us?"

THE CRY IS FOR BLOOD!

In view of this and state of affairs, there will be a Meeting of the Citizens of Iowa City, at the

STATE HOUSE, ON SATURDAY, MAY 31, 1856,

At half past Seven o'clock, P. M.

COME ONE! COME ALL!!

S. N. WOOD, Esq., whom Sheriff Jones failed to arrest at the time he was shot, has just arrived from Kansas, and will address the meeting.

SEATS RESERVED FOR LADIES.

Presented by J. S. Templin

March 31, 1856

Iowa City Republican Print.

MANY CITIZENS.

Fig. 4. In the wake of proslavery actions against the Free-State town of Lawrence in the Kansas Territory, numerous rallies occurred about Iowa and elsewhere. State Historical Society of Iowa, Iowa City.

grant aid organizations responded, answering Kansans' cries for hard-to-come-by supplies after scattered proslavery groups had interrupted deliveries on the Missouri River. They also began pressing to organize well-armed parties of settlers to cross Iowa. As one Kansas editor wrote, Free-State travel for the Kansas Territory would now have "fewer women and children, less house luggage, fewer agricultural implements; [and] more men, more arms, more ammunition."[14]

Aware of the northern reaction, Missouri proslavery leaders decided upon yet tougher measures as the only way to protect their gains in Kansas. They also had to act quickly in this presidential election year. If they waited to slow Free-State migration forcibly, proslavery men knew that the cautious national Democratic administration and its territorial officials would shrink from any more border ruffian behavior.

In February John Stringfellow's *Squatter Sovereign* paper had urged stronger action and specifically proposed that Lexington, Missouri, impose a quarantine "where all steamboats may be searched and the infectious political paupers be prevented from tainting the air of Kansas Territory with their presence."[15] In May and June the Missouri river towns were now ready to do it, pushed by proslavery leaders to act.

Abandoning occasional harassment of northern travelers, bands of armed proslavery men in early June began systematically to patrol landings and ferries of western Missouri towns, especially at Waverly, Lexington, Liberty, Parkville, and Weston, as well as Leavenworth in Kansas Territory. Lexington had cannon positioned onshore to stop fragile steamboats from making a run past the landing and to scare Free-State passengers into misgivings about entering the territory. Armed men boarded every upriver-bound boat—except ones carrying southern emigrants—and questioned passengers. What, they asked, was their destination and view of slavery? Did they show earmarks of antislavery settlers or New Englanders—a Yankee accent and a Sharps rifle or

Fig. 5. To offset their initial disadvantage in number of settlers, Free-State men turned to faster-firing superior rifles from the Sharps's Rifle Manufacturing Company of Hartford, Connecticut. These single-shot, percussion breech-loading rifles used a paper cartridge. Kansas State Historical Society.

a copy of the *New York Tribune* in hand? If so, proslavery militia detained them, confiscated their guns and sidearms, and took into custody anyone whose arms equaled or exceeded their baggage.

A priority was finding and seizing deliveries of the dreaded and coveted Sharps rifles. With a breech-loading Sharps, a man could load and fire several times before the poorly armed Missourians could load and use their muzzle-loaded muskets and shotguns. Free-State men fully used the Sharps rifle's famed long-distance accuracy to intimidate their opponents.[16] Proslavery leaders had known since the previous summer that Free-State forces were receiving such arms shipments through Kansas aid groups. Men at the river town landings kept an eye out for likely looking cargo. One news story told of a patrol group that boarded a steamer and spotted a long box. After the men unloaded it onto the levee and pried open the lid, they were chagrined to find it contained a rosewood piano destined for a woman at the territorial settlement of Osawatomie. What they missed on the boat was another box containing a cannon that one member of their group, actually a Free-State sympathizer, had opened and quickly closed with the comment that it simply contained cart wheels.[17]

The first arms shipment requested by a Free-State official had occurred after the "bogus" proslavery territorial legislature gained control in the spring of 1855. Feeling vulnerable, alarmed leaders in Lawrence took defensive steps within three days of the election. Charles Robinson, the principal Kansan agent of the Emigrant Aid Company, wrote its purchasing agent in Massachusetts, stating, "Our people have now formed themselves into four military companies . . . and we want *arms*." He asked the agent if he could please "send us 200 Sharps rifles as a loan until this question is settled? Also a couple of field pieces?" Six weeks later came the first installment, a hundred Sharps rifles disguised on the shipper's bill of lading as five boxes of books.[18]

Word of the shipment quickly spread. Proslavery spokesmen condemned its arrival as an attempt to scare restraint into western men and as an act of blatant resistance to the laws of the territory. Another installment of 117 Sharps rifles, "packed in casks, like hardware," arrived soon thereafter for use, if needed, against Missourians attempting to obstruct a planned Free-State October election of delegates to their Topeka Constitutional Convention.[19]

Not all shipments from Sharps, however, made it past the border ruffians' watchful eyes. David Starr Hoyt of Deerfield, Massachusetts, was on board the *Arabia*, a 171-foot side-wheeler, when it landed at St. Louis. In the mid-March chill of 1856 he oversaw the loading of thirteen unidentified crates from the Emigrant Aid Company. These crates contained two breech-loading cannons along with a hundred Sharps rifles. Despite the qualms of some about the danger of being discovered, Hoyt decided to risk the journey. As the steamboat made its way up the Missouri River, he took a moment to pen a letter to his mother. Hoyt told her that the trip was going well, after having left St. Louis successfully with the guns safe in the hold.[20]

Somehow the *Arabia*'s captain happened to open the letter, and while standing on deck before the passengers, who included proslavery partisans, he read it aloud. A gathering mob voted to throw Hoyt and his companion overboard. Hearing they were on their way, Hoyt quickly tossed overboard receipts and letters that incriminated others.[21]

The mob took Hoyt and his companion out on deck, where another passenger intervened and persuaded them to hold the two men until they arrived at Lexington. Though mob leaders threatened Hoyt with death unless he signed over possession of the weapons to them, he refused.

Members of the crowd then forced the issue; they entered the steamboat's hold and began carrying up the weapons. When they noticed that the breechblock to each of Sharps rifles had been removed, rendering the breech-loaders unusable, they demanded that Hoyt turn them over. He replied they were not on board but at Lawrence (while in St. Louis Hoyt had removed them, and others carried them overland by stage).[22]

Once moored at the landing in Lexington, a huge armed crowd gathered onshore, shouting for Hoyt to surrender possession of the arms. Again he refused. The mob leaders then seized the weapons and handed Hoyt a receipt: "Taken from D. S. Hoyt the following described property, to be delivered to the order of Wilson Shannon, governor of Kansas Territory, or his successor in office."[23]

Proslavery groups surveilling the Missouri River and trying to interfere with overland travel through Missouri increasingly turned to brigandage. Unorganized partisan bands, encouraged by political leaders, turned back northerners and supported themselves by plundering and shaking down passengers. It drew plenty of emigrants' complaints.

Two dramatic incidents by such proslavery bands spurred Kansas migration northward. They stopped the steamboats *Star of the West* and the *Sultan* in late June, with the results highly publicized. These events in one dramatic moment decided northern opinion that decisive actions had to be taken.

Fired by antislavery indignation, two emigrant aid groups had started for the Kansas Territory from Worcester, Massachusetts, in June. They reached Buffalo, New York, and continued via Great Lakes' steamers to Chicago. Thomas Wentworth Higginson, a radical antislavery minister in Worcester and a leading local agent of the Kansas Aid Committee who also penned articles for the *New York Tribune*, attended the send-off for the two armed Massachusetts parties. One group led by Dr. Calvin Cutter departed on June 17, and the second left on June 25 under Martin Stowell, who in 1854 had helped Higginson in the unsuccessful rescue of jailed Anthony Burns, who had escaped from a Virginia plantation and made his way north to Boston. The Kansas Aid Committee had advised both parties to go by way of Iowa.

Upon reading telegraphic news on June 27 that a party had been stopped and disarmed at Lexington on the Missouri River, a chagrined Higginson, fearing Cutter had decided instead to take the river route, immediately left for Chicago. Once there he learned it was not Cutter's party but one from Chicago. The group had gone upriver on the *Star of the West* from St. Louis only to be boarded, to have its goods ransacked for arms, and to be turned back downriver. News soon followed that Cutter's group traveling on the *Sultan* had suffered the same fate.[24]

Higginson headed for Alton, Illinois, to interview the disarmed Chicago group upon their return downriver.[25] He learned from the members that the steamer's captain had worked hand in glove with the proslavery men. Fifteen miles downriver from the next town the captain had set ashore a proslavery passenger, who dashed for Lexington on a fast horse. The exhausted horse died on arrival, but the man got word in time to roust a crowd, which waited for the boat onshore.[26] After docking at the wharf the travelers faced a large mob and leading men of the town who demanded the emigrants' rifles. They were boarded again at Leavenworth by proslavery leaders Senator Atchison, Benjamin Stringfellow, and others who pawed through their trunks and carpetbags, gathering up a bushel basket of revolvers and knives, and ordered them to return to Illinois or else be "responsible for useless bloodshed." Higginson forwarded a story on these "late outrages on the Missouri" to the *New York Tribune* as he awaited news of the Cutter party's fate.[27]

Meanwhile, the Chicago men told Higginson of how their steamer had met up with the *Sultan* on their way back downriver and that the two boats came together briefly for hurried warnings to be exchanged with Cutter's party of what lay ahead. When Cutter had three men shift steamers to make arrangements for his group to transfer from the *Sultan* to the *Star of the West*, armed proslavery men on board intervened, refusing to allow the *Sultan*'s armed Yankees to come aboard. The boats immediately separated, leaving Cutter's three men stranded and forced to return with the Chicago group to Alton.

While Higginson awaited more word of the *Sultan*'s fate, the second Worcester party under Martin Stowell arrived. Its members vowed their willingness to go upriver for Cutter, but Higginson said no. One and a half days later Cutter's company arrived in St. Louis. Higginson met them and chartered a steamboat to forward them all to Davenport via Keokuk, Iowa.

He also sent out another newspaper story about the emigrant party's treatment at the hands of the proslavery bands at Waverly, Liberty, Independence, Parkville, and Weston. Accompanying his piece was a lengthy article by Mrs. Eunice P. Cutter. She detailed insults received from "vile and motley militias" at the wharves that picked quarrels as a pretext for personal attacks and included "all classes in Western Missouri and the South" while their community leaders stood by and smiled their official approval.[28]

Higginson's dispatches told of the threats made upon gentlemen and ladies and of the courage shown by these victims of the proslavery militia. He praised Dr. Cutter, for example, for his "energy and courage" combined with "caution, prudence, coolness and discretion" and for bringing "back all his men safe, all his provisions, all his ammunition, some side arms, *and more good rifles than the Missourians have got from him*" [italics his]. Their other rifles they either "sunk in the river, or dismantled before they were surrendered."[29]

Proslavery editors John Stringfellow and Robert Kelley described the events far differently. In their *Squatter Sovereign* they wrote that the Chicago emigrants on the *Star of the West* were cowardly. "Like whipped dogs they sneaked up to Clarkson, and laid down their weapons to him." This earlier boastful "party of seventy-eight, all of them 'armed to the teeth,' surrendered to a company of twenty 'border ruffians.'" Subdued and shamed, the party has returned downriver, and "if this is the material we have to encounter in Kansas, we have but little to fear of the result."[30]

Joining them was the Leavenworth editor of the *Kansas Weekly Herald* (also known as *Leavenworth Herald*) who labeled those from Chicago a "piratical crew" that came to the area "to shriek for freedom, and would destroy the character of our institutions. Conservative men everywhere frown upon this movement of the Northern Aid Societies, and it should curse and politically damn every man in this Territory connected with the movement."[31]

As for the *Sultan*'s party under Cutter, Stringfellow and Kelley despised them as "cowardly Yankees, shipped out here from Massachusetts," and thought they "should meet a traitor's death." Indeed, Stringfellow and Kelley wrote, "we are of the opinion, if the citizens of Leavenworth City or Weston would *hang* one or two boat loads of Abolitionists it would do more toward establishing peace in Kansas than all the speeches that have been delivered in Congress during the present session. *Let the experiment be tried*." [italics his][32]

Ultimately it was the widely circulated and high-profile accounts by Higginson, with his tones of disgust about northern inaction, and Mrs. Cutter's stirring portrayal of what their party had endured that won the propaganda victory. Their skillful retelling of the experience reframed the thinking of leading northern emigrants, finally convincing them the Iowa overland route was the only feasible way to reach Kansas. On this score, Higginson's impatience with the lateness of this decision overflowed. "The South acts while we are talking," he grumbled. "Three weeks ago, $10,000, in the hands of the Chicago Committee, would have opened the Iowa route to Kansas. Five times that sum was, even then, subscribed in New England; but it was not *used* then—it is not used now. What is the consequence? The South sent hundreds, perhaps thousands, of fresh men into Kansas between the sacking of Lawrence and the eventful 4th of July. The North, so far as I can learn, *did not send a single party*. I have said enough."

Higginson sensed that changing the route would achieve something else as well; it would increase pressure by St. Louis and eastern Missouri commercial firms serving western upriver towns to reopen the river, for "the trade is all paralyzed." Only one steamboat was running daily from Alton to St. Louis whereas three had run the year before, and boats that carried the once "prosperous emigration up the Missouri River" no longer "pay their way, and are being laid up until peace returns."[33]

III

The Chicago caravan and those of Worcester's Cutter and Stowell companies headed for Iowa in early July to join others gathering to take the Iowa route, which was also called the northern route and the overland route and in years later would be commemoratively called the Lane Trail. The *Keokuk Daily Gate City* editor reported that the Chicago company "passed up by here on the 4th, on the way to Davenport," and that Captain Cutter's company stopped there on the afternoon next day and "will join the Chicago company at Davenport" for crossing over Iowa.[34]

On July 4, the Kansas Central Committee of Iowa officially announced to "The Friends of Free Kansas" a road being established across Iowa. The notice described the route as beginning at Iowa City, the westernmost limit of the railroad; proceeding through Sigourney, Oskaloosa, Knoxville, Indianola, and Quincy; and arriving in Sidney in Fremont County on the Missouri River. Furthermore the Western Stage Company agreed to add coaches for travelers on the route.[35]

Six days later came the road's endorsement at a meeting of Kansas aid organizations in Buffalo, New York, for they called it a better option than forcing open the Missourians' river blockade. To coordinate the aid for settlers, they created the National Kansas Committee, with headquarters in Chicago. During its six months of life it would distribute a large amount of provisions, arms, and money. At the top of its current to-do list was determining how to move emigrants across the overland trail through Iowa.

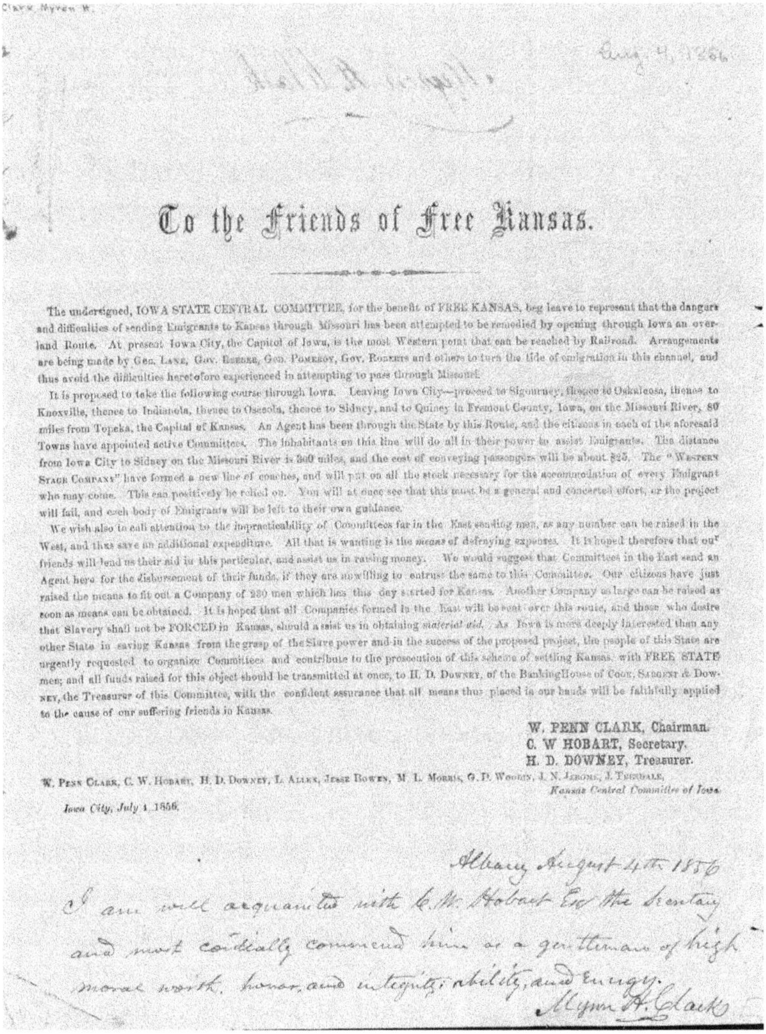

To the Friends of Free Kansas.

The undersigned, IOWA STATE CENTRAL COMMITTEE, for the benefit of FREE KANSAS, beg leave to represent that the dangers and difficulties of sending Emigrants to Kansas through Missouri has been attempted to be remedied by opening through Iowa an overland Route. At present Iowa City, the Capital of Iowa, is the most Western point that can be reached by Railroad. Arrangements are being made by Gen. Lane, Gov. Robinson, Gov. Pomeroy, Gov. Reeder and others to turn the tide of emigration in this channel, and thus avoid the difficulties heretofore experienced in attempting to pass through Missouri.

It is proposed to take the following course through Iowa. Leaving Iowa City—proceed to Sigourney, thence to Oskaloosa, thence to Knoxville, thence to Indianola, thence to Osceola, thence to Sidney, and to Quincy in Fremont County, Iowa, on the Missouri River, 80 miles from Topeka, the Capital of Kansas. An Agent has been through the State by this Route, and the citizens in each of the aforesaid Towns have appointed active Committees. The inhabitants on this line will do all in their power to assist Emigrants. The distance from Iowa City to Sidney on the Missouri River is 300 miles, and the cost of conveying passengers will be about $25. The "Western Stage Company" have formed a new line of coaches, and will put on all the stock necessary for the accommodation of every Emigrant who may come. This can positively be relied on. You will at once see that this must be a general and concerted effort, or the project will fail, and each body of Emigrants will be left to their own guidance.

We wish also to call attention to the impracticability of Committees far in the East sending men, as any number can be raised in the West, and thus save an additional expenditure. All that is wanting is the means of defraying expenses. It is hoped therefore that our friends will lend us their aid in this particular, and assist us in raising money. We would suggest that Committees in the East send an Agent here for the disbursement of their funds, if they are unwilling to entrust the same to this Committee. Our citizens have just raised the means to fit out a Company of 200 men which has this day started for Kansas. Another Company as large can be raised as soon as means can be obtained. It is hoped that all Companies formed in the East will be sent over this route, and those who desire that Slavery shall not be FORCED in Kansas, should assist us in obtaining material aid. As Iowa is more deeply interested than any other State in saving Kansas from the grasp of the Slave power and in the success of the proposed project, the people of this State are urgently requested to organize Committees and contribute to the prosecution of this scheme of settling Kansas, with FREE STATE men; and all funds raised for this object should be transmitted at once, to H. D. Downey, of the Banking House of Cook, Sargent & Downey, the Treasurer of this Committee, with the confident assurance that all means thus placed in our hands will be faithfully applied to the cause of our suffering friends in Kansas.

W. PENN CLARK, Chairman.
C. W HOBART, Secretary.
H. D. DOWNEY, Treasurer.

W. Penn Clark, C. W. Hobart, H. D. Downey, L. Allen, Jesse Bowen, M. L. Morris, G. P. Woods, J. N. Lemons, J. Trumale,
Kansas Central Committee of Iowa.

Iowa City, July 1, 1856.

Albany August 4th 1856

I am well acquainted with C. W. Hobart Esq the Secretary and most cordially commend him as a gentleman of high moral worth, honor, and integrity, ability, and energy.

Myron W. Clark

Fig. 6. To establish overland access to Kansas through largely unsettled Iowa, the Kansas Central Committee of Iowa laid out a route across the state that began at the westernmost railhead of Iowa City. Kansas State Historical Society.

Transportation planning moved quickly although route managers would make two changes. First, the Iowa Committee changed the Missouri River destination of Iowa's route from Sidney to Tabor in Fremont County after route planners discovered that the divided sympathies of Sidney residents made Tabor—the strongly antislavery community eleven miles north—a far friendlier place to seek rest and provisions. Second, by September 1856 the Burlington Railroad's arrival in Mount Pleasant (fifty miles south of Iowa City) would offer a closer and more direct option for overland travelers. From these two railheads the overland roads converged in western Iowa at Quincy (Adams County), and from there the trails continued to either Sidney or Council Bluffs.

But in July caravans were only congregating about Iowa City, with some ready and others still being organized. Shalor W. Eldridge, the national committee's route agent for Kansas emigration, soon arrived. Six weeks earlier during the "sacking" of Lawrence, he had watched helplessly as a proslavery posse set upon and destroyed his Free State Hotel, which in early 1856 he had leased and equipped for patrons' use. Now, having been delegated authority to bring about the successful movement of immigrant trains across Iowa to Kansas, Eldridge bought a horse and rode out to the first outer encampment three miles away. He came upon the Chicago company that had been turned back on the *Star of the West*, stripped of its arms and equipage, and with the passengers deposited onshore five miles from Alton, Illinois, by a fearful steamboat captain. Replacements for those disheartened passengers who had returned to Chicago had since reinforced the group, but jealousies among the leadership had demoralized the party of seventy-five emigrants. Eldridge presented his credentials, which authorized him to take charge of the various elements, and they accepted.

Provisions, such as tents, baggage, teams, and wagons, for the Kansas-bound groups were not easy to come by, however. Five Mormon handcart companies also were encamped on the western edge of town, and they competed for available supplies to make their sixteen-week trek to Salt Lake City before cold weather set in.

Once outfitted, approximately twelve Kansas companies totaling about five hundred emigrants set out one by one across the Iowa prairie.[36] The Stowell train carried something else as well, fifteen hundred muskets that Governor James Grimes secretly "gave" them after leaving his key to the state arsenal conveniently on his desk. Clearly, Governor Grimes's clandestine support for the Free-State cause went beyond oratory and letters.[37]

The time required to cross Iowa depended on the size of the company and on whether it was driven by horse teams, by oxen, or by stage. Eldridge's Chicago company, with good teams of horses, wagons, and gear, left Iowa City on July 4 and eight days out caught up with Dr. Cutter's Worcester, Massachusetts, company (which had also been sent back downriver on the *Sultan*). The well-supplied Cutter party had wagons drawn by ox teams. The two joined together under Eldridge and moved forward at the oxen's pace, making fewer miles a day.

Passing an Indiana party of fifty men, gradually, they also came together with a Milwaukee, Wisconsin, unit headed by brothers Edmund G. Ross and W. W. Ross. The substantial group included a two-horse surrey, followed by six covered wagons hauled by twenty-four oxen, and a smaller horse-drawn wagon.[38] Earlier the Ross caravan had faced a mixed welcome upon crossing the Mississippi River to Democratic-dominated Dubuque, Iowa. The Dubuque City Council had passed a resolution against the emigrant group, stating the council "most heartily condemned the banditti of armed men in their nefarious enterprise." Terming them "marauders," the council also urged that citizens avoid giving fellowship to such "rebels" and "traitors." A Davenport editor immediately castigated this resolution as "insulting interference" in the rights of people to immigrate to Kansas with their own political sentiments. But more than offsetting the council's action, others in town treated the entire caravan group to a supper at the Julien House with "toasts pronounced, speeches made, etc."[39]

Even for those riding across the state by stagecoach, without having to hitch up and drive teams or walk alongside the slow emigrant wagons, the trip was not easy. Samuel Gridley Howe—a prominent physician, a social reformer, and, like Shalor Eldridge, a leading member of the National Kansas Committee—had little good to say about the journey. It meant being "on horseback or in a cart, [and] sleeping in said cart or in worse lodgings, among dirty men on the floor of dirty huts." Similarly, Franklin B. Sanborn, a Massachusetts abolitionist inspecting the land route the next month, remembered "rumbling over the prairie roads in old and filthy stage-coaches, and catching naps by the way. Sometimes we would tarry for what was left of the night at new and filthy taverns, where the beds were shocking, and the food uneatable except for prairie chicken and wild plums, which could be cooked simply."[40]

A traveler with a Worcester, Massachusetts, company was highly impressed by "the broad and fertile prairies," the "luxuriant grass, high as a man's head," and "countless wild flowers." But he confessed that it was tough traveling the hundreds of miles across Iowa's expanse on foot in the July heat. And the food available was hardly what some were accustomed to eating. Their "rude fare" principally amounted to various "preparations of Indian meal 'corn bread.'"[41]

The best glimpse of a tedious stagecoach journey across Iowa came from Thomas Wentworth Higginson, the Worcester organizer of emigrant companies whom the Kansas Aid Committee also sent out to supply and arm the settlers. Lamenting the inaccurate stage route schedules, he concluded that

as each driver goes but ten or fifteen miles, and knows nothing beyond his own route, and as the agent at each end hardly knows *that*, it is impossible to state at any given moment what will be done. When the stage ought to go, it stops, and when it should stop, it goes.

At present no person, without actually traveling across Iowa, can appreciate the injury done by the closing of the Missouri River. Emigrants must toil, week after week, beneath a burning sun, over the parched and endless "rolling prairie," sometimes seeing no house for a day or two together, camping often without wood, and sometimes without water, and obliged to carry with them every eatable they use. It is no wonder that they often fall sick on the way; and when I consider how infinitely weary were even my four days and nights of staging, (after as many more of railroad travel,) I can only wonder at the patience and fortitude which the present emigrants have shown.[42]

IV

Despite the difficulties, the companies found people friendly and generous in the towns through which they passed. One exception occurred at a stopover in Osceola, midway across Iowa, where they encountered proslavery criticism. Arrangements had been made for Eunice Cutter to speak at a local meeting on issues of the time from a woman's standpoint. Hearing of the meeting a local blacksmith threatened to keep this New England lecturer from being heard. Learning of the blacksmith's plan, Shalor Eldridge made sure he stood next to him, and as the blacksmith rose to interrupt and cause a riot, Eldridge grabbed him. Others immediately forced him with fists to listen humbly and respectfully.[43]

After crossing Iowa's three hundred miles of prairie, creeks, rivers, and sloughs, the weary travelers needed rest and provisions before tackling the risks of Nebraska and Kansas. The small town of Tabor in Fremont County gave them a place to do just that.

Eldridge, the coordinator for Kansas emigrating bodies, saw "the choice of Tabor as a final point of rendezvous" as "especially fitting, being sufficiently near the crossing of the Missouri and distant from threatened border raids." Also, with Tabor being strongly antislavery and in full sympathy with the northern effort, it soon became the westernmost point in Iowa for Kansas-bound groups to rest and outfit themselves for the remaining trek ahead.[44]

Settled four years previously, Tabor had been founded by George B. Gaston after leading a Congregationalist group from the vicinity of Oberlin, Ohio. Having initially spent a year at Civil Bend on the Iowa side of the Missouri River, the group settled farther north in Fremont County on the uplands beyond the Missouri valley bluffs. George Gaston was the moving spirit behind town developments and, once an enterprise began, got things done.[45]

At Tabor in mid-1855, L. E. Webb stepped off a stagecoach in front of a simple new hotel. Webb recalled it had a dining room with a small post office tucked in one corner, where a couple of shelves held mail. Walking about the town in this vast western untamed prairie expanse, he saw it amounted to a dozen houses—mostly built of logs and a few of sod—and a schoolhouse. To buy something at a store, however, he had to travel several miles to Sidney or Glenwood.[46] Within a year, Tabor town activity and growth mushroomed with the arriving Kansas-bound companies.

Soon encampments spread out across the open prairie about Tabor. Tents dotted the town vicinity, on down the valley toward the mill, and near close-at-hand timber while a multitude of teams and accompanying livestock fed on nearby grasslands. It was exciting for townsmen to see their isolated antislavery haven now filled with people like themselves, sympathetic with the Free-State movement.

George Gaston's house served as unofficial headquarters for discussions. Mrs. Gaston recalled this exciting time of their lives, with houses "much overfilled and our comforts shared with those passing to and from Kansas." Moreover, "when houses would hold no more, woodsheds were temporized for bedrooms, where the sick and dying were cared for. Barns also were fixed for sleeping rooms. Every place where a bed could be put or a blanket thrown

Fig. 7. The Gastons' house. Tabor (Iowa) Historical Society.

down was at once so occupied. There were comers and goers all times of day or night, meals at all hours—many free hotels, perhaps entertaining angels unawares."[47]

Emigrants did not forget Tabor's generosity. "For the sympathy and ready helpfulness of its people in supplying the needs of the forces marching to the relief of the besieged free-state men," wrote Shalor Eldridge as the official coordinator of these emigrant bodies, "Kansas will ever owe Tabor a debt of gratitude." Undeniably, he continued, "we were most hospitably treated by the people of Tabor, who seemed never to tire of showing us sympathy and kindness."[48]

His thoughts were not alone. Thomas Wentworth Higginson, in one of his tour dispatches to the *New York Tribune*, wrote of the village's steadfast support in the face of Missouri threats: "The citizens of Tabor are entitled to everlasting gratitude for their unwearied kindness to our emigrants. The sick have been cared for, clothing has been made, and every house, stable, and melon-patch, has been common property. Let the Eastern States hold this thriving little village in grateful remembrance."[49]

Once rested and ready, emigrant trains slowly moved across the grasslands from Tabor to a ferry crossing at Nebraska City during the summer and fall of 1856. The Massachusetts column led by Martin Stowell was the first group to make the attempt, and it met resistance at the landing on the Iowa side of the Missouri River in July. Stephen F. Nuckolls—a Virginian, a slave owner, and the founder and leading developer of Nebraska City—owned the ferry and refused his operator to allow Free-State settlers passage.

A small group of three mounted men then rode down to the ferry and called for the ferry to let them cross. Once the boat arrived, the men refused to give it up until all sixty-five settlers with their three wagons could be ferried over. Nuckolls yielded in the face of their persistence, forceful words, and the generous ferriage paid, although he threatened to deny the Nebraska City ferry to other emigrants.[50]

The leading element of Kansas-bound emigrants—that is, the Eldridge and Pomeroy body (Samuel Pomeroy had joined Eldridge in Nebraska City)—comprised "fifty-three wagons, with teams of oxen or horses, some twenty-five horsemen, and over five hundred other persons on foot."[51] One member in the Stowell group wrote of the scene in his journal: "Walking across the prairies, the appearance of our train was remarkable. Extending from one end to the other, the distance was probably not less than three-quarters of a mile. If a person could have stood on some hilltop in the distance and watched our passage, he would have supposed us to have been at least a thousand strong. What a mighty movement did this seem to me, when viewing our route and calling to mind the primary cause of our being here!"[52]

Under General Superintendent Milton C. Dickey, the James A. Harvey, Calvin Cutter, and Henry J. Shombre companies began arriving in Topeka on August 13, but a few other companies (including Stowell's) had dropped off along the way to establish town sites. Trains coming up behind were scattered along a fifty-mile corridor stretching back to Iowa.

They traveled on a route marked during July by a Topeka committee of five under Dr. J. P. Root, chairman of the Kansas Free-State Central Committee, and A. A. Jameson. The team's designated route went up the Kansas valley and on to the border of Iowa by way of Nebraska City. On unbroken prairie away from old roads that were watched by proslavery patrols, the men installed poles in tall grass stretches, built stone stacks on ridgetops and on crests of short grass hills, graded means for wagon access at stream-crossing points, and blazed trees through widened timber trails. As the caravans moved along this route, portions of wagon parties split off to set up new villages: Plymouth, Lexington, Holton, Columbia, and others. In so doing the anticipated swelling tide of Free Staters would have the comfort of knowing safe settlements were nearby if marauding bands posed a danger to travelers crossing the broad, empty grasslands of Kansas.[53]

On August 13 the first wagon train in the caravans coming across Nebraska from Iowa arrived in Topeka. The local editor noted, "The organization and process of this train through the country has for a long time been a matter of considerable interest to the people of Kansas, as well as of the States. And with each successive train," he rosily foresaw, "the speedy pacification of our difficulties" in which "the last foothold of slavery in this land once consecrated to freedom, shall be rooted out."[54]

5

Ho! For Kansas

I

One man especially came to signify the northern land route, both in publicity surrounding its creation and in proslavery portrayals of it as an invasion. The Free-State answer to the Missouri River blockade came in a man of western spirit and with a compelling personality, James Henry Lane.

He traveled to Kansas in mid-1855 and became its most respected and admired yet hated leader in territorial and early statehood politics. Lane's appeal to beleaguered Free-State forces, wrote Rev. Pardee Butler, was that he "alone had military experience, and he alone had the daring, the genius and the personal magnetism of a real leader."[1]

Lane was a southern Democrat in Indiana, where, after training in law, he organized and as a colonel ably led an Indiana regiment of volunteers in the Mexican-American War and then entered politics. He served as Indiana's lieutenant governor, and while serving a term as a Democratic congressman in 1854, he voted for the Kansas-Nebraska Act. Forty-one years old upon arriving in Kansas, Lane—ever the opportunist—initially tried building the Democratic Party through which his political advancement might follow. Stories spread of his willingness to accept slavery if Kansas had good hemp-growing possibilities, and at a speech in Westport, Missouri, Lane had evidently stated that "he would as soon buy a negro as a mule."[2]

Lane's party-organizing efforts and promotions of President Franklin Pierce and Senator Stephen Douglas came to nothing, however. David Atchison and proslavery Democratic friends mistrusted them all. Besides, they already knew the proslavery direction they wanted to take and viewed Lane's national Democratic Party as soft on slavery. "Every National Democrat is an abolitionist in disguise," declared Benjamin Stringfellow, for "such a one might not steal a nigger himself, but would pat on the back those who do."[3] After all, they concluded, why embrace Lane when their own brand of proslavery men had already won control of the bogus territorial legislature and enacted strong slavery protections.

Lane could see that these angry proslavery radicals were driving many Democrats toward the Free-State position. At certain conferences and mass meetings and before an August 14 political convention in Lawrence, Lane voiced moderation and support for a Free-State Party so long as it excluded blacks and black settlement in Kansas. By fall he threw himself into Topeka's Free-State movement, which amounted to an insurrection against what the members called the bogus proslavery government.[4]

Proslavery forces feared his shrewd, daring, and persuasive abilities while the Free-State Kansas leadership among New Englanders loathed him. In their eyes Lane bore the odium of having voted for the Kansas-Nebraska Act and amounted to nothing but an opportunistic chameleon and "black-law" Democrat who favored laws to keep Negroes from settling in Kansas. But Lane's strenuous, intense, and impulsive nature, combined with his military background, attracted western men among Free-State elements while his rival, Dr. Charles Robinson—cool, argumentative, cautious, clearheaded, calculating, and wily—spoke for the antislavery New England contingent.[5]

Making full use of his "peculiar, flashing, and exciting oratory," Lane was unrivaled in his mesmerizing ability to sway "these men of the prairies." An 1857 observer wrote that Lane defied "every recognized rule of rhetoric and oratory, at will he made men roar with laughter, or melt into tears, or clench their teeth in passion."[6] "He was at his best," wrote another, "when he stood before a frontier audience with a cause to proclaim or an opponent to denounce." Six feet tall and with a lean, wiry build, he wore his restless energy and personal magnetism in shabby attire. "His usual habiliment comprised an old straw hat, cowhide boots, calfskin vest, woolen shirt, grey or butternut brown . . . and a bearskin overcoat." And "whether in pursuit of border ruffians or public office his attire was the same. His beard was variegated but not luxurious; his hair, like his beard, was usually unkempt. If he wished to disguise himself he had only to acquire a shave and a haircut, and don a regular uniform or a respectable suit, and few recognized him."[7]

Thomas Wentworth Higginson witnessed Lane's captivating character at Nebraska City. After making his way across Iowa, the antislavery organizer rested during one mid-September evening, grumbling about his filthy hotel conditions. Suddenly Higginson saw that "Lane's rough riders, forty in number, booted blanketed spurred & full armed came dashing in—Lane among them—one of the men of the age, spare, gaunt, . . . with a hard fine enamel of the Napoleon air the old Demagogue; living a life of breathlessness, eagerness & plenty of scamp Jupiterism."[8]

Higginson walked over to the schoolhouse to hear Lane's address and came away amazed at his flamboyant gifts. He noted, "Never did I hear such a speech; every sentence like a pistol bullet; such delicacy & lightness of touch; such natural art; such perfect adaptation; not a word, not a gesture, could have been altered; he has every hearer in his audience at the end of his muscles; not a man in the United States could have done it &

72 .. Ho! For Kansas

Fig. 8. In numerous addresses about Iowa, James Henry Lane publicized the overland route to bring settlers and aid to the beleaguered Free-State residents of Kansas Territory. Kansas State Historical Society.

the perfect ease of it all, not a glimpse of presentation or effort; & yet he has slept in his boots every night but two for four weeks."[9]

Lane had captured Iowans' sympathies in the summer of 1856 when, by force of his personality, he pressed for opening the northern overland route. His Iowa days began after Congress rebuffed his attempt to obtain recognition for the unofficial Topeka government's request for statehood. Lane launched a series of blistering Free-State speeches to rouse northern states' indignation. At Chicago, before the mass meeting excited by the sacking of Lawrence and the closing of the Missouri River to Free-State travelers, came forth one of Lane's greatest extemporaneous performances on the evening of May 31. There, he tapped the intensity of his fiery and impulsive nature—his husky voice alternatively "harsh and raspy" and ranging from "shrill tenor to a tragic bass" in loose, disjointed sentences—and brought the immense crowd repeatedly to wild enthusiastic applause.[10]

Nine days later in Davenport, Iowa, he played the same themes. Tumultuous applause greeted his introduction before the courthouse, whereupon he launched into exposing the outrages perpetrated "upon the citizens of Kansas, merely because they dared to say that Kansas ought to be a *Free State*." In what the newspaper editor described as a "masterly and stirring speech" that was two hours long and "frequently interrupted by heartfelt shouts," Lane confessed that he himself had voted for the Nebraska bill so people of the territory could "make their own laws and to mould their own institutions," but the bill had turned out to be "a sham and a lie." Instead, "the administration pro-slavery party said to the people of Kansas, make your own laws but you must make them to suit Slavery, or we won't admit you as a State." Slashing away, he pulled out a copy of laws enacted by the proslavery bogus legislature and read how it "imposed a penalty of *two years* imprisonment in the penitentiary for kidnapping a white baby into slavery, and for kidnapping a negro baby, the penalty *was death*—who [here] were the nigger worshippers." [italics original][11]

The next night in Burlington, Iowa, he similarly swayed the audience. He concluded his "brilliant" speech at midnight "in the presence of thousands, in the open air; the ladies thronging the windows of the neighboring houses, and manifesting their sympathy by the waving of handkerchiefs."[12] Throughout Lane's speaking tour he skillfully stoked public support for armed emigration. Lane told an editor a few months later that "in passing though Iowa I addressed the citizens upon the subject of politics at every prominent point—often speaking three, and sometimes four times a day—making during the march seventy-two speeches."[13]

Lane may have thrilled audiences, but his actions across Iowa also attracted trouble. Even while organizing to leave Iowa City for Civil Bend near the Nebraska line, local Democratic papers portrayed him as leading a band of rogues. One Iowa City editor castigated "the organization of armed ruffians in our midst" for the sake of ambitious "scoundrels like James H. Lane and his co-conspirators. How long will citizens of Iowa City feed and clothe the dupes of Col. Lane?" These men, the editor contended, are nothing more than "a band of brutal outlaws; many of them more fit to adorn the hangman's scaffold, than the rolling plains of Kansas."[14]

No sooner did they reach Oskaloosa seventy-five miles away then several teamsters refused to go further without pay. In an angry exchange a teamster grabbed Lane by the throat, shutting off his wind. Once released, Lane found arms to finish the dispute, but others held him back. And to charges that Lane and his men had stolen oats from a widow lady without paying for them, an Iowa City editor denied it on grounds that the teamsters were not emigrants but our own citizens who "find their own feed, and are paid by the day." To that a Democratic editor replied: "We have the more direct testimony of the teamsters who acknowledge that the oats were taken by *them*, but positively affirm that Lane knew about it and was under contract to pay for them. *He didn't do it.*" At any rate, by the end of the first week, eight of Lane's teamsters had quit and returned to Iowa City.[15]

II

Despite troubles, Lane's pending arrival in Kansas disturbed proslavery bands that had held the upper hand in Kansas-Nebraska violence. Even though the men under Lane's command amounted to less than one-fourth of those in emigrant companies making their way across Iowa, his personal notoriety and rumors about him exaggerated his influence in the minds of proslavery Missourians. They were mortified with thoughts that all of the companies amounted to Lane's "army of the north" and, while well armed, were on the march and heading their way. Amid the fears, one editor who opposed the Free Staters wrote tongue-in-cheek reports that "the notorious Lane and his armed band of '*Freedom Shriekers*' passed through Nebraska City a few days ago," the men "armed with Sharpe's rifles and Colt's revolvers, and their loins girded with the *New York Tribune*." As to their purpose, "they desire agitation—it is their very breath and life."[16]

Lane's readiness to enter the territory distressed leaders in the National Kansas Committee. The last thing they wanted was the emigration to be viewed as a military invasion rather than merely as a group of settlers traveling a new route across Iowa to peacefully reach Kansas. If the group was characterized as an invading army, it would justify proslavery foes' demands that President Pierce authorize U.S. soldiers to stop Free-State caravans from entering the territory. The Keokuk Free-State editor protested that proslavery partisans were fabricating "bloody fights and fiendish conduct" by Free-State emigrants "to bring a large amount of force and means to their assistance." Conversely, the Democratic editor in Iowa City charged that James Lane, when in Washington, DC, had connived with Republicans to delay passage of the army appropriation bill, by which "the

President could at once send a force to Kansas, drive out the intruders, and restore peace."[17]

The National Kansas Committee sent two of its most prestigious emissaries—committee chairman Thaddeus Hyatt and its financial manager Dr. Samuel Gridley Howe—to catch up with Lane and transfer command of the emigrants to a civilian. "Pity that such a man as Lane is at the head," wrote Howe to Senator Sumner, but "we shall do all we can to keep a bit in his mouth." They arrived at Tabor, Iowa, at the end of July. With the guidance of Rev. John Todd, they connected with the trail coordinator Milton Dickey in nearby White Cloud and rode down to the large emigrant encampments near Nebraska City, where Lane was reported to be.[18]

It turned out that Lane instead was encamped on the Iowa side of the river at Civil Bend, eluding the U.S. marshal who was after him for bringing armed men into the territory. Meanwhile, Capt. Samuel Walker arrived with fifteen Free-State men from Topeka, seeking to establish communication with Lane. Meeting with Howe and other leaders, they prepared a letter for Walker to deliver to Lane, his close friend. With the strength of the National Kansas Committee footing the bills for much of the expedition, the letter stated that, by unanimous consent, its leadership was being placed in the hands of Milton Dickey, the acting coordinator of supplies and subsistence for the expedition as general superintendent. Further, Lane should remain out of the territory for the time being.[19]

Walker found the restless James Lane in Civil Bend at Dr. Ira Blanchard's house. He handed Lane the letter. Lane read it and then sat down for some time, "his head bowed and the tears running down his cheeks." Then looking up he said, "Walker, if you say the people of Kansas don't want me, it's all right, and I'll blow my brains out. I can never go back to the states and look the people in the face and tell them that as soon as I got these Kansas friends of mine fairly into danger I had to abandon them. I can't do it."

Walker stated that "the people of Kansas would rather have you than all the party at Nebraska City." He offered, with his fifteen men, to deliver Lane safely to the Kansas Territory. Accepting the idea in light of the situation, Lane quickly readied himself.

Dr. Blanchard and his neighbor Elvira Platt set about disguising Lane to pass him off as one "Spanish Joe." Blanchard prepared a solution of nitrate of silver and Elvira helped slather it on, "washing his face and neck, arms and hands" so that he might "return to Kansas as a half breed cook for a company of men about to return to the seat of war."[20] Adorned with the solution, which had mixed results, and some of Blanchard's old clothes, Lane was ready. Blanchard first pulled Lane across the river by canoe to join Walker and his men and then returned to his Civil Bend home while Lane and Walker's men all rode for Lawrence. Despite hunger, fatigue, and accidents along the way that gradually reduced the group to but a few, thirty hours later Lane entered Lawrence, Kansas. Meanwhile, Samuel Howe could accurately report that the emigrant expedition "is now rid of Col. Lane's presence and the disadvantage of the military aspect which that presence gave it."[21]

Upon Lane's arrival in Lawrence on August 11, events soon turned aggressive. Within five days he and other Free-State volunteers took the offensive and soon drove proslavery men from three strongholds in the Lawrence vicinity.

Rumors spread of threatened destruction to western Missouri towns and counties. Leaders at a proslavery rally at Westport, Missouri, issued a call for men and aid, boldly stating, "LANE'S MEN HAVE ARRIVED!—CIVIL WAR IS BEGUN." Another call to meet at Lexington, Missouri, claimed that "four hundred Abolitionists under Lane have actually come into the Territory and commenced a war of extermination upon the Pro-Slavery settlers." Their intention "is to drive us from the Territory and carry the next election and get possession of the reins of government. This we *must not submit to*. If we do *Kansas is lost to the South forever*—and our slaves in upper Missouri will be useless to us—and our homes must be given up to the Abolition enemy." [italics original] Similarly, appearing in the *Leavenworth Journal* with exaggerated hysteria were fearful headlines, including: "Citizens to Arms!! Our Country is invaded! And hired minions are massacring our people in all parts! Now that the Government troops have turned TRAITORS! and COWARDS! we are forced to act for ourselves."[22] A few days later Territorial Governor Wilson Shannon was removed, and his replacement, John W. Geary, was due to arrive in three weeks.[23]

Terrified, Missourians pleaded with their own governor Sterling Price to call out militiamen for the protection of western counties. Over in Kansas Territory, many panic-stricken proslavery inhabitants fled. Daniel Woodson, as secretary of the Kansas Territory appointed by President Franklin Pierce, became acting territorial governor. Being an arch proslavery man, he issued a proclamation on August 25 declaring Kansas to be in a state of insurrection and called upon militia to put down the rebellion (essentially an invitation for armed proslavery Missourians to enter Kansas). Their incursions followed, bringing face-offs and skirmishes.

As of early September Lane was awaiting reinforcements for an assault on Hickory Point when the newly arrived Governor Geary issued a proclamation on September 11. The announcement demobilized Woodson's militia operations and commanded all bodies without government authority "instantly to disband or quit the territory, as they will answer the contrary at their peril." Geary, a decisive man with a strong executive ability, had been an officer in the Mexican-American War. His intent now was to bring Democratic success in the fall presidential election by suppressing disorder and ending outside influences.

III

Lane's force of some fifty men skedaddled north, first to Civil Bend, and after a few days they went on to Tabor, Iowa. Lane said the move was to allow Geary time to establish peace and "open the road" free of proslavery militias trying to block or hinder emigrants arriving from Iowa. Upon their arrival at the end of September, Lane's men found shelter in the various homes and buildings of townsmen. Their horses were likewise split up among them for feed and care, with Rev. John Todd housing some fifteen horses in his new barn. Cavalry drills in the public square occupied their days amid the comings and goings of other settler trains.[24]

With Geary's bold steps making travel safer, Todd recalled, emigrants who were still waiting about Tabor began to depart: "[Luke] Parsons and [radical journalist James] Redpath and their companions in travel struck their tents, and left their camps near Tabor, on the morning of September 13, 1856, for Kansas. Several from Tabor joined them." They went with a recently arrived company of armed emigrants whose leader was nineteen-year-old Preston B. Plumb. He had assembled a company of ten at Iowa City and left about September 3, adding others along the way. They pulled into Tabor with three wagons: one contained relief supplies and travel provisions; another, seventy-one Sharps rifles, ninety-three revolvers, other rifles and muskets, bowie knives, and ammunition; and the third, a dismantled brass cannon and carriage boarded up to be unseen.[25] Tabor residents had provided a welcoming dinner to the arriving party.

Next the wagon group entered Nebraska Territory and, between Nebraska City and Nemaha, met up with General Lane's retreating company. Lane delivered an inspiring speech, and then he and his fifty mounted men continued on their way to Iowa. Plumb's company, by forced marches and evading U.S. troops, delivered their stores safely at Topeka several days later.[26]

"The wants of Kansas constitute the absorbing topic of interest here now," wrote Todd to a fellow Congregational minister in Burlington, Iowa. Indeed, "it was much feared that our friends in the territory would be reduced to a state of suffering before a sufficient force could be raised to conduct safely to them the provisions which were here waiting to be conveyed." His mid-September letter indicated that "Kansas forces had been congregating here for more than three weeks until yesterday."[27]

As Lane's troops moved toward Tabor, one in the company remembered that Lane stopped them before entering the village. He "admonished the men that in regard for the moral and religious principles of Tabor people, the men of the company were to conduct themselves with utmost decorum." They camped on the public square, drilled daily, and engaged in various sports, but they did not speak profanity or steal chickens.[28] Upon hearing that troubles had subsided in the territory, they moved to near Archer, Nebraska, before reentering Kansas.

While in Tabor they were met by another large company of emigrants coming from Mount Pleasant, Iowa. Cutting fifty miles off the overland trip from Iowa City to Tabor, rails of the Burlington and Missouri River Railroad now reached Mount Pleasant, which made it the new rail hub for Free-State westbound emigration. Col. Shalor Eldridge, the national committee's agent for emigration across Iowa, led the eighteen-wagon company, a train supported with greater funding and organization than Eldridge had for the first expedition from Iowa City in July. Now crossing Iowa in September, Eldridge had two hundred volunteers—mostly men—equipped with a field gun and wagons loaded with small arms, edged weapons, munitions, tents, and provisions. Also in the wagons, with the help of Eldridge's lieutenant, Robert Morrow, were two hundred more state arsenal arms made secretly available from Iowa governor James Grimes.[29]

Reverend Todd well remembered the Eldridge train's arrival in Tabor on October 1: "They proceeded directly to the southwest corner of the public square, where they proceeded to pitch their tents. They camped in front of the parson's gate, placing the mounted cannon in the center, and hoisting on it the stars and stripes. The 18 covered wagons were arranged in a circle, around the national banner. Outside the wagons was pitched a circle of tents, and outside the tents campfires were built, and still outside of the fires were placed armed sentinels. . . . On the next day about 200 men drilled on the public square."[30]

Lane's presence also prompted anger among the eastern Free-State emigrants, Todd remembered, because Sharps rifles had been promised them at various stops along the way but not received. To calm down the men, Lane stepped forward and, climbing atop a cannon carriage, spoke to them along the following lines:

> I know you have borne much already, since you left your homes. You have endured with fortitude the perils, inconveniences, and privations of the way as good soldiers. Now you want Sharps rifles. Well, let me tell you, a Sharps rifle is a good weapon to use on an enemy at a distance, but it is good for nothing in a close encounter. If you come into a close fight (and I hope to God you may), a Sharps rifle is worthless. It is far inferior to a weapon with a bayonet. If I had my choice of arms, I would not arm more than one in ten with a Sharps rifle. As the arms you want are not here, I hope you will conclude to go on and see us through.

The men continued on to Kansas, departing on October 4.[31]

IV

As the Eldridge party moved into Nebraska another smaller group passed it while going the other direction. The second group included John Brown, accompanied by several of his family members, who was leaving Kansas and headed toward Tabor and then east to raise funds. Inside their mule team wagon were numerous arms and munitions that Brown intended to store in Tabor.[32] Arriving there on October 10, his sons continued on their way east while Brown—sick with dysentery—spent a week in Tabor, recuperating among friends.[33]

It was Brown's first recorded visit to Tabor, which would become his clandestine outpost during parts of the next two years. Kansas was quiet for the moment, but Brown expected conflict to reignite in the spring. He wanted to be ready for it.[34]

Col. Milton C. Dickey (superintendent of the main caravan through Nebraska to Topeka in August) and Dr. J. P. Root (leader of the July party that marked the emigrant trail from Iowa's border down through Kansas and Nebraska) led the last wagon group across Iowa in 1856. The wagons contained freight, Sharps rifles, and goods on its way from Mount Pleasant, Iowa, toward Tabor and Kansas. In the caravan were John Brown's sons Salmon and Watson, intending to repay those who had recently killed their brother Frederick. When John Brown learned of it in Chicago, he sent word for his sons to wait for him at Tabor and set about returning to Iowa.[35] On October 30, while stopping at St. Charles, Iowa, Watson penned a note to his family that they were well and "in the company of a train of Kansas teams loaded with Sharps rifles and canon [*sic*]. I heard a report that Father had gone east. The travel very slow. You can write to us at Tabor."[36]

This particular shipment of Sharps rifles in the Dickey and Root caravan would become important, for the rifles eventually ended up in John Brown's hands. The Massachusetts State Kansas Committee originally had donated the two hundred Sharps rifled carbines and a field piece (about a six pounder) to the National Kansas Committee in Chicago. From there the committee's general agent, William F. M. Arny, shipped them to a warehouse in Iowa City to be held in reserve. About late August, however, the agent received a report that the warehouse had been broken into and goods taken, whereupon he went immediately to Iowa City.[37]

Finding the arms still there but judging them insecure, Arny retrieved the fifteen boxes. Every box held a dozen Sharps carbines, and he addressed the wooden lid of each to "T. B. Eldridge, Mt. Pleasant, Iowa." Arny hired teamsters to load and haul the boxes—each about four feet long and one foot square—fifty miles south to Mount Pleasant, where waited Thomas B. Eldridge (brother of Shalor Eldridge, whose large wagon train had left

Fig. 9. John Brown emerged as a leader while urging that the fight be taken to proslavery aggressors. Kansas State Historical Society.

there in late September). Thomas Eldridge was the current agent of the National Kansas Committee outfitting emigrant trains to Kansas. Now he arranged horses and wagons to haul the Sharps rifles, ammunition, and camp equipage in the next caravan led by Dickey and Root.[38]

This wagon train reached Tabor in early November 1856. John Brown's sons separated at this point, with Watson staying to wait for his father while Salmon went on to Kansas. As for Dickey and Root's cargo, they received information that "the troops are watching and stopping every one who goes in over the new road." Deciding the risks were too great for what they carried, they made their mind up to store the Sharps carbines, ammunition, cannon, and supplies in town.[39]

Their materials added to goods the National Kansas Committee already had in storage along with the miscellaneous arms that John Brown had recently brought from Kansas.[40] Although they heard Governor Geary had neutralized the situation in Kansas, the wary Free-State men decided to store their accumulated arms here in case troubles erupted in the lead-up to the next year's autumn elections. Consequently, the arms, equipment, and other goods filled every conceivable storage place about Tabor.[41]

The Reverend John Todd housed the two hundred Sharps rifles and ammunition in his cellar that winter along with many boxes of sabers, rifles, muskets, accoutrements, boots, and clothing. The field piece he kept in his barn. George B. Gaston's accommodations for storage were also all in demand.[42]

Once unloaded and put into storage, Dickey and Root's train pressed on for Nebraska. Upon their arrival in Topeka on November 15, the local editor welcomed the train. He noted their reporting that "a large number of emigrants are preparing to start for Kansas early in the spring."[43]

V

While Kansas bled during the summer of 1856 and more Iowans joined in the relief effort, Governor Grimes of Iowa added his state's support for the Free-State cause. Angry that the national government failed to protect adequately those former citizens of Iowa who moved to the territory of Kansas, Grimes wrote President Franklin Pierce in late August. The situation was deteriorating, he warned, and his state would not stand by idly if conditions worsened. Three Iowans had already been slain by outlaw bands. Indeed, wrote Grimes,

> some have been compelled to flee from the Territory for no offense save that of having emigrated from a free State, while others remain there, stripped of their property, and appeal to their fellow-citizens of Iowa for sympathy and protection. While I write, an army raised in the State of Missouri is marching into Kansas, with the avowed purpose of driving out all those citizens of the Territory who emigrated from the free States, and who express a preference for a free State constitution. Another armed body of men have placed themselves on the emigrant route from the State of Iowa, to prevent at the point of the bayonet any further emigration from this state.
>
> The State of Iowa cannot be an indifferent spectator of these acts of lawless violence. She will not submit to the closing of the emigrant route through her domain into that Territory.

If military forces obstructing immigration into the territory were not dispersed, Grimes held it to be the states' duty, similar to James Madison's argument in his Virginia Resolutions of 1798, "to 'interpose to arrest the progress of the evils' in that Territory." Grimes's forceful letter prompted howls from Democratic newspaper editors. The Free-State editor in Lawrence, however, thanked him for writing a "manly letter" that "breathes the spirit of freedom" unlike the "*cant* issued by the Executives of some other States."[44]

Grimes would eventually take heat for his Free-State assistance in 1856. In early 1858 the editor of the *Des Moines Iowa State*

Journal asked what happened to muskets taken from the Iowa arsenal. "The State Arms—Where Are They?" read the headline, hoping to shed light on Grimes's covert aid of supplying weapons for Free-State forces. Did these arms, the editor snidely inquired, go "to Kansas under Jim Lane's escort or were they all used up in opening the Missouri River?"[45]

His probing bore little fruit because by that time Grimes was off to the U.S. Senate and his successor, Governor Ralph P. Lowe, said he knew nothing about it. Also the Republican legislative majority suppressed an investigation.

The story nearly came up again at the time of the congressional investigation into John Brown's Harpers Ferry raid when it looked into evidence that the Sharps rifles he used were brought to Virginia from Iowa. Senator Grimes wrote a letter to Governor Samuel Kirkwood asking the exact facts of the matter.[46] Likely he wondered if the Sharps rifles had traveled together with the missing state arsenal muskets carried on Eldridge's September caravan and traceable to the same origin, a warehouse in Iowa City. Grimes notified Kirkwood that the U.S. Senate's investigating committee would endeavor "to identify some of these arms with those arms belonging to the State of Iowa." Of this effort Grimes disingenuously recalled that when Iowa's share of federal weapons first arrived in early 1856, a person "came to Burlington to get me to let some of them be taken by the Kansas emigrants to defend themselves against the Missourians, which I refused to do." Instead, he had sent them "to Iowa City and placed them in [the] charge of [George] McCleary who was Adjutant Gen'l of this state." "Of course," he wrote, "if any arms were taken they were taken clandestinely and in violation of law." Immediate justice, he postured, demanded answers about "were they taken and how, by whom, when and for what?" His sleights of hand to cover things up and escape inquiry in advance of a congressional investigation worked, and the committee did not question further.[47]

Although the Free-State cause trembled in dire straits through the summer and fall of 1856, by early 1857 interference with Kansas-bound emigrants had subsided and travel returned unchecked to the Missouri River. Free-State emigrants, though with difficulty, had nicely outflanked the western Missouri proslavery men who had closed the river to all but those travelers with southern sympathies. This effort coupled with Governor John Geary's actions to defuse violence—in particular, convincing a large advancing Missourian militia under David Atchison not to attack near-defenseless Lawrence before the impending presidential election—had quieted organized proslavery aggression.

Large-scale incursions by proslavery Missourians ended. In southern Kansas, however, acts of revenge and plunder persisted as marauding bands from both sides continued to attack those thought to have wronged them.

By late 1856 Atchison and the Stringfellow brothers saw ultimate failure ahead. Despite their pleas, too few southern state settlers had arrived to offset the northern current entering Kansas. Dr. John Stringfellow—the virulent proslavery editor of the *Atchison Squatter Sovereign*—grew disheartened by the weak southern support. In March 1857, he gave up, and he and his partner, Robert Kelley, sold the business. A year later John returned to Virginia while his brother Benjamin Stringfellow turned increasingly to his Kansas law and business interests.[48]

Senator Atchison, bleak and seeing futility in southern resolve and now writing in June 1857 to a South Carolina mayor, wondered "whether an earthquake—a moral and political earthquake, shaking the institution of slavery to the earth, and bringing ruin upon the whole South, would rouse her to action." Although Atchison urged "one more effort" for the territorial legislature in the October 1857 election, which the Free-State Party then won, he had pretty much "come to the conclusion to curse Kansas and quit the cause of the South."[49]

VI

If "history is the unfolding of miscalculations," as writes one historian, the proslavery strategy in Kansas offered such an instance.[50] Atchison, Stringfellow, and the others, recklessly driven to succeed, had overreached in closing the Missouri River. Antislavery Iowa and northern newspapers made the most of it, dramatizing events for their readers. Perhaps equally important, proslavery leaders' actions to create a neighboring slave state had angered St. Louis interests and the local merchants in western Missouri as they lost money when Missouri River traffic dwindled and northern papers capitalized on Free-State fury.

Part of proslavery's undoing was the new telegraph and quick railroad express that sped news continuously of events in Kansas. The immediacy and intensity of the reports brought an exaggerated urgency to the Kansas imbroglio. Few southern reporters were in Kansas nourishing a public thirst for news, but plenty of northern ones were present. They included such radical correspondents as James Redpath, John Henry Kagi, William Addison Phillips, Richard J. Hinton, and Thomas Wentworth Higginson.

Behind all this, New Englanders' literary dominance upon northern and western thought and an energetic, rising Republican Party gave power to the storied uproar of "Bleeding Kansas." As the compiler of the history of Vernon County, Missouri, put it, "Throughout the contest the Free Soilers had the advantage. There were many men of real literary ability among them, book writers and newspaper men. Every prominent Northern Republican paper had its special correspondent, who fought and wrote about it, giving his own version of matters." The South, on the other hand,

> always deficient in printing material, and with not one writer where the North had ten, contented itself by establishing in the Territory three or four small newspapers edited by blusterers and swaggerers, who did their cause more harm than good. These sheets were

assisted by other blusterers and swaggerers in Missouri and elsewhere, whose brutal and insane shriekings were caught up and republished by the Republican journals with considerable profit to the Free Soil side.[51]

Simultaneously, verses extolling Free-State deeds written by such northern poets as John Greenleaf Whittier, Henry Wordsworth Longfellow, James Russell Lowell, Ralph Waldo Emerson, and William Cullen Bryant helped shape public sympathy behind the cause.

Free-State propaganda lauded settlers when they stood up and took the fight to proslavery bands and militias. Conversely, slavery sympathizers, who had seen themselves as hard-boiled westerners able to push around weak-kneed antislavery emigrants, now found violence at their own front door. They themselves were turned upon and plundered or driven out by the likes of Charles Lenhart, Jim Lane, James Montgomery, John Brown, and other Free-State bands.[52]

By December 1856, the Free-State editor of the *Herald of Freedom* in Lawrence observed that proslavery aggressors found "the Free State settlers made of sterner stuff than they expected, and their expulsion a more difficult task than they anticipated. So, they have concluded to leave, for a more genial climate, and a less resolute people."[53]

Now with river traffic reopened, stories of Iowa's part in the Kansas struggle changed focus. Coverage shifted to events of Iowans and Kansans cooperating to help enslaved people flee western Missouri via Kansas and Nebraska. Proslavery prophecies that Free-State settlement would "abolitionize" the land and lead to "underground railroads" everywhere were coming to pass.

6

Scramble to Freedom

I

As the hold of proslavery men over the Kansas Territory loosened and Free-State settlement grew, Lawrence and other Free-State communities became home or temporary refuge to escapees from Missouri slavery. Odds of continuing north to Free States were yet slim, however; runaways had to cross vast empty stretches of prairie with little chance to find food or shelter when needed.

Ira D. Blanchard in southwest Iowa saw these impediments could be overcome by converting the emigrant trail running from Kansas through Nebraska and across Iowa to the Underground Railroad's use.[1] No sooner did the last emigrant caravan leave Iowa for Kansas during the late fall of 1856 then Blanchard left his home at Civil Bend (a thin cluster of farms across the Missouri River and north of Nebraska City in Nebraska Territory) and headed for Topeka. There he discussed his idea with some antislavery men, who agreed to pursue the scheme for aiding runaways.[2]

The first attempt was nearly disastrous. Two black men from Jackson County, Missouri, had reached Topeka and were then directed northward according to plan. When they failed to appear at Civil Bend, some Kansas men staying at Elvira and Lester Platt's place, located next to Blanchard's farm, went in search of them. They reached the prearranged location to the south but found no

Fig. 10. Ira D. Blanchard of Civil Bend, Iowa, worked to establish Underground Railroad connections with those assisting escaping slaves in Kansas and operated a station point to guide runaways toward their next Iowa destination. Kansas State Historical Society.

one there. Unbeknown to them, slave catchers had reached the black men first and taken them to Missouri. At Linden, a hamlet twenty-five miles from Civil Bend, the captors housed them in a small log jail. That evening they escaped by making a hole in some of the rotting logs, and they lit out for Iowa through the Missouri River bottoms. Though they became lost and separated in a snowstorm, searchers rescued one and the next week found the other. The two companions were reunited at Tabor, Iowa.[3]

This attempt was soon followed by the early Underground Railroad effort for Judy Clarke. She drew special notice because of her escape from George W. Clarke, a dangerous proslavery man and the notorious killer of well-liked Free-State settler Thomas W. Barber near Lawrence in 1855. Clarke—a U.S. agent for the Pottawattamie Indians and described as "a thick set man about five feet three inches in height"—was highly talkative, influential, and violently disposed against Free-State people. He lived on a rise of land two miles outside the proslavery town of Lecompton.[4]

The agent shared ownership of Judy Clarke with an equally notorious proslavery guerrilla leader named Col. H. T. Titus. The man lived nearby, about a mile and a quarter south of Lecompton, where he had built a fortified log cabin with portholes. By the summer of 1856, however, Titus had plenty else to think about as Free-State groups retaliated for the depredations of him and his men. On August 16, Free-State forces attacked and burned his "Fort Titus" and captured the wounded leader. A cannon ball had passed through a trunk on which Judy was sitting inside the building, but she was uninjured.[5] By December Titus departed for Nicaragua with a hundred men.

Judy then stayed at George Clarke's place although he was preoccupied that fall leading men attempting to drive out Free-State settlers from Linn County. When at home, he treated Judy poorly. The final straw came when, angered by some oversight or disobedience, he grabbed a chair and beat Judy over the head.[6]

As soon as possible she ran off toward Topeka. Some twenty miles out Judy reached the Howard family farm southeast of town, where she stayed for about six weeks. Meanwhile, George Clarke had advertised a reward for her return, identifying her as a heavy black woman in her late thirties.

One day some proslavery men detected Judy. Seeing that they noticed her, she "pretended she was glad they had found her; said she had had a hard time, and made no fuss about going back, pretending she was glad to go home." They stopped for the evening at a hotel at or near Lecompton and sent word for Clarke to bring his reward for her retrieval. As she recounted a few weeks later,

> The servants in the hotel were very busy getting ready for a great occasion, and she went right into the kitchen to help. Talking, and working, and laughing, they had a gay time. In clearing up the kitchen after the supper dishes were washed, she managed to get her bundle outside the door without exciting any notice. Then they went to work dressing turkeys, after which they had to wash their hands, of course. She washed hers outside by the kitchen door, as the others had done, then came in with the wash-pan for some warm water and soap; and stepped out to give her hands a thorough cleaning.

At this unguarded moment she bolted away with her bundle and ran up a nearby brush-filled ravine. Though "she was missed in a very few minutes," they saw no more of her. Hiding in the densest bushes until first morning light, she worked her way up the ravine, which brought her to a hilltop at the prairie's edge.[7]

In advancing daylight she spotted a man coming her way on a road leading southwest of Lecompton and, noticing that he carried a book, surmised he might be a Free-State man. Judy approached him. He identified himself as Dr. Barker and said that he was returning from a visit to a sick woman. Though he was a neighbor of her slaveholder Clarke, she asked the doctor for help by allowing her to hide at his place and for his assistance in gaining her freedom. He replied she should continue walking south to the next ravine and follow it to the rear of his house.

After remaining there for a day or two, Dr. Barker took Judy by wagon to Lawrence, a few miles away. He dropped her off at the father-in-law of George Earle, a member of the Stubbs militia company organized to protect Lawrence and Free-State Kansans. He in turn moved her to an active Underground Railroad organizer, John Armstrong, living just south of Lawrence at Washington Creek.[8]

As Armstrong worked out arrangements over the next six weeks to move her toward Iowa, Judy hid at the residence of Mrs. Scales, who kept boarders. In the cellar, Mrs. Scales and Armstrong pulled onto its side a large barrel and put in straw, clothes, and blankets, and there Judy stayed when people were awake upstairs. During the day, when the boarders were away, Judy came up and helped out in the kitchen. At the end of the first week, however, Capt. Henry Scales—a proslavery man who did not know she was being hidden in his home—discovered her one morning in the kitchen. Mrs. Scales convinced him to "keep a secret," and what went on there Scales never exposed.[9]

In late February 1857 Rev. Henry B. Burgess, an antislavery man in Lawrence, loaned Armstrong his closed carriage for the trip north, and another man lent a team of mules. Several others donated money. By the time all was ready, the carriage now also contained a second woman runaway, as well as a Topeka man to assist Armstrong.[10]

Traveling often at night, they stopped along the way at Rochester, then Holton—where they got stuck crossing the creek and had to unload the passengers to free the buggy—and New Albany. In making the trek north over the brown winter prairie, Armstrong followed for much of the way the three-week-old track of John Kagi, a newspaper correspondent who had recently traveled to see his father near Nebraska City and in a few months would join up with John Brown. In crossing the Missouri River to Iowa above Nebraska City at Wyoming, the water was filled with large pieces of ice that carried the ferry downriver a half a mile before reaching shore. After delivering the runaways to Dr. Ira D. Blanchard at Civil Bend, Armstrong's part in the venture ended (his journey there and back took three weeks). The runaways stayed the night at Blanchard's house, and the next morning Blanchard had Judy climb up behind him on a horse and they rode to Tabor. She stayed at George Gaston's house for two weeks, and Rev. John Todd took her to another stop, where others helped the runaways on toward Chicago.[11]

Judy did not forget the help. "I had several letters from her afterwards," recalled Armstrong, that she sent from Chicago, where she lived several years. "She had a daughter living in Lawrence County, Missouri and offered me $500.00 to go and get her." For Armstrong, this first trip to Iowa was but the beginning. "We afterwards sent several women up," he commented. "Some came from Missouri, some from Kansas."[12]

With these early Underground Railroad initiatives having some success, two Fremont County settlements became prime receivers of runaways escaping Missouri via Kansas and Nebraska. One was Civil Bend, a rural hamlet in the southwestern part of the county, and the other was Tabor, near Fremont County's northern border. Both sites were largely Congregationalist. One-time missionaries to tribes in unorganized territories—Ira and Mary Blanchard to the Delawares and Lester and Elvira Platt to the Pawnees—had settled across the Missouri River at Civil Bend in the late 1840s.[13] Soon they were joined by a group of Congregationalists from the Oberlin, Ohio, area led by Elvira Platt's brother, George Gaston.[14] The Gaston group left shortly thereafter for drier and higher ground and founded the town of Tabor in northern Ross Township. With members of these two communities being either related or familiar with one another, establishing an Underground Railroad route from Civil Bend to Tabor did not take long.

II

Assisting runaways could be dangerous. In these frontier borderlands could be found an assortment of armed fugitives, black and white alike, along with various slave catchers and kidnappers of free blacks. For wagon drivers carrying concealed black people, there lurked in proslavery neighborhoods numerous settlers on the watch for strangers passing through with escaping slaves. There was no telling when something would go wrong on the trail. Encounter the wrong persons and a tense situation, mixed with fear, anger, and adrenaline, could go quickly out of control.

The enslaved of western Missouri, assumed today to have been unarmed, were in fact living in a frontier area where arms were commonplace and easily accessed. In one such Missouri town on a mid-March morning in 1856, citizens noticed a black man running down the commercial street of Independence with a derringer pistol in his hand. He had just been sold, but before the city marshal could lodge him for the time being in jail, the black man broke free and ran into the street with the marshal close behind. The marshal discharged several shots while Mr. Smith, the black man's previous master, jumped on horseback and caught up with the man to run him down. The man jumped a fence as Smith fired his own pistol and missed.[15]

Finally overtaken, the runaway fired his pistol at one of his chasers, grazing the man's head. The others, thinking his pistol was now empty, rushed at him. But he pulled out another gun and was raising it to fire when another pursuer felled him with a shot. Upon his body they found two single-barrel pistols, a large bowie knife, and a pocketknife. With this incident in mind, the town's newspaper editor urged a greater need for "effective steps to enforce the law to prevent negroes from carrying arms. We believe that at least half the negroes who parade our streets, are in the habit of carrying weapons of some kind. Let this be a warning of the danger in permitting such things."[16]

Eight months later with suspicions aroused about possible "insurrectionary movements among the slaves," a citizens' meeting took place in New Madrid and Scott Counties, Missouri. Among the recommendations connected with prohibiting any public gatherings of Negroes was an appeal for "every slave owner to disarm his slaves."[17]

Then there were armed runaways hiding out in western Iowa's Missouri River bottoms near Civil Bend. On September 5, 1857, the *Brownville (Nebraska) Advertiser* reported that three men—perhaps slave hunters—had heard that three armed Negroes had been spotted in the willows below town. Seeing the chance to earn some easy money, the trio rode to the site, dismounted, and moved through the brush to catch their prey. Coming upon the runaways, a gunfight began at once. One of the runaways straight away killed the slave hunter named Myers while a second man wounded one of the runaways in the arm. Two runaways escaped, managing to ride off on the slave hunters' horses, while the wounded man ran to the nearby farm of William Kelly, where he gave himself up.

The fugitive was taken to Brownville—a small town of mixed Free-State and proslavery sentiment—where two doctors examined his wound. They decided they had to amputate the arm before placing him in the custody of the deputy sheriff. That night a group of Missourians came across the river and threatened to hang the recovering captive for having dared to defy white men. But Deputy Thompson, guarding the prisoner at the American House, twice refused the mob's entry during the night and warned he would shoot anyone who tried breaking in to take the man. Finally a town slaveholder convinced the men to return home, and soon the deputy took the recovering runaway thirty miles north to the Nebraska City jail.[18]

Meanwhile, the two fleeing runaways rode upriver from Brownville some twenty-five miles and crossed over to the Iowa side of the Missouri River opposite Nebraska City. There they hid out for two months. By chance a Missouri slaveholder from the vicinity of St. Joseph, Missouri, discovered them while searching for other runaways. The slaveholder had been to Iowa while fruitlessly tracking five of his escaped slaves. He knew that his slaves had first run off to Topeka in Kansas Territory and had followed them there. Frustrated in Topeka, he went to authorities for help, but those Topeka citizens who had hidden the runaways had already helped them escape north.[19]

The exasperated slaveholder then shrewdly turned to a freedman from Jackson County, Missouri. Traveling to Topeka and representing himself as a fugitive, the freedman tricked abolitionists into telling where he might join up with the five escapees and even received a horse to get there. The slaveholder, once his decoy informed him of the direction the runaways had taken, set out in pursuit along with three other men.

The slaveholder's group overtook his runaways, in company with six others, hiding out on the Iowa side of the Missouri River in a bend near Nebraska City. The eleven included the two runaways from Brownville. Spotting the hunters approaching their hideout, the runaway who had killed the slave hunter in the thicket near Brownville, took aim at the intruders and fired three shots. All missed their target. The chasers then shot him down while screaming at the others to throw down their arms, and they did. The captors gathered up "thirty-odd revolvers" and conveyed their captives back through St. Joseph, Missouri, to the farms from which they had escaped.[20]

III

Such incidents near territorial or Iowa borders seemed to show slaveholders' control weakening and their slave property growing more insecure. Slave traders were busy. In 1859 the steamer *New War Eagle* pulled up to a St. Louis wharf with about fifty Negroes, twenty-eight of them owned by Major Adams of Clay County, Missouri, and being taken south for sale. The slave owner lightheartedly remarked how "Greeley, Seward, Dorris, of Platte County, and himself, are rapidly making Missouri a Free State." George P. Dorriss, a Platte City merchant, was heavily into the slave trade locally, "taking large gangs South every few months" for sale.[21] The editor of the *St. Joseph Weekly West* saw a conspiracy afoot between slave traders and Free-Soil newspapers. The "abolitionist" newspaper warns slave holders their property is not safe, and then a buyer shows up to find a frightened farmer willing to sell his slaves for whatever he could get before losing them all.[22] Whatever the cause the effect was noticeable. By August 1859 in Jackson County, a comparative statement of its county assessors' books showed "the number of negroes (slaves) in that county has decreased 500 in the past year, which is about 17 per cent."[23]

Slavery supporters thus grew increasingly nervous while Free-State confidence rose. Meanwhile, Topeka's Underground Railroad activists continued to hide and funnel runaways north toward Iowa.

At a Sunday morning service in Topeka's First Congregational Church on July 11, 1858, Rev. Lewis Bodwell heard murmurs that "a family of 'emigrants' had arrived." They were being concealed, he learned, at the stone cabin of John Ritchie near Shunganunga Creek.[24]

These runaways were not the typical adult group. Rather it was a family of five light mulattoes: George, Fanny, and their three children—a six-year-old, a four-year-old, and a baby of four months. Their fine looks and well-mannered behavior left all who saw them in Topeka thinking the family would be highly valued as house servants and that strong efforts would be made to recover them. George, described as a bright man of "alert, soldierly manner," had served a U.S. Army officer, and Fanny, his attractive wife of "modest ways" and quiet demeanor, had belonged to an Alabama woman and had worked as a laundress.

Favorable circumstances had enabled their escape. With "the master far west, the mistress far south, some good friends near, and their only responsible keeper" distracted with higher-priority "cares and duties," the family had seized a chance to leave. Friends had guided the young family, which traveled at night, to Topeka. Now Reverend Bodwell volunteered to go with a driver named Emerson for the journey north.

By Wednesday (July 14) they were on their way, seven people riding in the canvas-covered wagon pulled by fresh young horses splashing a muddy course through the rain. Within a day the slow-moving party had crossed creeks and navigated over ruts and roots of an unsteady forest road to arrive thirty miles north of Topeka at the Holton settlement. With rain continuing to fall, "the little mother and her children found shelter in a small log cabin." The others spent their night in the wagon near the rising waters of the nearby creek.

The next day back on the road, they had a scare when they spotted "on the next rise and coming towards us, five hard looking fellows." Had the slave owner somehow pursued and caught up with them by another route? Bodwell told Emerson, "They have us, but keep moving. Don't let them look in. Don't let them have the first shot." And to George and Fanny he said, "Lie close and don't let the baby cry." The riders divided, passing on the right and left of the wagon. The wagon mates were highly relieved, to say the least, when they heard the men ask as they passed, "How far to Holton?"

Reaching the Nemaha River only to find its banks full and impassable, they went upstream several miles over the rain-drenched prairie searching for a place to cross. Having no luck, they made camp and ate rations of half a biscuit each. The mother then nursed her baby before she and the children moved into the wagon to sleep. The others slept on the ground. By July 18—the fifth day out—their provisions were nearly exhausted, and they drove across the prairie in search of a place where they might find food. Their hopes rose in coming upon a train of three wagons that had also been cut off by the Nemaha's high water. Though they worried about the train having come from proslavery Leavenworth, Emerson went down to the camp and returned in little over an hour with welcome supplies. They continued their slow trek toward Central City in hopes of spying a place to cross the river. Finding nothing they pulled up in a brushy hiding spot for the night.

For the next four days the group struggled to find a way across the swollen Nemaha. While crossing a creek in plain sight of a cabin as its occupants watched from shore, one of the horse team balked, suffering from horse collar sores and weariness. To lighten the load, Bodwell and Emerson shielded the fugitives from sight as they left the wagon, waded to the bank, and climbed the slippery slope. At another stream, even with the help of three mounted Yankee settlers, they had to abandon one impassable ford and trudge through dense brush–lined paths and marshy land back to higher ground for the remainder of the night. Their Yankee friends returned after hearing an upper ford might be passable at the small hamlet of Central City. So all loaded up again and on they went. In the early morning hours of July 23, they crossed over into Nebraska and, with bright sunny weather, drove more comfortably on "fairly dry roads along the high prairies."

By Sunday evening of the twenty-fifth, the seven reached Nebraska City. To reduce risks of detection, the party followed the Missouri River up to a less-frequented settlement of Wyoming. There they and the wagon team crossed by ferry to Iowa, twelve days after having left Topeka. At that point Reverend Bodwell began walking behind the wagon so that Emerson could drive the wagon more easily across the rain-soaked, almost impassable bottoms first to Civil Bend and then on to Tabor.

As it happened, George Gaston of Tabor had ordered a door and windows for the town's schoolhouse then under construction, and they had recently arrived by steamboat at "the Bend." Gaston's teamster and an antislavery stalwart, Sturgis Williams, loaded the supplies along with the fugitive passengers and, by late afternoon, drove into Tabor, with the four-horse team "bringing the door and windows" and "underneath them the father, mother and the three children."[25]

The family went to the house of George and Maria Gaston to spend the night, but with the great amount of rain and swollen rivers, they ended up having to wait there several days. The Gastons had gone to Ohio, and their neighbors Abby Cummings and her niece were keeping house. They helped the black family rest and prepare for the journey ahead. The niece found them "the most interesting company of fugitives that ever passed through Tabor." She was especially impressed by the mother, whom she described as "*very beautiful*" and "lady-like and intelligent." She also related "a most touching" scene when she took the woman upstairs to show her where they were to sleep: "I stood talking with her while she undressed the little girl and boy; when they were ready for bed without any word from their mother, they knelt down, with folded hands, to repeat their evening prayers. [Despite their travails of recent weeks] those little children had not forgotten the home training, but knelt as simply and naturally for their evening prayers, as the children of safe and sheltered homes, who have never known danger.

"Do you wonder if my eyes were dimmed with tears as I bid her 'Good Night.'"[26]

After a few days, another townsman drove them by wagon toward the Nishnabotna River, with the woman riding beside him with a veil over her face and the baby in her arms and the others beneath the materials in the rear. But the family with their soaked belongings was forced to return to Tabor when the water proved too high to reach the bridge. While at the Nishnabotna a man offered to take them by boat to the bridge if they removed the wagon wheels for loading. He seemed to grow suspicious when the driver refused, so the next day they instead went north, where the family was concealed at Mr. Nashe's place in

Silver Creek. From this point it is uncertain where they traveled east and whether they safely reached their destination.[27]

This episode was hardly the end of runaways entering Civil Bend and Tabor on their way to points east. An event that shook these antislavery communities commenced only four months after Reverend Bodwell and Emerson returned to Topeka. On Thanksgiving, aided by John Williamson, a black man living in Civil Bend, two servants named Celia and Eliza Grayson escaped from the house of Nebraska City's founder and leading developer, Stephen Nuckolls. Their flight inaugurated a series of incidents associated with Nuckolls's efforts to regain his enslaved girls. Confident, determined, and no man to irritate, the hard-driving town leader sent out search parties through Civil Bend and Tabor, and then he led a mob to scour Civil Bend. The searches all resulted in lawsuits for destroyed property and personal injuries. The next year Nuckolls learned that Eliza was living in Chicago. He traveled to the city and captured the girl, but a mob of supporters rescued Eliza. He left the city embittered.[28]

While Underground Railroad operations gradually receded, the northward flow of enslaved persons from Missouri continued into the Civil War. John Brown's actions, however, soon eclipsed Iowa's memory of these events.

7

Raising the Stakes

I

As numerous Free-State parties moved across Iowa toward Kansas in 1856, two young men from Springdale, Iowa, had joined the emigrants. George B. Gill and seventeen-year-old Barclay Coppoc climbed aboard the first major Kansas-bound wagon train from Iowa City led by Shalor Eldridge, trail coordinator for Free-State overland operations.

A lean twenty-four-year-old of freethinking bent, Gill had already worked on a whaling ship in the Pacific and now was joining the Free-State cause in Kansas. In late August 1856 he and a friend happened to be in the vicinity of the Osawatomie battle and joined the fight against a large proslavery force of border Missourians that attacked, looted, and burned John Brown's family's home community. While Brown and some thirty men fought to stave off the attack, the day's events cost the life of Brown's son Frederick. Though at that time Gill had no acquaintance with John Brown, in less than two years he became one of Brown's close comrades in arms.

Gill's reminiscences in his letters tell a good part of what is known about John Brown in Iowa and of his last trip through the state. Though only formally schooled to age ten, George had a gift for expression and was a quiet but sharp, independent observer of persons and events. Gill stayed in Kansas in

Fig. 11. George B. Gill of West Liberty, Iowa, who rode with John Brown during 1858 and early 1859, wrote informative letters about Brown and his men in their Kansas and Iowa actions. Kansas State Historical Society.

1856, becoming part of a Kansas Free-State militia company for a time.[1]

None of the men who went with Brown to Harpers Ferry in 1859, apart from his sons, had fought with him in 1856, the year when Brown stepped up to resist proslavery intimidation. The men with Brown in 1856 had endured plenty of hard living, sleeping rough out in the brush. Brown had one son shot dead and another wounded and saw his eldest son driven to near insanity from imprisonment. For his tough actions, Brown himself became a reputed guerrilla chieftain although those who stood with him in Kansas did not remain. In fact, twelve of the twenty-one men who would join Brown at Harpers Ferry had been with him less than a year, and most of their experience together occurred in Iowa.

The earliest of his followers helped make his reputation, and the later enlistees admired Brown for the reputed aggressive pursuit of his antislavery convictions. The Pottawatomie killings committed in late May 1856, however notorious, showed border proslavery invaders that they faced a determined and fearsome adversary. Salmon Brown later repeated a comment of his uncle Rev. Samuel Adair, who lived in the Osawatomie vicinity, that "he never did approve of the killing but admitted that it nearly cleared the country of border ruffians."[2]

The events of 1856 soon made Brown, with his hard convictions and willingness to fight, a figure who was both dreaded and a target of proslavery hatred. Numerous bands of guerrillas on both sides roamed eastern Kansas in 1856, but Brown's Pottawatomie killings followed quickly nine days later by his success at the Battle of Black Jack set him apart from the others.

His willingness to embrace violence separated Brown and other radical Free Staters from the conservative Free-State men who wanted the movement's actions kept defensive and lawful. More important, Brown and the territory's other foremost guerrilla leader, James Montgomery (in southeast Kansas), aimed not simply to make Kansas a Free State but also actively to undermine acceptance of slavery and make its profitability insecure. Their hard-hitting methods attracted followers in Kansas, mainly young and adventurous unmarried men such as Charles Lenhart who were keen to join Free-State battles and spread hostility to slavery.

The young enlistees of Brown's and Montgomery's had come from northern states—Ohio, Maine, Iowa—and gravitated to groups of Free-State partisans. William Henry Leeman, for instance, had come west in 1856 with Dr. Calvin Cutter's party from Massachusetts. After proslavery forces turned them back at Lexington, Missouri, on the Missouri River, he joined Martin Stowell's group from Massachusetts at Keokuk, Iowa, and made it across Iowa to Kansas. Within two months the eighteen-year-old was in the thick of it, joining John Brown's "Regulars" in September for the defense of Lawrence. As with several of Brown's enlistees, the antislavery excitement affected him, merging with his "adventurous disposition" and desire to do something.[3]

For the less restrained on both sides, guerrilla operations also gave them an opportunity for thievery and plunder whether for revenge or personal gain. It happened often enough to tarnish Free-State and proslavery guerrilla operations and to undermine public opinion.

II

The men in Brown's group who followed him to Harpers Ferry began to come together in Iowa during the fall of 1857. Brown had spent the first half of the year in the East, trying to raise financial support for his plans. While there, he had met and hired an Englishman named Hugh Forbes as a military instructor to train his anticipated small body of men in Tabor, Iowa.

But at Brown's western sanctuary in Tabor, where he spent July to October, his efforts had been disappointing. Only he and his son Owen were there to read Forbes's pamphlet "Manual of the Patriotic Volunteer"; to target shoot; to clean up the arms stored in Rev. John Todd's basement that the guns' original owners, the Massachusetts State Kansas Committee, had helped transfer to Brown; and to discuss military matters with Forbes. Disagreement regarding Brown's notions for attacking slavery in Virginia soon divided Brown and Forbes. Forbes's seemingly more realistic plan, based on inciting local slave revolts rather than bringing on a general insurrection by direct assault, went nowhere with Brown. His mind was fixed on stirring a general insurrection. Anyway, he never did take well to working with others.

When in early November Forbes departed Tabor, Brown and Owen quietly reentered Kansas in their single-team wagon. At Lawrence and Topeka, Brown set about finding men of antislavery passions who wanted to resist proslavery agitation and were willing to join "a company for the purpose of putting a stop to the aggressions of the pro-slavery forces."[4]

The young men he found were unmarried with an antislavery bent who had come to Kansas without families and, caught up in the excitement of a great cause, soon were spending time with like-minded companions looking to support the Free-State struggle. As he got to know them, George Gill described his companions as fellows with "a moral basis" and not simply "adventurers." To be precise, he thought these men were the kind "who didn't know how to settle down and earn an ordinary living," and being unsure of "what to do with themselves," they "were ready for anything that was interesting."[5]

Service in antislavery militias and guerrilla outfits had given the young companions organized outlets for exploits where men ate together, became friends, and were radicalized in their forays. They had all grown up in a time when antislavery talk was increasingly in the air and when events in Kansas sparked moral outrage against proslavery injustices. These young men highly regarded the older men like John Brown, with his reputation and links to outside financial support. And now, in late 1857, he gathered the small, informal groups of friends together.[6]

Near Lawrence, Brown first visited with John E. Cook, who had studied law before coming to Kansas and was an excellent marksman. They had met in early June 1856 after the Battle of Black Jack. During that fight Brown's nine men and fifteen other Free-State volunteers killed four militia men, wounded some others, and captured twenty-five men, all of whom were commanded by Missouri militia captain and deputy marshal Henry Clay Pate. Shortly thereafter Cook arrived with Charley Lenhart, the young guerrilla leader, to help guard Brown's prisoners. Now in the fall of 1857 Cook listened to Brown and, interested in what he proposed, went to the boardinghouse of Cook's English friend Richard Realf and suggested that Luke Parsons and Richard Hinton become possible recruits. Cook, Realf, and Parsons followed Brown to Topeka, where he met with a former soldier named Aaron Dwight Stevens. Stevens, in turn, urged friends Charles W. Moffett and John Kagi to consider joining the cause. Brown also visited with a black runaway from Lexington, Missouri, named Richard Richardson.

By early December, three men who had initially agreed to meet Brown in Tabor could not make it: journalist Richard Hinton, Col. Charles W. Leonhardt, and Charley Lenhart, the young, bold Kansas fighter from Iowa. Ten of the men did arrive on time, however. The December group consisted of Owen Brown, Aaron Stevens (also known as Col. Charles Whipple in Kansas), John Kagi, Charles Plummer Tidd, Charles Moffett, Luke Parsons, William Leeman, Richard Realf, John Cook, and Richard Richardson, the black runaway. Seven of this group became the nucleus for what would be Brown's twenty-one-man band at Harpers Ferry.[7]

Nearly all the men who gathered in Tabor were in their early to mid-twenties, and some were already veteran guerrilla fighters. Stevens, who became Brown's trusted lieutenant, had once been a soldier in the Southwest. He had first met Brown in August 1856 when, with Capt. Samuel Walker's small Free-State force on their way north to help escort James Lane from Iowa into Kansas, he had overtaken the lean and weather-beaten man then carrying his wounded family members to Iowa. John Kagi, who would become Brown's closest associate, was Ohio raised, well read, and idealistic. Now a young lawyer and news correspondent, he had entered Kansas with one of Lane's groups and had joined Stevens in the Second (Topeka) Kansas Militia company. Kagi and others in the group had been captured in 1856 after taking horses from a proslavery town and were imprisoned four months, assaulted, and later wounded. After recovering, Kagi undertook census work in the Kansas Territory and turned to newspaper correspondent work, reporting for the *New York Evening Post*, *New York Tribune*, and *Washington (DC) National Era*. Also in Brown's group were Charles Tidd, a quick-tempered friend of John Cook's who had come west from Massachusetts with Dr. Cutter and Martin Stowell's caravans across Iowa, and Charles Moffett, an Iowa man from Montour (Tama County). Moffett had drifted to Kansas in 1856, and during the armed engagements in August and September, he had been captain of a detachment under James Lane's command encamped at Topeka. There was also Luke Parsons, a young wagon maker who had come from Illinois in May 1856, quickly fell in with Lenhart and Cook, and joined in the Free-State fights at Fort Titus, Osawatomie, and Franklin.

Though at the initial meeting in Tabor John Brown provided few details of what he had in mind for the organized company other than to stop proslavery aggressions, his small group presumed it concerned Kansas. Richard Realf, before leaving for Tabor, told a friend that Brown intended "to prepare a fighting nucleus for resisting the enforcement of the [proslavery Kansas] Lecompton Constitution" as a prelude to "a movement against slavery in Missouri."[8] So at Tabor he was surprised along with Cook and Parsons when Captain Brown informed them that his "ultimate destination was the State of Virginia."[9]

Argument immediately flared. Cook had supposed Brown's plan would only concern Kansas and Missouri rather than somewhere out east. Realf and Parsons agreed with Cook, but without money to return to Lawrence and hearing the others' pleas to stay, they consented to go on.

That issue resolved, the party stayed briefly in Tabor while Captain Brown prepared to move operations to Ashtabula, Ohio, where all would spend the winter in military training. He obtained teams for two covered wagons in which they would load the stores of material at Tabor: "blankets, clothing, boots, ammunition, and about two hundred revolvers of the Massachusetts Arms patent." The main goods, however, were fifteen boxes containing two hundred Sharps carbines. They distributed their weight between the two wagons along with the other materials.

While at Tabor they learned of a Missouri runaway slave's plight in Nebraska City. Having fled to the territory, the man had been jailed after his captors shot him and broke his arm, which a doctor then amputated. Threatened by proslavery men at Brownville, he was transferred to a jail in Nebraska City. Brown told the people of Tabor that if they would cover their actual expenses, he and his men would travel the twenty-five miles, cross the Missouri River, rescue the man, and place him in their hands. But the townsmen ultimately refused, fearing it might lead to unforeseen consequences.[10]

So on December 4, 1857, Brown's men departed for Springdale, Iowa, from where they intended to continue by train for Ohio. Their two wagons were heavily loaded, and those not driving walked across snow-covered ground. They moved slowly on the poor roads, nearly freezing from the bitterly cold weather, and stayed away from towns lest the arms and ammunition aboard their wagons be discovered.

At night they set up camp near the side of a road or trail and found feed for the mules. They fought the chill with a fire and a large canvas, which they put up in lean-to fashion, fixing it to the ground on the side against the cold wind and slanting it up poles toward the fire. Under it, wrote Parsons, "we all slept there side by side and were tolerably comfortable, barring the smoke." Owen Brown's diary entry from one evening on the trail described the wintery journey: "Very cold night; prairie wolves howl nobly; bought and carried hay on our backs two and a half miles [to feed the mules]; some of the men a little down in the mouth—distance travelled 20 miles."[11]

On this trip during winter nights, they got to know each other better. Four personalities stood out. They all considered Aaron Stevens, a onetime soldier in the western territories and guerrilla band operator out of Topeka, a generous and brave man who was impulsive but with a great sense of humor. Gill saw in him "one of nature's noblemen" who attracted the confidence of the others, often so much so as to "weigh heavily upon him at times." Everybody liked John Cook, with his social and hearty informality. Talkative though suave when he needed to be, he was a well-meaning man of good principles whose sharpshooting ability with firearms was envied.[12]

Charles Tidd stood out as a reliable, fearless, and affectionate man. He and Stevens had the finest singing voices of the group, but Tidd, who was also notorious for his sexual pursuits, had a quick and sarcastic temper, which often led to quarrels. Indeed, the impulsive natures of both Stevens and Tidd—the two most physically athletic among the men—made for occasional testiness between them.[13]

Then there was John Kagi, a regular *New York Tribune* writer and the man closest to Brown. Gill felt him to be "the most thoroughly educated of the party." Standing before others in discussion with his "long and angular build" slightly bent and hands behind his back, Kagi spoke in a way that appealed to thoughtful listeners. A man of "unruffled serenity" and an agnostic—being uninterested in religion's "useless problems"—his optimism found "no day so dark that he did not see somewhere the sun peering through the clouds." Richard Realf, an Englishman who had traveled to Kansas across Iowa in the fall of 1856 and worked as a correspondent with the *Illinois State Gazette*, caught everyone's attention with his precocious personal charm and poetry writing. His brilliant public talks enthralled listeners, though those closer to him noticed a sort of unstable mix of highly imaginative and melancholic personality.[14]

Among these conspicuous ones were quieter personalities. Owen Brown (John's son), considered one of the best of Brown's men, who had a lame arm and a "calm, philosophical way of speaking" that was not easily brushed aside; and William Leeman, age nineteen with a bit of a wild streak, who had fought with Brown at the Osawatomie in 1856 and later had served with Aaron Stevens. Leeman, who was socially likable and felt himself part of a noble cause, smoked much and drank some, but Gill also noticed he "would go around a section rather than go past a dog that would bark at him." Also with the bunch were Charles Moffett of Montour, Iowa, and Luke Parsons of Byron, Illinois, who had both participated in the Kansas Free-State fighting in 1856 with Parsons at the Battles of Black Jack and Osawatomie, and Richard Richardson, an intelligent man who had escaped from slavery in Lexington, Missouri, the previous year.[15]

The men knew their leader, John Brown, in a general way as a fearless, tough-minded Kansas fighter with eastern financial backers. Looking at him they saw what an antislavery man from Grinnell, Iowa, had witnessed: "a quiet, resolute, keen eyed old man of about sixty years," with "nothing of the ruffian in appearance," who seemed motivated "by high moral and religious principles." As to his appearance, George Gill described Brown as a man "about five feet ten or eleven inches tall, very bony and sinewy."[16]

Brown's followers recognized other personal qualities in their daily contacts with the Old Captain. His personal magnetism for enlisting men drew from his low-key, casual, and friendly way without being forceful. He was quiet and charismatic while encouraging his men that "if they believed as he did, he would be glad to have their assistance in freeing slaves" and together fight for their common goal. Getting there would not be easy, Brown acknowledged, and he, like his men, would need to shoulder a willing acceptance of hardship.[17]

After several weeks of living together and observing daily routines, the men glimpsed other sides of Brown as well. A mix of bravery and caution, Brown was easygoing but not very talkative, clipped in expression, and with his own share of odd habits. To outsiders who thought him to be a Bible reader and a praying man, Gill commented, "I never heard him pray in my life. Nor do I know that he carried a bible. He carried the 'philosophy of Confucius,' which [a financial backer] Gerrit Smith gave him and which he promised Gerrit that he would read and which he did a very little occasionally simply because he had promised to do so." Though he told Gill he "could not comprehend why God permitted the sin of slavery to exist," he saw himself as an instrument of God and "that he need have no fear for as long as God needed him, he would protect him. And if no longer needed his life was not worth preserving."[18]

Brown did not, however, push his own religious convictions on his men, who had their own wide-ranging thoughts on the subject. Kagi and Gill were nonbelievers, others were of spiritualist or unknown religious bent, and men from Quaker households soon joined the band. Stevens once stumped Brown on God's active intervention in human affairs with the question that "'if God controls all things, and dislikes the institution of slavery, why does he allow it to exist.' 'Well,' answered Brown 'that is one question I cannot answer.'" Brown, however, was "always much given to moralizing," which made his personal company "rather depressing. The boys were always *perfectly respectful* to him," stated Gill, but waited to "have their fun" until he was not there [emphasis his]. And his men were hardly ignorant puppets, for Kagi, Realf, and Cook were well-read newspaper correspondents with pronounced views of their own. What held them together was not leader worship, philosophy, or religion, but their mutual hatred of slavery and their wish to strike blows against it.[19]

When not in tents and outdoor shelters, recalled Gill, Brown "did not stay very much with his men, and kept out of sight as much as possible." But when living in close quarters, they also saw a few of his lesser aspects or foibles. "He was intolerant in little things and in little ways," Gill remembered. Although the Old Captain's diet included no butter or cheese and he did not insist others avoid it, it was another matter when it came to his drink, tea. Disregarding their wishes "he would wrangle and compel them to drink tea or nothing, as he was cook and would not make coffee for them."[20]

More irritating to his rather rambunctious crew was his rigid manner. They had heard he was especially tough with his family, but here, wrote Gill, "I have known Stevens to sometimes raise merry hell when the old man would get too dictatorial. He was iron and had neither sympathy or feeling for the timid or weak of will." And yet, although Brown did not much like Tidd, he liked Stevens, perhaps because he did not raise a fuss against Brown's dictation "in situations where it was a captain's right."[21]

Gill summed up John Brown's lesser qualities as his being "very superstitious, very selfish and very intolerant, with great self esteem." Indeed, a part of him was "essentially vindictive in his nature," being unable to "brook a rival." Further, "at first he was very fond of [guerrilla leader James] Montgomery"—a man of mirth who was not disposed to impose his will on others— "but when he found that Montgomery had thoughts of his own, and could not be dictated to, why, he loved him no longer. Montgomery, Lane and all others went down before his imperial self." He was delighted when at a church meeting in Grinnell, Iowa, Josiah B. Grinnell referred to him as "Moses."[22]

But in early 1858, these traits were but irritants to his men as they encamped across Iowa. At day's end their hard living vanished in moments of companionship. During various evenings around the fire, to relieve the chilly tedium they joined in singing or debating issues, all presided over by Captain Brown. As Luke Parsons recalled, the Old Captain "used to name the pieces that he wanted sung & very frequently 'The Slave has seen the northern stars' [and] 'From Greenlands Icy Mountains' & c. &c," all of which he "joined with a harty [sic] good will." And when enjoying himself in song and other activities, according to George Gill, Brown would habitually spread "his hands out in front of him, palms down and going through an undulating motion." Parsons noticed that Brown's "favorite posture was standing with his hands clasped behind him under his coat. He was a man of few words, but was a good listener." And there was plenty of discussion of issues, as Owen Brown entered in his diary four days out on the road: "Cold, wet and snowy; hot discussion upon the Bible and war . . . warm argument upon the effects of the abolition of slavery upon the Southern States, Northern States, commerce and manufactures, also upon the British provinces and the civilized world; whence came our civilization and origin? Talk about prejudices against color; question proposed for debate,—greatest general, Washington or Napoleon."[23]

The relief and break from travel on Sundays helped keep spirits up in the twenty-one days' journey to Marengo, Iowa, which they passed on Christmas Day. They walked the final forty-five miles to Springdale within a couple days. By the twenty-ninth John Kagi wrote his sister from there about the journey having been "very long and tedious." A few days later Kagi wrote that he expected they would take the train to Chicago. But this plan was not to be.[24]

Brown had assumed he could sell his mule teams and wagons for cash in Springdale and continue their journey by train to Ohio, but he found ready money tight from the deepening effect of the nation's financial Panic of 1857. So he struck an arrangement with William Maxson, who was a nearby farmer though not a Quaker, and bartered the teams and wagons in exchange

Fig. 12. William Maxson sheltered and fed John Brown's recruits when they trained at his farm during the winter of 1857–58. State Historical Society of Iowa, Iowa City.

Fig. 13. The Maxsons' house, where nine of John Brown's men stayed with the Maxson family of seven over the winter. State Historical Society of Iowa, Iowa City.

for Maxson putting up Brown's men at his place for the next three months (based on a rate of $1.50 per week for each man). By January 11 the men had settled in at Maxson's place, a grout house three miles north of Springdale. "Tidd and Realf slept in the parlor bedroom, Cook and Kagi in a room off the kitchen, and the other six men and the darkey in the east room upstairs."[25]

Before leaving town Brown arranged with John H. Painter, a Quaker, to haul the fifteen boxes of Sharps rifles plus two hundred revolvers to the rail depot at West Liberty. From there Painter shipped them marked as "carpenter's tools" and addressed them to John Brown, Jr., at Conneaut in Ashtabula County, Ohio. John Brown, Jr., first took the arms to a nearby village and stored them at a furniture place beneath some coffins, and he later transferred them to a haymow room built in a farmer's barn in an adjoining township. Meanwhile, once Brown had worked out the arms shipment arrangements with Painter, the Old Captain departed Springdale on January 15 for the East. Painter had consented to send the arms out of his belief that it was God's service for the rights of man, but it came at a cost: he was "unchurched" by the Friends' Yearly Meeting.[26]

In the East, Brown spent time visiting with his New England–based financial supporters. He wanted their aid to launch a spring campaign against slavery east of the Allegheny Mountains. Simultaneously, he pondered how to how to deal with the behavior of Hugh Forbes, the drillmaster he had hired the previous summer to train his men. Forbes had departed Tabor following disagreements with Brown. Still angry, Forbes now attempted to expose Brown's plans in letters sent to Brown's benefactors and to leading political figures. Meanwhile, Brown also took a reconnaissance trip to Canada, looking to encourage blacks to become involved in his plans, and then made three trips to the black community of Chatham (some fifty miles from Detroit in western Ontario).[27]

In the meantime, his little band at Springdale spent three hours every day doing military exercises in a field near Maxson's house and taking day jobs close by such as husking corn or cutting wood. With his rich bass voice and passionate manner, Aaron Stevens took Hugh Forbes's place as drillmaster, instructing the men in tactics and target practice and in lessons drawn from Forbes's "Manual for the Patriotic Volunteer." Cook, with his love of firearms and exceptional marksmanship, also led the men in target practice, and Stevens's ability as a swordsman, using wooden swords fashioned by Owen Brown, drew the trainees' wide interest.[28]

The military drills, performed openly in daylight with no effort to disguise them, did not go unnoticed and did not sit well with some of the locals. While the Springdale Quakers, most of whom were intensely antislavery, thought the training was intended for some kind of Kansas operations, a few in the area suspected the boarders were Mormon spies. Maxson's non-Quaker neighbors to the east had their own dark suspicions. His Iowa Township farm abutted the eastern border of Springdale Township, and most folks in the township staunchly opposed abolitionists. Upon seeing the strange goings-on, indignant citizens of Iowa Township met and passed a resolution excluding Maxson from their township, a declaration he proudly accepted.[29]

Group discipline remained strong despite the close quarters, the boisterous activity, and to the consternation of a few local parents, the pursuit of an occasional romance with neighborhood sweethearts and one resulting pregnancy. Mainly, however, the Quaker community enjoyed winter diversions provided by the young men, including a mock legislature held at the village schoolhouse a mile away. Topics included introducing and debating bills to nullify the Dred Scott decision and Fugitive Slave Act, to appropriate fifty thousand acres to divide into farms for those liberating themselves from slavery, and to design the ideal "State of Topeka." In these gatherings, three men stood out: the brilliant Richard Realf, the gregarious John Cook, and the analytical John Kagi. Realf and Cook also gave lectures in school districts of nearby towns during these winter months.[30]

George Gill, watching and listening, admired how "Realf, with fiery eloquence would hold his audience spellbound; Kagi with calm, logical deductions would be invincible, and Cook would hold an intermediate position—comic, poetic, or mirthful, as the occasion demanded." In private conversations, however, others also carried influence: Owen Brown "with his calm, orderly, and honest ways, Stevens with his fine, rich voice, and passionate thoughts [that] made life worth living in their boarding-house and all around them." Such fellows Gill saw as "earnest men, as liberal towards others as they were positive in their own convictions," which to a stranger's eyes looked one minute like a boardinghouse fight about to break out and minutes later having evaporated in "a cheery, hearty laugh."[31]

All the men welcomed Brown's return in April 1858. With so many crowded in at William Maxson's place, the tight quarters invariably led to occasional frayed nerves and bickering. Impatient to get on with their mission, the men's personality differences, such as Tidd's sarcasm and known intimacy with a neighbor girl, were bound to grate on one another. Tidd's and Stevens's impulsive styles also found them at odds.

Offsetting any irritability was the welcome news that Brown had added two local men to the small group. Then living a few miles away in West Liberty and probably kept up to date by his brother, Dr. H. Gill, at Springdale, George Gill knew about the group's wintertime activities in Springdale. When Brown returned to Springdale for two days in April 1858 and rejoined his men, George brought Stewart Taylor to meet John Brown at John Painter's house. Taylor, a friend of Gill's who worked at a West Liberty blacksmith shop, was a practical-minded fellow with a "wonderful tenacity" in his notions of what was right. Gill had known Brown slightly in Kansas, and Brown recognized him upon his introducing Taylor. Brown welcomed the two men to join the group. By the time Brown's men departed the next day, Taylor had quit his job, and both he and Gill climbed aboard the train bound for Chicago to Detroit and on to Chatham, Canada.[32]

III

Traveling in the guise of a company of surveyors returning east, two incidents targeted the black member of their group, Richard Richardson. When changing cars at Rock Island, some onlookers moved to have him arrested as a "runaway nigger." But before the bystanders could act, Gill wrote, "we were speedily relieved of this by the conductor taking him by the arm and pushing him into the car and immediately starting the train." They arrived at Chicago at dawn the next morning and ate breakfast at the Massasoit House without incident, but upon returning for afternoon dinner, "the landlord informed the old patriarch that our colored man would have to wait and eat with the servants." Giving "the landlord a little of his terse logic," Gill recalled, Brown got up and left. The others followed. They walked to the Adams House to dine, where everything went well, "caste and color, accidental and otherwise, not being considered."[33]

Soon they crossed to Chatham, Canada, some fifty miles east of Detroit, Michigan. At this town of six thousand persons, one-third of them black runaways, Brown conducted a secret constitutional convention, one aimed to fashion a provisional government for a black state in the southern Appalachians. Only thirty-four blacks and twelve whites participated in the two-day schoolhouse meeting. The small turnout disappointed Brown as did the failure of any influential American blacks or his eastern financial backers to attend. The best Brown got was the participants' heartfelt support for the ideals expressed in the preamble to his provisional government's constitution.[34]

Within a few weeks, Brown (now growing a long white beard as disguise), along with John Kagi and Charles Tidd, was back in Kansas via St. Louis. George Gill and Aaron Stevens arrived through Iowa, with Gill entering the territory in early August and Aaron Stevens shortly thereafter.

What prompted Brown's return to Kansas and postponement of his raid was Hugh Forbes's letters, which claimed that John Brown and his conspirators were about to take reckless actions in the East with Kansas arms. When Brown met with his men in Cleveland, he told them that "the friends on whom he relied for money were, as he expressed it, in a panic on account of Forbes." By going to Kansas and making, "if possible, . . . some demonstration as an offset to Forbes's revelations," Brown believed the betrayer's allegations would be discredited.[35]

With this announced change in plans, the rest of Brown's disappointed group split up to find work. While Richard Realf went to New York to keep an eye on Forbes and Richard Richardson continued to Canada and worked on a grain farm, Owen Brown journeyed to his brother Jason's place in Akron, Ohio. William Leeman, Stewart Taylor, and Luke Parsons worked on the farm of E. Alexander Fobes (brother-in-law of John Brown, Jr.) in Ohio until Parsons returned at summer's end to his folks' place in Byron, Illinois. Charles Moffett did odd jobs as he traveled back to his Tama County, Iowa, home. John Cook went to Harpers Ferry, where he found work and scouted out the surrounding area. He tried hard to convince George Gill to go with him, but Gill at the time "did not have entire faith in the scheme being carried to a successful conclusion" or how soon an attempt to do it would ever be made.[36]

8

Heaven Sent

I

Back in Kansas, John Brown and a few of the men—George Gill, Aaron Stevens, John Kagi, and Charles Tidd—briefly stayed around Lawrence and in early July moved on to southeast Kansas, where they hung about into the fall. These southeastern counties lay below the big bend in the Missouri River where no natural boundaries separated Missouri and Kansas. The area was still in turmoil, having been relatively untouched by Free-State successes in 1856.[1]

The situation was especially unsettled in Linn and Bourbon Counties, which bordered on Missouri. After proslavery guerrilla bands had driven them out earlier, Free-State settlers began coming back during 1857. Soon violence erupted in land disputes, as proslavery public officials intimidated and harassed Free-State arrivals. Trouble centered about Fort Scott in Bourbon County and Paris, the Linn County seat where proslavery leadership dominated. Radical Free-State partisans rallied behind James Montgomery, who lived near Mound City in Linn County. The guerrilla chieftain in 1857 stood where John Brown had been the year before, the object of arrest warrants and attacks but highly regarded by Free-State settlers looking for protection.

In early July 1858 Brown, Kagi, and Tidd visited James Montgomery at his log cabin with the thought of joining forces. Only six weeks earlier thirty proslavery men under Charles A. Hamelton (spelled Hamilton by some writers) retaliated for Montgomery's men having driven them into Missouri. Hamelton and others crossed back to Kansas near the Marais des Cygnes in northeastern Linn County and, grabbing whatever Free-State settlers they came upon, forced eleven men into a ravine. Standing above, they shot them down, killing five and wounding five, and one lay uninjured after feigning being hit. In response Montgomery raided West Point, Missouri, in search of two proslavery assassins, but they escaped.[2]

With such disorder in the border counties, Kansas territorial governor James Denver conducted a personal inspection and wrote: "We passed through a country almost depopulated by the depredations of the predatory bands under Montgomery, presenting a scene of desolation such as I never expected to have witnessed in any country inhabited by American citizens. . . ." Brown, while doubtless disagreeing that Montgomery was the sole cause, did see all around that "deserted farms and dwellings lie in all directions for some miles along the line, and the remaining inhabitants watch every appearance of persons moving about, with anxious jealousy and vigilance."[3]

The Hamelton massacre hung as a shroud over the area when John Brown encamped about 220 yards from the deep ravine where the widely reported murders occurred. Here, within a quarter mile from the Missouri line, he began to enlist men under the assumed name of the Shubel Morgan Company. Soon his company contained ten men, including six of the previous winter's trainees at Springdale, Iowa, plus four others who had escaped Hamelton's clutches. Brown's own men included his son Owen, John Kagi, Aaron Stevens (Charles Whipple), Charles Tidd, William Leeman, and George Gill. Though Brown kept quiet about being back in Kansas, his presence soon became known, increasing local residents' fears in this part of Kansas and adjacent Missouri. Soon, Territorial Governor Denver placed an armed posse on the adjacent quarter section at the Kansas-Missouri border.[4]

Brown's thought of joining together with James Montgomery's force, which was larger in number than any Brown had commanded, did not last long. His praise for Montgomery as a gentlemanly, brave natural leader of integrity and purpose gradually bumped up against Montgomery's own headstrong ideas, which led Brown—rankled at any thought of serving under another—to go it alone. This choice was not so for his men, who went back and forth between the two "captains" and served depending on the excitement of the moment.[5]

The Old Captain's bouts of the ague, a malarial-like condition with alternating chills, fever, and sweating, reduced his active leadership in southeast Kansas. His plain, frugal encampment had likely brought it on, he thought, for "I had lain every night without shelter, suffering from cold rains and heavy dews, together with the oppressive heat of the days." He first came down with ague July 23, and it continued until well into November. Throughout, his letters were regularly sprinkled with comments of "very feeble," "very weak, and write with great labor," "still weak," and "not quite recovered." His health grew worse in August. At Osawatomie, John Kagi, Brown's half sister Mrs. Adair, and the Adair family attended him as he lay for four weeks in a corner of Reverend Adair's cabin. Even as late as December 2 he reported, "My health is some improved" although "still I get a shake now and then." Milder attacks also had struck George Gill and John Kagi. Not surprising, the initiative in guerrilla activities fell to Montgomery with Brown only intermittently involved.[6]

In these operations, "Kagi was with Montgomery a good deal of the time," wrote Richard Hinton. "In the beginning of November, the latter's cabin was fired into. Kagi, a guest there at the time, assisted in its successful defense. Tidd was also on hand. Gill mainly remained with the Captain [Brown]. Stevens held 'Snyder's Fort' [Brown's modestly reinforced encampment]. Jeremiah G. Anderson and Albert Hazlett were usually under Montgomery's command, the former having been several times under arrest. Leeman remained with Stevens."[7]

The guerrilla struggle heated up during mid-December when Montgomery with a hundred men attacked Fort Scott to rescue Benjamin Rice, a Free-State settler who many believed had been wrongly arrested for murder. Brown's men participated, and though he attended the advance rendezvous, Brown stayed back when Montgomery was chosen to lead the effort. Montgomery's group succeeded but not before John Kagi had received a load of buckshot in his back, which his heavy overcoat protected from serious injury, while a member of Montgomery's party in turn had killed the shooter. The affair inflamed proslavery feeling, angered the new territorial governor Samuel Medary, and embarrassed moderate Free-State leaders, who wrongly accused Brown of committing the outrage.

Four days later, however, came a greater test for those trying to contain the turbulence.[8]

II

George Gill, reconnoitering the Kansas-Missouri border on December 19, happened upon a black fellow presumably selling some brooms. "I found that his name was Jim Daniels; that his wife, self and babies, belonged to an estate, and were to be sold at an administrator's sale in the immediate future, and that his present business was not in selling brooms particularly, but to find help to get himself, family and a few friends in the vicinity away from these threatening conditions."

Gill considered the thirty-year-old Daniels "a fine looking Mulatto." White residents around his proslavery neighborhood knew him as a cheerful man of "fun and mischief" although "a little tricky and a most astonishing liar."[9] Gill, after parting from Daniels, rushed to locate Brown, and they quickly arranged to assist the Daniels on the following night. Up to this point Brown had been "just waiting for something to turn up; or in his theo-logical way of thinking was expecting or hoping that God would provide him a basis of action. When this came he hailed it as heaven sent."[10]

Likely for mutual protection, Gill and Brown, Kagi, Tidd, and Stevens were living in the log building that housed Montgom-ery's mother-in-law a short distance from Montgomery's place. The men had thrown up an earthwork around the building and punched a few "concealed loopholes between the logs in the house."

As Gill, Brown, and the other men discussed how best to enter Missouri, a two-part scheme developed. Brown would lead one party of about a dozen men to the James Lawrence farm on the north side of the Little Osage River (running through the cen-ter of Vernon County). There Lawrence's son-in-law, Harvey G. Hicklin, and his family lived as tenants along with the Daniels family. Leading a second smaller party of eight—Tidd, Hazlett, and five others—Aaron Stevens would ride south of the Little Osage to retrieve a friend of the Daniels family.[11]

Recruits for the raid in Brown's group were a mixed lot. Along with John Kagi and George Gill were two undesirables associ-ated with James Montgomery—Charles R. Jennison (known as "Doc" Jennison), a stridently aggressive antislavery man will-ing to plunder foes, and Samuel "Pickles" Wright, a known horse thief and reckless young man. A good addition was Jeremiah G. Anderson, a twenty-five-year-old Iowa man from Kossuth in Des Moines County who later would join in Brown's Harpers Ferry raid. He had come to Kansas in 1857 and settled on the Little Osage in Bourbon County. Twice arrested by proslavery men, then imprisoned at Fort Scott, Anderson by 1858 was a reliable Montgomery lieutenant.[12]

Vernon County, Missouri, had comparatively few slaves, but Free-State "Jayhawker" parties now and then entered its border counties. By 1858, as a Vernon County historian put it, "the Aboli-tionists were no longer despised; they were feared and dreaded."[13]

The evening of December 20 was chilly with some snow on the ground. The two raiding parties gathered together and mounted their horses at "Bain's Fort," a large log house a little northwest of the present town of Fulton in northern Bourbon County. They moved out toward the state boundary a few miles away. Crossing the open border they wended their way a few miles over rolling prairie lands toward Hicklin's place while Aaron Stevens's group broke right and moved south to cross the Little Osage. Long about midnight Brown's group rode into Hicklin's farmyard.[14]

The farmer awoke to a shout of "Get up and make a light!" He peered out the window to see in the bright moonlight a yard full of armed men. Thinking they might be robbers, he grabbed the $52 in gold and silver from his pocketbook and quickly stuffed it into the straw tick of his two children's trundle bed in the middle of the room. He scarcely stepped back from the bed before men battered in the east door. Stepping through the doorway, they demanded Hicklin's surrender as one of the men, James Steele, immediately began searching for money and reached into the straw ticks of the bed of Hicklin's wife but left the children's bed untouched. Harvey Hicklin and Jim Daniels—his father-in-law's slave—were friends, and Gill believed Hicklin to be "a very fair man and perhaps a very good one."[15]

Daniels wanted none of the Hicklins' personal belongings taken. But despite orders to leave the Hicklins' items untouched, some ignored this direction. Brown intended they consider "all personal property belonging to the estate . . . as being owned by the slaves, having surely been bought with their labor." The Brown rescue party further seized "a conveyance and also something to dispose of for funds to defray costs of the long overland trip." Anyway, with his hands full inside, Gill acknowledged that "some of our number proved to be more adventurous, ready to take from friend or foe if opportunity offered." Once Gill discovered men taking watches and other articles, he informed Brown, who "caused an immediate disgorgement" of at least the most visible items. As George Gill summed it up, "The party was hastily gathered and the selections [of men] were not perfect."[16]

While Daniels handled arrangements on the outside, Brown entered the house and, looking at Hicklin, said, "'Well, you seem to be in a pretty tight place. But you shan't be hurt if you behave yourself,' etc."

Hicklin recalled what happened next: "He said he knew I was only a tenant there, but he was going to take off all the negroes and free them, and he was also going to take provisions for them and property enough to bear their expenses to freedom. He talked with me rather pleasantly for thirty minutes or more. He said he was doing the Lord's will and was not ashamed, etc. At last a man came to the door and said, 'Captain, the wagons are loaded and all is ready.'"

Brown directed two of his men to stay with the Hicklins for two hours and to shoot them if they attempted to escape. The party left about two o'clock, and the guards remained about an hour before departing. Accompanying Brown's party were three enslaved adults—a man named Sam Harper, Jim Daniels, and his wife, Narcissa, pregnant and close to giving birth—and the two Daniels children. The party also took two horses and a harness, a yoke of oxen, and an old large Conestoga wagon, plus some provisions: pork, lard, tallow, saddle, shotgun, overcoat, boots, and blankets.[17]

They went south three-fourths of a mile to the farm of John Larue, who had five persons enslaved at his place. Finding the family asleep, Brown "awoke them with the usual voice of 'Hallo,' which when replied to by 'What's wanted,' was answered by the old man . . . 'We have come after your Negroes and their property. Will you surrender or fight?'" Perhaps expecting trouble John Larue had plenty of arms inside, as well as his father and a boarder, and replied, "We'll fight." "All right," said Brown, "we'll smoke you out, then," which "would have been attempted forthwith, as there was plenty of fire in the negro quarters."

Then Larue, his father, and boarder quickly reconsidered and surrendered.

Meantime, once Harvey Hicklin's guards left, he ran to his neighbor's house at about half past three, and the two rode together to John Larue's. They "found the old gentleman, Isaac Larue, sitting by the fire," who told them Brown had taken John Larue and Dr. A. Ervin, the boarder, as prisoners. They figured Brown's group had departed only a short time ago because all could still hear "the rattle of the caravan" in the distance. Larue had lost five Negroes—two were named George and David—six horses, a wagon, eight hundred pounds of pork, and considerable bedding and clothing.[18]

While Brown's raiding party moved slowly toward Kansas, Aaron Stevens's smaller party reached the Little Osage River only to find its banks full. The flooded river slowed their crossing, but once across, they moved quietly down the valley toward the farm of David Cruise, the owner of an enslaved woman named Jane whom the Daniels wanted freed. The sixty-year-old Kentucky-born Cruise had lived on the farm for more than twenty years. He had built a farm of several hundred acres and owned a sizable amount of personal property and livestock. On his place were Lucinda (his second wife), two boys (the older one was away), and two enslaved workers—George and Jane. To his proslavery neighbors David Cruise seemed an esteemed gray-headed pioneer, not a "border ruffian," but antislavery men saw him as "one of the most active enemies of the free-state cause, and having accumulated much property through raids into Kansas."[19]

When Stevens's men pulled up to the Cruise house, Stevens called out and asked to stay the night. The men represented themselves as proslavery friends from north in Bates County who had found the Little Osage full and impassable on their trip back from Fort Scott. At their first shouted "halloo," David Cruise reached for his revolver. His thirteen-year-old son, Rufus, later recalled, it "was in the scabbard with a string over the hammer," and Rufus "moved the string so it would come out of the scabbard." The men outside repeated, "We can't cross the river, and it's too cold to camp." Though his son urged his father to not let them in, David Cruise relented and said, "'I guess they are all right,' and then he opened the door, drove away the dogs, which were barking furiously, and told them to come in."[20]

Moving toward the door, Cruise had handed off the revolver to his son, who passed it to his mother in bed. Stevens and two others stepped inside, and as the two sat down to warm their hands in the fire, suddenly Cruise's son saw that Stevens "drew his pistol and cocked it, and said to [the] father, 'You are my prisoner.'" Seeing it, the father softly asked his son where the pistol was, but the frightened boy was already starting to break for the door. He ran onto the porch, where one of the raiding party shouted at him to stop.

Momentarily falling down, he then heard a single shot go off inside the house as he got up and ran into the darkness. Stevens's shot struck Cruise as he stood in his nightclothes at the end of the fireplace, and he fell to the floor dead. Stories differ about what had happened, with neighbors having heard Cruise was unarmed and that his revolver was out of reach on his and his wife's bed. George Gill, however, later heard returning members of Stevens's party say that, in the half light of the cabin as the boy ran out the door, Cruise had reached for a nearby revolver, but it had a string on it that entangled its use and thus enabled Stevens to save himself by firing first.[21]

The Cruises' boy, who got away in his nightclothes and barefoot in the cold night, ran four miles to Allen Mitchell's house in snow six inches deep but, he recalled, "felt no pain until after I got to Mitchell's by the fire, although my feet felt as big as bushel baskets." The next morning he was taken home, where his frozen feet were dressed. How his father's loss touched him is unknown, but evidently Cruise's wife was "seemingly not much surprised" at her husband's fate. According to what Stevens's hardly disinterested friend Gill heard—perhaps from Jane, the Cruises' enslaved woman—the wife "had often told him that if he didn't behave himself he would get killed sooner or later."[22]

From the Cruise farm, Stevens's party liberated the Daniels' friend Jane. Rufus Cruise heard later that when the two men with Stevens had sat down inside by the fireside, Jane was seen looking "through the window at them and laughed and then went back to the kitchen and began to pack up. She told my mother 'good-bye' and took with her $60 in money, part hers and part my mother's, and all her own clothing, bed and bedding; all these were put in one of our wagons and hauled away, with many other things." Overall the party took away two yoke of oxen, a wagon loaded with numerous items and clothing, eleven mules, and two horses, but the only money they had found was $30 in gold from the pants of David Cruise (the main family money, buried in the saddle house, went undiscovered). Leaving the Cruise farm the raiding party went a half mile east and took a mule from the farm of Hugh Martin, though he was not a slaveholder.[23]

As Stevens's group got under way, John Brown's larger caravan north of the Little Osage continued its unhurried late-night return to Kansas. They carried hostages John Larue and his boarder, Dr. Ervin, to a half mile west of Barnesville in Kansas Territory, where they were set free to return home.[24]

The eleven now liberated enslaved persons exuded "genial warmth" that broke the "very cold night." Gill recalled with pleasure: "One of the women pitied poor Massa! He's in a bad fix; hogs not killed; corn not shucked, and niggers all gone." When one driving the oxen asked how far it would be to Canada and heard back fifteen hundred miles, he yelled, "Oh golly; we never get dar before spring!" He brought the whip down on the oxen, shouting, "Git up dar, buck; bung along." Jim Daniels remained quiet through the journey, more aware of "the dangers of the situation" than the others were with "implicit confidence in their protectors."[25]

Fig. 14. Sam and Jane Harper, liberated in John Brown's raid of December 20, 1858, upon two farms in Vernon County, Missouri, were wed by a justice of the peace in Springdale, Iowa, and spent their remaining years in Canada. Kansas State Historical Society.

III

By morning both parties were back at Captain Bain's fort, where Brown learned "to his sorrow" that Stevens had killed Cruise. Thereafter Stevens never could shake the killing from his mind, and just before the Harpers Ferry raid when asked about what had happened, he replied he did not like talking about it. "'You might call it a case of self-defense,' answered Stevens, 'or you might also say that I had no business in there, and that the old man was right.'"[26]

Uncertain about who might be coming after them, those raiders who did not return to their homes moved "into a deep ravine" away from the road for the day. At night they shifted to the house of Augustus Wattles north of Mound City. Arriving about midnight, all at first gathered inside the house. It so happened James Montgomery and a few of his men were sleeping in the loft. Soon, as told by Mrs. Emma Wattles Morse, the men in the loft were roused "by the chattering and laughing of the darkies as they warmed around the stove while Mrs. Wattles was getting supper. Montgomery put his head down the stairway, exclaiming: 'How is this, Capt. Brown? Whom have you here?" Brown then introduced them as "'*a part* of my family' from carrying 'the war into Africa.'" After supper the women and children were taken to the house of J. O. Wattles, only a few steps away; the men went to their wagons while Brown and two of his men lay on the floor for the two or three hours remaining of the night."[27]

If Brown did not know it at the moment, Montgomery knew that the operation and the killing of Cruise would result in a general uproar as had happened the previous week after his own controversial raid on Fort Scott.[28]

Back in Vernon County, Missouri, the raid's victims and twenty-two frightened north-county residents immediately petitioned their governor, Robert M. Stewart, for protection. "We are unorganized, without arms, ammunition, or the means of subsistence in case of a border war," wrote the petitioners, whereas "this lawless band in Kansas is organized, armed with Sharp's rifles, [and] threaten our whole border, causing life and property to be insecure." Governor Stewart quickly responded with a proclamation deploring the acts and, acting beyond his authority, offered $3,000 for the arrest of Brown and $1,000 for each of the murderers and their delivery to Missouri authorities. The General Assembly, however, failed to appropriate any money. Only the James Buchanan administration soon offered a reward of $250 for the arrest of Brown and Montgomery.[29]

Meanwhile, Missouri border citizens had responded at the first alarm of the raid. At Duncan Creek 250 men from surrounding northern Vernon and Bates Counties came together the next day. They lingered about the Kansas border for a time but did not cross to attack Bain's fort, where they could have successfully captured or killed Brown's entire group. Inflated fears about whom and what they might face shrank their resolve, and in ones and twos the men drifted off.[30]

On the Kansas side of the line, rumors flew about Missourians coming across at any moment. Upon reaching the ears of conservative Free-State leaders—defensive-minded men who opposed offensive incursions into Missouri—they began organizing a force that would either kill John Brown or hand him over to Missouri. But when they learned others to their rear stood ready to defend Brown's group, and judged that James Montgomery would likely support Brown, the leaders backed off.[31]

The controversial rescue only grew in the hands of newspaper editors. George W. Brown, editor of the *Herald of Freedom* (organ of the New England Emigrant Aid Company) whose destroyed office from the sacking of Lawrence had been rebuilt, had no time for the guerrilla actions of John Brown and James Montgomery. In his view the turmoil of 1856 was over, and southeastern Kansas's conflict had now "degenerated from a contest to secure civil rights, into a mere strife for plunder." Appealing to the majority of Kansans weary of the struggles, the editor urged "peace and quietness" for Kansas settlers to prosper. "The mass of the Pro-Slavery men of '56 have disappeared," he contended. "The slavery issue is dead." It was all too apparent, wrote the editor, that "*radicals* of the Free State party were laboring to bring on a civil war" through "the hireling correspondents of Eastern newspapers" and by the fire-eater "portion of the Kansas press." He warned them, "Don't magnify our difficulties in the East and thus keep away many of those otherwise desirous to make homes among us."[32]

Meanwhile, Brown, Montgomery, and radical antislavery men and newspapers saw George Brown and other Free-State "moderates" as lacking spine and as "having abandoned its antislavery principles, [and being] more interested in Kansas development than the slavery issue." John Brown counted as friends the opponents of George Brown's *Herald of Freedom*. The Old Captain reciprocated by shunning the likes of the editor and his associated Charles Robinson wing of the party, which he saw as "cowardly" and "old-granny," and its newspaper as "one of the most mischievous, traitorous publications in the whole country."[33]

But even Kansan newspapers that were ordinarily friendly to Brown and Montgomery had little good to say about the foray into Missouri because of the Cruise killing. Happening as it did on the heels of the Fort Scott tragedy with its fevered public excitement, the raid magnified Kansans' worries. "All last week," wrote a Kansas editor about the exaggerated coverage, "the dreadful telegraphic and newspaper tragedy was on the boards again. Fort Scott was taken and destroyed—men, women, children, donkeys, haystacks and all, sharing alike the dreadful fate. Missouri was invaded, and dear only knows how many whole counties are now in desolation. By next week we expect . . . to learn that all Kansas is to meet a terrible doom at the hands of Missouri." Because of the exaggerated newspaper reports, the editor acknowledged that "the East thinks that all Kansas is involved in one vast incendiary blaze, awful to think of."[34]

The Brown party, meanwhile, stayed with the Wattles on Wednesday night, December 22, and resumed their journey early the next morning. Two of Brown's men escorted the liberated slaves while Brown himself remained behind with the Wattles. Thereafter, often only George Gill was with the freed blacks who were driving the team on toward Osawatomie. Arriving near sunset at the door of Reverend Adair (Brown's brother-in-law), he and his wife after a brief moment's talk decided they must take in the pitiable band.[35]

The group stayed at the Adairs' place through Christmas, and at two o'clock in the morning on December 26, the refugees were moved to a less noticeable location immediately south of Osawatomie. The secreted group settled in at an uncompleted preemption cabin "neither chinked nor daubed, without door, floor, or windows," that its owner had abandoned. Supplied with arms and food, the liberated group built their own chimney of prairie sod and remained at the cabin for nearly three weeks, going undetected by Missourians searching timbered areas along streams. Brown, though most anxious to get on his way north with the liberated group, judged it could not be done until Daniel's pregnant wife gave birth. The Daniels would name the boy John Brown Daniels.

Soon after the delivery of Narcissa Daniel's baby at Dr. James G. Blount's place in Garnett (twenty-five miles from Osawatomie), the group prepared to leave for Lawrence on January 20. While Stevens and Tidd went to obtain horses for the journey beyond Topeka, Brown and Gill yoked and hitched the oxen to an old, heavy broad-wheeled wagon. Once loaded with their passengers, they were on their way.[36]

Before leaving, John Brown made a final visit at the Wattles' home, where he penned a letter of his thoughts about the raid to the *New York Tribune*. Though usually he left newspaper writing to his man John Kagi, this time he gave his views directly. The resulting article was widely published under the title "Old

Brown's Parallels." The essay underscored that when Hamelton's men came from Missouri and massacred Free-State men, the authorities did little, whereas when he and his band went into Missouri to liberate slaves, the authorities raised all hell.[37]

Weather—both bad and good—dogged Brown and Gill's northward trudge across the winter prairie. They ran into tough going during the first leg of their journey from Garnett to the house of Maj. J. B. Abbott on the Wakarusa River south of Lawrence. First through mud, next slush, and then over the rutted frozen ground of the evening, they walked beside the slow-moving oxen pulling the Conestoga wagon filled with their freed slaves. The drive took a toll on Gill and Brown for neither had good shoes or winter wear.

The group rested the next night with the Ottawa tribe at Ottawa Jones's place, but upon arrival at antislavery fighter James B. Abbott's house on February 24, Gill's feet were frozen and old Brown had frozen fingers, nose, and ears. The next day they transferred to the nearby farm of Joel Grover, whose large stone barn offered shelter. During this one-day stopover, while Gill watched over their liberated party, Kagi and Stevens went to *New York Tribune* writer William A. Phillips to give him "all the particulars of that adventure." He soon published the story. And Brown found in Lawrence a buyer of the oxen for butchering and replaced them with two teams of horses. Also, from Samuel F. Tappan, a leading antislavery man, they received the loan of a two-horse wagon with a driver.[38]

On the night before their departure, Dr. John Doy came to visit Brown. A citizens meeting had decided to help a group of thirteen endangered free and escaped slaves to Iowa, and they were ready to depart the next day. Doy had agreed to take them to Iowa because, having been preyed upon by a gang of kidnappers, they were asking for protection.[39] Dr. Doy knew well the roads to Holton, at which point they would connect to the main Free-State emigrant route to Iowa. He had one wagon and team for his twenty-five-year-old son to drive and another provided by a contributor with a driver to carry passengers.

What brought Doy to Brown's that evening was, as Doy explained, the previous understanding the two men had for his wagons to join Brown's so that there would be sufficient protection for all. But Brown had now changed his mind, thinking he needed the whole escort to protect his group because, after all, some of Doy's party "were known to be free-born, while the others, having free papers, had lived, some, months, some, years, in the Territory, and were not supposed to be sought for." Doy pleaded with Brown long into the evening, expressing fears that the members of his party on their own would be left defenseless if discovered. But the Old Captain's mind was made up, to his often-expressed later regret.[40]

The disappointed Doy returned to Lawrence for an early morning departure and started his two Iowa-bound wagons on their way as planned. He anticipated reaching Oskaloosa twenty miles to the north, where a guard could be found to protect their way to Holton. By that evening, however, when John Brown's two-wagon party was leaving the Grovers' farm and heading west for Holton via Topeka, the Doy party had already been captured. Unknown to Doy, slave catchers had followed his every movement and the night before had gathered at the nearby proslavery town of Lecompton.[41]

Doy was hardly twelve miles out of Lawrence on that January 25 morning when an armed group of ten to fifteen slave hunters, including the notorious kidnapper Jake Hurd (also spelled Herd), rushed from a low ravine and swooped upon his party. The slave catchers put their own drivers into the wagons and made a dash for Missouri with scouts a mile ahead and behind. Soon the captives were locked up first at Weston and then in the Platte City jail. The slave catchers accused Doy of stealing enslaved persons from Missouri, and after a trial, Doy languished in the St. Joseph jail. The kidnapping, reported in the news as fully as accounts of Brown's movements were, aroused great northern indignation. Finally in July 1859 James Abbott led ten Lawrence men who broke into the jail and rescued Doy. As for the captured blacks, none ever reached Iowa. All were re-enslaved although two reportedly escaped again.[42]

IV

With Doy's fate unknown to John Brown's group, the drivers of their two wagons, tightly packed with passengers and provisions from the Grovers and Abbotts, approached Topeka in the faint morning light on January 25. George Gill went on ahead to awaken the Daniel Sheridan family at their farm on a rise two miles southeast of Topeka. The wagons arrived to find the Sheridans waiting to receive them and unloaded the wagons of passengers in the cold morning chill. All crowded into the small stone house and quickly edged toward the warmth of the fireplace, for the shivering escapees were poorly clothed and wearing worn-out shoes. After breakfast the passengers were distributed among nearby antislavery homes while John Brown remained with the Sheridans.

Before their departure the night of January 26, Sheridan's neighbor Jacob Willits went to other houses and some stores to obtain several pairs of shoes for the liberated blacks. The evening of their departure, Willits helped take Brown and his group down to the Kansas River crossing. There he recalled, "I noticed Brown shivering, and that his legs trembled a good deal." Willits reached down from his horse and "felt of his pantaloons, and found they were of cotton, thin and suited to summer, not to the cold weather we had then." Upon crossing the river Willits convinced Brown to take the new underclothing he wore, and "we got down beside the wagons on the boat; I took the drawers off, and he put them on."[43]

Aaron Stevens again joined Brown and Gill as they moved northward across the bleak January winter scape. Four miles out of Topeka they took a break and unloaded their passengers, who cooked up some of their provisions for lunch at Cyrus Packard's house. They then proceeded another twenty-eight miles to Holton, a county seat town created recently by Free-State emigrant company members from Milwaukee under Edmund Ross, who had traversed Iowa in 1856. But the town's initial antislavery dominance had eroded as new emigrants with more general western attitudes arrived and grew the town to nearly a thousand residents. So Brown's small, slow-moving caravan went six more miles to his intended stop, the vacant cabins of Dr. Albert Fuller on Straight Creek.[44]

During these last miles the mild weather turned for the worse, and on Friday morning, the twenty-ninth, the caravan reached Fuller's place in a blinding prairie snowstorm. Some Holton residents, however, had seen in the blowing snow a suspicious wagon group and riders. Thinking it might be Brown, word quickly spread.[45]

The weather stopped Brown's party from going farther, not because of the snowstorm, but because the past month had been unusually mild, with frequent rains and little snow. In fact, farther north near the Nebraska border, an editor at White Cloud had reported three weeks earlier that "the protracted warm spell" had loosened the Missouri River ice and the river was running clear. At Fuller's cabin in the Holton area, Straight Creek, fed by rain and snowmelt, had nearly overflowed its banks and was temporarily impassable. Because of the soft roads and the horses' needing a rest from hauling their heavy loads, the group waited for the creek to subside. Brown sent Tappan's driver with his emptied wagon back to Topeka to retrieve Kagi and Tidd, who had stayed back to gather provisions.[46]

Before long Brown learned they were not alone. Stevens, who was staying alone in a small empty cabin about a hundred feet from the others, had walked toward the creek to check the water level. Eight men suddenly approached him and asked if he had seen any Negroes in the area. Stevens "told them if they would come with him he would show them some, and conducted them to his cabin where he had left his rifle." Stepping in to reach it, he immediately swung it up and pointed directly at the leader and demanded his surrender. He did while his companions dashed off. The group following Brown's caravan up until then had done nothing because, according to Stevens's captive, they had doubted it was the one they were looking for because it had no oxen and no guards.[47]

Fearing other tracking parties might be on the way as soon as darkness settled in, either Stevens or Gill traveled that night to meet a neighboring antislavery farmer named Wasson. He was asked to hurry to Topeka and alert John Ritchie that Brown's group had been discovered and needed help. Wasson arrived in Topeka early the next morning as Reverend Bodwell's small Congregational group was about to begin service.

Ritchie, hearing a commotion at the back of the room, turned to find an antislavery friend hurrying toward him to whisper the news. Soon the service was canceled. A body of sixteen available men gathered with arms, ammunition, and provisions and moved north out of town, with some walking and some riding horses. The Topeka men reached Brown's location at Fuller's cabin at ten o'clock the next morning. Kagi and Tidd had also returned with a wagon of provisions. Meanwhile, serving as sentry, Stevens could see men hovering about north of the creek but keeping out of Sharps rifle range.[48]

As word spread of Brown's presence, various proslavery bands searching for Brown joined forces. The largest group amounted to an assorted collection of twenty-five men led by John P. Wood, a bogus deputy U.S. marshal from Lecompton. Another led by J. T. Hereford—a young lawyer and devil-may-care fellow from Atchison—comprised fifteen town boys who had responded to Marshal Wood's appeal for help.

These vigilantes clearly outnumbered Brown's few men, but they hesitated to attack in fear of the noted guerrilla chieftain's reputation as "a terror throughout the whole border of Missouri."

Brown, meanwhile, received information that the proslavery forces were massing north of his location with the likely intent of cutting off his march beyond Spring Creek.[49]

Within four hours of the Topeka boys' arrival, which brought the total number of defenders up to twenty-three white men, Captain Brown put into practice his rule of "going to close quarters when in the presence of the enemy." According to Gill, Brown placed the men "in double file, in front of his two emigrant wagons, and said, 'Now go straight at 'em, boys! They'll be sure to run.'" Indeed, wrote Gill, "the closer we got to the ford the farther they got from it." Marching toward the fording point at the creek they scarcely had entered the water when Marshal Wood mounted his horse and rushed off. His men immediately ran for their horses also, "but they were not all so lucky as he was in untying their horses from the stumps and bushes." In their panic a bizarre scene unfolded: "Some horses were hastily mounted by two men. One man grabbed tight hold of the tail of a horse, trying to leap on from behind, while the rider was putting the spurs into his sides; so he went flying through the air, his feet touching the ground now and then." The skirmish came to be called the Battle of the Spurs.[50]

As soon as those of Brown's men who had horses reached the other side of the high-water creek, they took off after their fast-running foes. Following about six miles, they captured five horses and four prisoners, all of whom—including Hereford—were Atchison fellows. While the chase was under way, the rest of Brown's entourage successfully used long ropes to move the mired emigrant wagons across the creek.[51]

As the refugees and their escorts resumed the journey, Sam Harper, one of the liberated men, recalled that Brown told him and four other black men to mount the captives' horses. The prisoners following behind had to slog through the mud of the early spring thaw that went up over their ankles and made for tough walking.[52]

Guarding the prisoners that evening, Gill overheard one shouting obscenities. John Brown advanced to the shouter and said, "Tut, tut, you are not doing right, for if there is a God, it is wrong to speak his name in that way; if there is none it is certainly very foolish." And when one of his men started abusing one of the captives, "the old man read him a lecture on the cowardice of insulting a man unable to defend himself." The next morning he released the captives to find their way home as best they could and gave the captured horses to the "brave Topeka boys who had walked so far to help us."[53]

All members of the caravan knew they must press on for the Nebraska border and Iowa because troops were reported to be in their rear. Consequently the mounted members among their Topeka protectors, including John Ritchie, remained and accompanied Brown's group another forty-five miles to within six miles of the Nebraska line. A few went all the way to Tabor, Iowa.[54]

The last night that Brown's groups spent in Kansas was at Albany, an antislavery settlement of Congregationalist New York immigrants located two miles north of Sabetha at the head of Pony Creek on the emigrant trail north to Iowa. Brown stayed at the cabin of local leader Elihu Whittenhall, who with a few others had organized an Underground Railway branch that they called League No. 40. The next day, February 1, 1859, local Underground Railroad operator William Graham went with Brown's party over the border into Nebraska to help them cross the Nemaha River.[55]

The weather turned very cold, recalled Graham, and with the river too high to cross they sought shelter at the log house of Tessaum, a half-breed Indian. By morning, with the ice now getting stronger, "they took the wagons to pieces and pushed them across; then [cut trees and] laid poles across [from the shore to center ice], with rails and bushes and boards on them, and over this bridge they led the horses."[56]

The cold weather persisted while they trudged over snow-drifted roads the next fifty miles toward Nebraska City. George

Gill began to fall behind the others, being quite crippled from his previous episode of frostbite. As night fell, soon three men on the lookout for Brown's caravan stopped Gill, who succeeded in persuading them that he was traveling south. The encounter effectively delayed his arrival at Nebraska City. Unable to catch up with his companions, he searched for and finally found the cabin of John Kagi's older sister, Barbara, and husband Allen Mayhew. He stayed overnight with them on the north side of South Table Creek. The next day, he later learned that within fifteen minutes of his leaving Mayhew's place, "the house was surrounded by about fifty men; a posse in search of Brown and his men or contrabands."[57]

When George Gill caught up with the Brown and the caravan, they had already crossed the Missouri River to the Iowa side. In the words of a proslavery editor at Nebraska City, they were now considered to be "safely on 'tother side of Jordan,'" doubtless to the joy of the liberated blacks. The editor had little good to say about it, however. The Old Captain, he wrote, had passed through this city "at the head of a herd of stolen niggers taken from Southern Missouri, accompanied with a gang of horse thieves of the most desperate character." To the writer's way of thinking, "there is an appropriateness and fitness in nigger stealers being associated with horse thieves," even though "the profession of the horse thief is the more liberal and dignified calling."[58]

V

When during the night of February 4 the two-wagon caravan pulled into the rural hamlet of Civil Bend, Dr. Ira Blanchard saw to the overnight distribution of the travelers between his place and that of Lester and Elvira Platt, his neighbor to the south. John Brown stayed with the Platts.[59]

From there they took the usual Underground Railroad track twenty miles through the Missouri bottoms and on up to Tabor. This Congregationalist settlement was of course well known to

Brown, for it had served as his safe western headquarters during late 1856 and much of 1857.

Expecting a strong welcome and several days' rest for them and their weary teams, Brown's group instead was met with a courteous chilliness. Though antislavery to the core, Tabor's Congregationalists were bothered by Brown's Missouri raid. They willingly aided escapees from Missouri but did not approve of going into Missouri to liberate them, especially when it involved killing slaveholders. Part of their chagrin undoubtedly traced to a few weeks previous when Stephen Nuckolls and his men from Nebraska City had roughly searched through Tabor houses in a fruitless search for his two runaway girl servants.

While the blacks occupied a small schoolhouse outfitted with a stove, John Brown, John Kagi, Charles Tidd, and Aaron Stevens were dispersed among the settlers' cabin homes. The next day being Sunday, Brown wrote a note to Rev. John Todd and asked that the church service include an expression of thanksgiving for what his group had done to accomplish the deliverance of slaves from their wicked masters. The reluctant parson instead said he would acknowledge the note and announce that a public gathering to discuss it would occur the next evening.[60]

The resulting schoolhouse meeting did not go well. After considerable discussion, during which the dismayed Brown left the meeting, all but four attendees in the packed room adopted a final resolution: "That while we sympathize with the oppressed, and will do all that we conscientiously can to help them in their efforts for freedom, nevertheless we have no sympathy with those who go to slave States to entice away slaves and take property or life when necessary to attain that end."[61]

Upset and hurt by the action, Brown and his group left town within four days. They proceeded north to the Charles and Sylvia Case Tolles cabin on Silver Creek (near present-day Malvern). The couple had been in pre-territorial Kansas at the Baptist mission with Ira Blanchard in the 1840s and now provided a station point for runaways coming through Tabor. The next morning with snow falling Brown's wagon party moved off northeast. Five days later, after several overnight stops with antislavery supporters along the way, Brown's party reached the western outskirts of Des Moines, where James C. Jordan lived.[62] Brown had previously stayed with the state senator and antislavery man, and he readily sheltered the group out back in his nearby timber.

The next morning Brown sent John Kagi into Des Moines to locate John Teasdale, who owned and edited the *Des Moines Citizen*, which would soon be renamed the *Iowa State Register*. Teasdale and Brown had attended the same church when they lived in Akron, Ohio, and the editor was an antislavery radical. Kagi told Teasdale that Brown would be coming through the city at a specific time and would be pleased to visit him where the bridge crosses the Des Moines River. Teasdale later wrote that the ordinarily clean-shaven man he had known earlier now sported a "long snowy beard" and said "he was on his way to Virginia, where he meant to begin a conflict for freedom that would fire the whole country." Teasdale "deprecated the struggle as madness that would probably cost him his [Brown's] life without benefiting the poor blacks. [But] his soul was on fire" and convinced that the hour was right to strike for the fate of the country. Bidding Brown farewell, Teasdale paid the toll fees for the wagons to cross the bridge.[63]

Beyond the crossing Brown's party drove the heavily loaded wagons up the bluff line. After two days of mild weather that caused them to struggle through the thawing swamp bottoms of the Skunk River, they reached higher ground. Gradually they made their way to the Congregationalist town of Grinnell.[64]

The Old Captain had not been there before, but he had been told of it. Leaving the wagon group in a nearby grove, he rode in to the recently built grouping of ninety houses and knocked at the door of Rev. Josiah B. Grinnell. Brown, with his plain suit and wide-brimmed hat, introduced himself as an acquaintance of Deacon Chauncey Chapin, Grinnell's father-in-law. The vigorous town founder welcomed Brown, saying he had been reading recently about Brown's Missouri doings in the latest *New York Tribune*. Soon the covered wagons were brought into town, the arms stacked in Grinnell's parlor, and the room made ready for sleeping arrangements, which were augmented with nearby hotel rooms for the remainder of the tired escorts and refugees.[65]

Grinnell's friendly welcome stood in contrast with that of Tabor, and the town held a reception the next night for Brown, his men, and their liberated companions. The event drew many curious people to see the Kansas travelers who were portrayed in the news either as courageous rescuers or as Brown's "robber gang." Both Brown and John Kagi spoke and answered questions, and at the next evening's Sunday meeting for them, prayers were given and a hat passed for money to aid the travelers.[66]

Brown, his men, and their passengers departed the next morning with plenty of provisions in the wagons to last them for several days. Hardly had they disappeared from view down the soggy, mud-rutted tracks of their route than Democratic newspapers attacked Grinnell citizens for sheltering and giving ovations to scoundrels on the run with a price on their heads.[67]

The going was tough for the horse teams, which strained to pull the bulky wagons through the heavy, sticky soils. Steadily, however, the roads improved, and they made good time, driving their wagons through Iowa City about noon on February 24. Further, according to George Gill, they took no effort to conceal their movements.[68]

The Quaker hamlet of Springdale lay about seventeen miles east of Iowa City. Though but a few years old, it was familiar territory to Brown and his men from the previous winter's guerrilla training camp. While the others rested, Brown could not resist sending a note back to Tabor founder George Gaston, crowing about how well the Grinnell residents had treated them.[69]

Fig. 15. Josiah B. Grinnell, the outgoing Congregational abolitionist and founder of Grinnell, Iowa, aided runaways from slavery and sheltered John Brown, his men, and twelve slaves they had liberated and were escorting to Canada. State Historical Society of Iowa, Iowa City.

VI

While the ague still troubled him some, Brown nevertheless kept busy making arrangements for what would come next—namely, organizing railroad transportation to move his men and passengers to Chicago. For help he got in touch with his friend William Penn Clarke, a vocal antislavery Republican and noted lawyer in Iowa City.[70]

Over the next twelve days Clarke put together everything the group needed, including arranging for a boxcar to be delivered at West Liberty, the nearest rail connection eight miles south of Springdale, and persuading the railroads to look the other way about what they wanted to do. He received some initial help from Josiah Grinnell, who went to Chicago and visited with General Superintendent of the Chicago and Rock Island Railroad John F. Tracy. Tracy balked at giving them a boxcar, but he did give Grinnell a fifty-dollar draft made out to John Brown. Next, Clarke contacted Hiram Price of Davenport. Price sat on the board of directors of the line through West Liberty and provided a helpful letter. With Tracy's draft and Price's letter in hand, Clarke used them to impress the West Liberty stationmaster that higher-ups knew of, and allowed, the boxcar arrangement.[71]

Before long the boxcar permit for Clarke arrived from the Chicago and Rock Island office in Davenport via telegraph to the *Iowa City Republican* newspaper. On March 9 Springdale citizens took Brown's group to Keith's mill at West Liberty. The boxcar was scheduled to be delivered to the mill, where the group would stay overnight. The rail station was located nearby. An early morning eastbound train from Iowa City dropped off a boxcar at the mill siding, and by mid-morning a crowd of townsfolk had gathered to see Brown, the black refugees, Tidd, and Stevens climb inside the boxcar. John Kagi closed the car door and moved the car into position with the help of George Gill and some townsmen. When the postmaster, who had been appointed by the Democrats, put his hand on the car to help push and other antislavery bystand-

Fig. 16. William Penn Clarke, an ardent abolitionist and well-known lawyer in Iowa City, arranged for John Brown and the twelve liberated slaves to reach Chicago by train. State Historical Society of Iowa, Iowa City.

ers booed him, he offered the excuse that he had only put his hand against the car to keep from falling.[72]

George Gill remained in West Liberty, as his health gave out from the two-month journey. John Kagi and William Penn Clarke chose to ride in the passenger car to keep watch on a man who had threatened to divulge the goings-on.[73]

When the next Chicago-bound train arrived, the engineer placed the boxcar between the engine and express car, and by early afternoon the train was on its way to Davenport. Upon arrival Kagi and Clarke kept the untrustworthy passenger from talking about the boxcar. When the train was ready to leave for Chicago, Clarke quickly took a room at the Burtis Hotel. From there he watched the string of cars cross the bridge over the Mississippi River into Illinois.[74]

They had also successfully evaded U.S. Marshal Laurel Summers in Davenport who had been informed that Brown and his entourage were at Springdale. The marshal's posse, some say, had mistakenly watched a road and ferry crossing while others thought Summers's posse failed to spot them because the posse had done only a cursory examination of the train.[75]

The train reached Chicago late at night, and Brown's party awakened Allan Pinkerton at 4:30 a.m. on March 11. The detective kept some of the weary group at his house and sent the others to the house of a black friend named John Jones. While Mary, Jones's wife, was none too happy to receive such a rough-looking crew, she fed them and did note that they behaved themselves well.[76] The group stayed that day while Pinkerton attended a scheduled lawyers' meeting that afternoon and convinced some to give funds that could help see the liberated refugees to Canada. Upon his return, the group caught a late afternoon train for Detroit.[77]

One day later, on March 12, the tedious journey of the weary blacks ended when they crossed the narrows, the water gap separating Detroit from Windsor, Canada, where their lives would begin anew. Upon reaching the landing the entire group first went to one of the farms of the Refugee Home Society. Frederick Douglass, who witnessed the March 12 crossing into Canada, wrote, "Here was a company of peculiar interest, who had been forcibly emancipated . . . not for the purpose of stealing, but to restore twelve human beings who had been stolen, to the full possession of themselves." Moreover, Douglass rejoiced, "Here they are, beyond the reach of slaveholders and kidnappers," and "acknowledging no master but God, safely landed on the free and glorious shores of Victoria's dominions."[78] Three days later the *Detroit Tribune* followed up by asking that the humane "furnish them an outfit for commencing life in the land of freedom. They are without a dollar, poorly clad, and have neither household comforts nor tools for farming."[79]

News of how the black arrivals were doing came in early November. Seven of the twelve were in Windsor, where two of them were sawing wood and working general jobs, a twelve-year-old was doing general work, and two women were hired to turn ground for planting potatoes and corn. At their dwellings they grew vegetable gardens and had three hogs among them. One family of five lived nine miles outside Windsor and worked the farm of an owner in return for a share in the farm's income.[80]

VII

With the long trek completed, Brown's attention turned to his Harpers Ferry plans. While Stevens and Tidd sought work for the time being, Brown and Kagi went to Cleveland and stayed for a week with the sister of Charles Moffett, an Iowan who had been a member of the group during the winter of 1857-58. Brown and Kagi spoke at two poorly attended meeting hall lectures. During this time Brown sold a horse and mule shipped from Springdale, Iowa, and mailed the proceeds—$150—to his family at North Elba, New York. Brown remained in Ohio until early April, visiting his son and speaking before the congregation of Joshua R. Giddings, a prominent antislavery congressman. After coping with a return bout of malarial ague, during May and early June John Brown went to Boston, where he met several times with his secret committee of six benefactors about money for his Virginia plans. Kagi, meanwhile, was in Cleveland, working with the jailed Oberlin rescuers who had taken runaways from slave catchers.[81]

Kagi's main job, however, was to begin gathering together the Iowa and Kansas men who had joined them in the past. While John Cook waited at Harpers Ferry, having found work there the previous summer while doing reconnaissance, Kagi sent off a flurry of letters to old comrades. He corresponded with Luke Parsons, Charles Moffett, William Leeman, Richard Hinton, Charles Leonhardt, George Gill, and friends he had made among Montgomery's men, such as Iowan Jeremiah Anderson, and others who might be interested in joining Brown's group. Brown enlisted a few members of his family and other relatives. He also tried to recruit freedmen he knew in Cleveland and Oberlin and sought his son John's help to attract those living in Canada.

The first to arrive was Jeremiah Anderson. During the second week in April he became the ailing Brown's traveling companion on his trip from Ohio to Rochester, New York, and thereafter. Formerly with James Montgomery, the Iowan had joined Brown in his Missouri raid and helped escort the liberated blacks on toward Lawrence. Anderson had in mind to continue with them all the way to Canada, but something came up that kept him in Kansas.

Anderson was youngest of a family of eight and was immersed in the strong antislavery views of Wesleyan Methodism. He had grown up in Des Moines County, Iowa Territory, at Round Prairie near where the village of Kossuth developed. His reserved and quiet manner contrasted with his outgoing easiness when among friends. Resolved to be a part of things in Kansas, he had gone in 1856 to Bourbon County, where he ended up imprisoned twice for his antislavery activities.[82]

While Anderson accompanied Brown on money-raising efforts, Kagi faced long odds from May into August while trying to bring

Fig. 17. Jeremiah G. Anderson went from Yellow Springs, Iowa, to the Kansas Territory and participated in antislavery efforts there. He joined John Brown in his Harpers Ferry raid and died in the effort. Kansas State Historical Society.

back their old comrades. Charles Tidd, Aaron Stevens, Albert Hazlett, and Leeman all replied they were ready to join the excitement when needed. And Stewart Taylor—George Gill's old roommate at West Liberty, Iowa, who went with them to Canada in April 1858—was elated to receive Kagi's letter. The twenty-two-year-old Taylor, a constant reader and friendly fellow of a spiritualist and rationalist bent, had written Kagi the same day his note arrived: "The pleasure that it affords me in receiving your token is unbounded," having removed "suspense and doubts with bright hopes." Indeed, he continued, "it is my chief desire to add fuel to the fire."[83]

Others, however, Kagi could not find or they failed to reply or simply did not turn up. Richard Richardson, the runaway who stayed the winter at Springdale and went with them to Chatham in April 1858, was evidently "away harvesting." In 1858 Richard Realf had returned to England. Then Kagi learned he was back in America but did not know his whereabouts (Realf had gone first to New Orleans and then to Tyler, Texas, during this period). Leonhardt, a military-trained Polish fugitive from the 1848 revolution and immigrant to Kansas, had been an antislavery partisan and a friend of Brown's. But he did not answer Kagi's or Brown's letters sent to him in Cincinnati, where he was a law student.[84]

Two antislavery comrades declined because their current lives now outweighed the companionship they had enjoyed the year before. Charles Moffett of Montour, Iowa, and Luke Parsons of Byron, Illinois, had both been Kansas guerrilla fighters, had participated in the winter drill at Maxson's place in Springdale, and had attended the Chatham Convention. They had found odd jobs as they drifted back home. Gradually they lost faith in, or their zeal for, the movement although they continued to be highly interested in what "the boys" were doing.[85] Moffett replied to Kagi's letter that present "difficulties in the way" would prevent him from coming "tho I feel as deap an interest for the caus as ever and hope yet to do more for it than I hav." When Parsons found out during the summer of 1858 that "Brown, Kagi, Stevens and Tidd were in Kansas keeping up the racket," he had sent off a testy letter to Brown and asked "why he took care of part of the crowd and left the rest of us to shift for ourselves." Brown replied, "You have a good trade and can take care of yourself anywhere; Kagi is supporting himself by his pen, as to Stevens and Tidd, they had to be cared for. Hope you will keep in correspondence with the rest of the boys. Think all will be well in the spring." Unsatisfied, Parsons later admitted, "I was mad and did not reply."[86]

Instead, during that winter Luke Parsons and four others got together oxen and a covered wagon to head west in the spring of 1859. Without money, still peeved at not having heard from Brown or Kagi, and putting up with home complaints to pay a $230 debt he owed, he and the others left Illinois for the Pikes Peak gold fields. "When at Council Bluffs waiting for grass to grow on the plains," recalled Parsons, "I got letters from Brown and Kagi saying they had been to my home in Byron, 'that I must surely turn back, sure go, we depend on you, etc., etc.'" Then "I also got a letter from mother saying, 'You have fooled away time and money enough with Brown, keep on to Pike's Peak. Brown will come to some bad end, and then you and I will be glad you are out of it.'" Luke wrote back to Kagi that if he had the debt paid and could tell his folks "to kiss my foot, then I should go immediately" to rejoin Uncle Brown. Too bad the "others are not with you that you expected," he wrote, but the fact the "you have some new ones" he hoped would make up for the deficiency.[87]

Then there was George Gill, Brown's close companion during the journey after the Missouri raid, whom both Kagi and Brown urged to join them. Lingering health problems and personal skepticism had kept him back in West Liberty, Iowa, however. "I had been sick much of the spring and summer previous," Gill would write, "and in my last interview with the old man I would not promise to follow him farther, being worn out physically and not feeling any more sanguine of the necessary funds being raised, and having been east the previous year on a wild goose chase I could not see the necessity of going further at present." More to the point, Gill told Brown, "Captain, I fear I have not moral courage enough to go with you. It seems to me that we should do no good and that it will be only useless suicide." And yet Brown continued to hope that "George G. will so far redeem himself as to try: & do his duty after all. I shall rejoice over 'one that repenteth,' [for] I think the best way for every man is promptly to straighten up whenever he sees his wrong."[88]

Despite Kagi's many letters to comrades, the final results showed that five of the twelve men from the 1858 Springdale training had bowed out. Kagi and Brown, however, did gain two new recruits—Edwin Coppoc and his half brother Barclay Coppoc, both young Quaker men from Springdale, Iowa. Their antislavery enthusiasm had been fired in seeing and talking to Brown and his men during their two stays there. In midsummer Edwin and Barclay sold off their stock, and Edwin arranged with a black man to handle the farm. Hiding their ultimate destination, they traveled back to their old Ohio stomping grounds and stayed until August. But their mother, Ann Raley, saw through their plans and knew their larger intent was to join Brown.

Twenty-four-year-old Edwin and twenty-year-old Barclay were temperamentally quite different. George Gill, who knew both local men well, admired Edwin as having a strong business ability and as being a decisive man but with a winning and magnetic personality that gladdened people to be his friend. Barclay's wonderful magnetism worked mainly with the girls, as he had several marriage engagements and in all probability had intimate relations with them all. Intelligent but more cautious than his brother, Barclay displayed a nonaggressive spirit and suffered from asthma. John Brown perhaps also sensed a lack of strength in Barclay for, during the actual raid, he assigned Barclay a support role in helping Owen Brown move weapons from the farmhouse to a school near Harpers Ferry.[89]

Fig. 18. Edwin Coppoc, a Quaker from Springdale, Iowa, enlisted in John Brown's Harpers Ferry raid, where he was captured, tried, and hanged. State Historical Society of Iowa, Iowa City.

Fig. 19. Barclay Coppoc, brother of Edwin Coppoc, joined John Brown in the failed attempt at Harpers Ferry, but he was able to escape capture and returned to Iowa. State Historical Society of Iowa, Iowa City.

VIII

Ultimately by the time of the October 16–18, 1859, raid on the Harpers Ferry arsenal, Brown and Kagi had gathered—counting themselves—twenty-two fighters. Ten had come out of Brown's Kansas and Iowa experiences: John Cook, John Kagi, William Leeman, Jeremiah Anderson, Barclay Coppoc, Edwin Coppoc, Albert Hazlett, Charles Tidd, Stewart Taylor, and Aaron Stevens. The others included his three sons; two neighbors; five black men he came to know in the East or at Oberlin, Ohio; and one "erratic and unbalanced" but "generous, brave, and devoted" recruit, Frank Meriam, who donated $600 in gold to the cause.[90]

In the weeks leading up to mid-October, the twenty-two men assembled at the Kennedy farm, a small place that Brown rented near Sandy Hook on the Maryland side of the Potomac and a mile downstream from Harpers Ferry. John Brown worried that the highly talkative John Cook, who had arrived much earlier to scout out the Harpers Ferry situation, might have let details of the operation slip. While there Cook had become a part of the community as a teacher and a lock keeper and had married a woman from Chambersburg, Pennsylvania.

Another danger to Brown's plans came from his Quaker friends back in Springdale, Iowa. A local leader, Moses Varney, having failed to talk Brown out of his Harpers Ferry designs and worrying about what might befall the local young men who had joined Brown, solicited the help of Quakers in another Iowa community. They came up with the idea of mailing letters of warning to Secretary of War John B. Floyd in hopes that he would send reinforcements to Harpers Ferry and discourage Brown from making his intended assault. Mailed from two different locations, they waited and hoped for good news. The secretary of war, however, did not believe the warnings and did nothing. The letter writers learned they had failed when they received a copy of the *New York Tribune* reporting the attack.[91]

Brown moved up the date of the raid after Cook brought news that the sheriff, perhaps at the request of suspicious neighbors, was about to come and search the Kennedy place. This schedule shift surprised not only John Brown, Jr., who planned to join them, but also those of Brown's men who were already there and soon expecting the arrival of George Gill and Elazar Maxson, who had recently left Iowa. Kagi rushed off a letter to Charles Moffett, stating, "We hear that a warrant has been issued to search our house, so we must move eight days sooner than we had intended. Start at once, study map, will try to hold out until you come."[92]

Brown's men sensed a bad situation developing when the Old Captain announced his intent was to capture Harpers Ferry. Up to this moment his men had thought the aim was only to temporarily seize, not hold, the arsenal; in essence, they would repeat the Missouri raid but on a larger scale. Not only that, Cook's news of the sheriff's impending arrival to search the premises prompted several of the men to urge that they get away at once.[93] A turbulent argument ensued between them and the Old Captain. Cook favored Brown's idea; Stevens, Jeremiah Anderson, and Leeman said they would support it; and Kagi would go along but wanted all of them to get out of Harpers Ferry as soon as possible. Four others, however, strenuously objected. Brown's sons—Owen, Oliver, and Watson—saw capturing Harpers Ferry as a deathtrap. Doubtless they were reminded of their brother Salmon's warning that Brown would insist on order, on "getting everything arranged just to suit him" before acting. It would lead him, Salmon cautioned, to hesitate and delay, for "you know father. You know he will *dally* till he is trapped!" Joining the objectors was George Tidd, who temporarily walked out of the fight against Brown's scheme to cool his temper. But when the Old Captain pressed the argument to the limit by proposing they select someone else to command, the hot discussion ebbed when one of his sons remarked, "We must not let our father die alone." One by one all acquiesced, having seen what lay ahead but choosing not to look.[94]

IX

Leaving the farmhouse after sundown on October 16, Brown and his men reached Harpers Ferry after ten o'clock. By midnight they had cut the telegraph lines east and west of town, seized the armory, and followed up by taking the arsenal, the Hall Rifle Works, and several hostages. The unsuspecting townsmen gave little resistance until morning, but once alerted local citizens began to exchange gunfire with Brown's men. Militias from nearby towns quickly organized to participate in the defense of Harpers Ferry. By noon local militiamen were driving Brown's men to the safety of the Engine House on the armory grounds, and soon the militiamen had taken the Hall Rifle Works, killing three of Brown's men. By day's end the rest had retreated into the Engine House.

Though now trapped, Brown refused to surrender at dawn the next morning. With that Col. Robert E. Lee signaled his company of ninety U.S. Marines to storm the building. Breaking down the doors, it took but a matter of minutes before the assault was over and the raiders vanquished.[95]

As the resulting three-day debacle became hopeless and bore out the forebodings of Brown's sons, seven of Brown's men— essentially elements of his rear guard—escaped in the confusion. The men included Barclay Coppoc, Owen Brown, John Cook, Charles Tidd, Albert Hazlett, Francis Meriam, and Osborne Perry Anderson, one of Brown's five black comrades. Anderson and Hazlett found a rowboat that they paddled across the Potomac River to Maryland and headed for Pennsylvania. Hazlett was captured near Newville in southern Pennsylvania and extradited back to Virginia.

Leading the others' flight north was Owen Brown, a calm, experienced woodsman and occasional Underground Railroad operator. After running back to their boarding place at the Kennedy farm to grab some provisions—biscuits, sugar, and blankets—they began what would become a monthlong walk northwest over the mountains. Each man also carried two long-range guns, two revolvers and a full cartridge box, and other supplies.[96]

Owen's plan for survival was to "follow the mountain ranges, making to the northwest when we could; traveling only at night upon the edges of the clearings; sleeping and hiding by day in the thickets on the uninhabited mountain tops; shunning all traveled roads at all times; except as we were obliged to cross them in the night; building no fires; buying or stealing no provisions; in fact, not speaking aloud till we should, at least, get beyond Chambersburg, Pennsylvania."[97]

As provisions ran out, however, they turned to picking up dry, hard corn or raw potatoes in fields and dried apples in orchards as they moved farther into Pennsylvania. John Cook was captured when, after their provisions were gone, he was designated to walk down from their hiding place to buy more. There, eight miles from Chambersburg, manhunters who were thirsty for the $1,000 reward issued by the state of Virginia caught and returned him to Virginia. Owen lingered about twelve hours, confidently expecting Cook's return because he was "the quickest and best shot with a pistol that I ever saw." Finally they resumed their northward trek.[98]

The four remaining men grew ever weaker from the icy rain and a good share of sleet and snow, plus feeling the strain of constant danger. Fatigued and gaunt, the men took greater risks to eat, stealing here and there a chicken at night from a hen roost or occasionally milking a cow. When the exhausted Frank Meriam could go no farther, Owen—leaving their hiding place in a midfield briar patch—walked him through the falling snow to a northbound train outside Chambersburg. Coppoc, Tidd, and Brown then continued their slow trek toward northwestern Pennsylvania. A woman from whom they bought doughnuts ferried them across the Juniata River, and from there they followed the towpath of the canal and the main road some fifteen miles toward

Bellefonte. They first stayed in an empty house, then took the risk of knocking at a small farm house.[99]

A friendly farm couple warmly received them for the night. Sitting about the fireplace, the men perked up when the farmer mentioned his recently arrived newspaper. They could now read news of what had happened at Harpers Ferry. Feigning unconcern but then casually picking up the paper, they learned that Brown and his men had captured and held the arsenal for two days and three nights. Tidd read aloud to the others of how, when the operation was over, a wounded John Brown had been captured with Iowa members Stewart Taylor killed in the engine house, Jeremiah Anderson bayoneted in the final assault, and Edwin Coppoc disarmed and captured.

As they listened to Tidd and the farmer read aloud the stories, Owen remembered that "Coppoc sat gazing thoughtfully into the blaze of the great fire-place, and I happened to be looking at him when our farm-host went on to say that the very latest news was that the man Coppoc had been tried, too, and found guilty." Barclay "did not speak, but a little while after, he stealthily brushed away a tear from one of his cheeks, and sighed in a half-choked way."[100]

Forty miles farther on their journey, at Halfmoon, a village in west-central Pennsylvania, Owen Brown and Charles Tidd started northwest toward Townville in Crawford County, where they found work. Owen put Barclay Coppoc aboard a stage to a railroad line where he could rejoin his Quaker relatives in Salem, Ohio. Coppoc took with him a box filled with the men's guns, cartridge boxes, blankets, and other items for safekeeping at an Ohio destination.[101]

His days on the run were not over, however. In little more than a week a proslavery informant wrote the Virginia governor that Barclay Coppoc was back in Iowa. This news set off a series of disputes between the two governors over Virginia's effort to return Barclay for trial. Iowa's governor Kirkwood leaked news of the extradition request to antislavery friends, who saw to it that Barclay was warned to leave the state, and he did.

X

Exceeding the press attention given to Barclay Coppoc, however, was the massive coverage across the country about the capture, trial, and execution of John Brown. At 11:15 a.m. on Friday, December 2, 1859, as the rope was adjusted around his neck and the scaffold trap fell, thousands were attending sympathy meetings across the northern states. Church bells tolled, and many in sympathy hung black crepe. Large assemblies took place in many cities in the East and Midwest, with smaller gatherings elsewhere. A recorded list of the substantial number in eastern states appeared in five small-print columns of the *New York Herald*.[102]

In Kansas Territory a handbill drew many to a meeting of sympathy regarding John Brown on Saturday evening in Lawrence. The meeting planners also brought folks together to organize antislavery sentiment. With Joel Grover as chairman, the "densely crowded" meeting "continued to a late hour" as the group listened to speeches and passed resolutions. The Old Captain, read one, "has been cruelly maligned by the Democratic Press of Kansas and the North generally"; therefore, the organizers "affirm our full confidence in the integrity of his character, and the nobleness of his motives."[103]

At another meeting in Lawrence on January 20 at Miller's Hall, people listened to a lecture by William A. Phillips, the well-known territorial correspondent of the *New York Tribune* and author of *The Conquest of Kansas* (1856). About Harpers Ferry, he said, oh how "we hastened to deprecate it when the telegraph first brought us the news." But now, "shall the timid and soulless get up 'Union' meetings, to denounce the old Puritan?—to persuade the South that *they* are not John Browns?" Kansas, "thank God," Phillips said, "has not been guilty of any such nonsense" Today "the country is so much under the influence of its South-

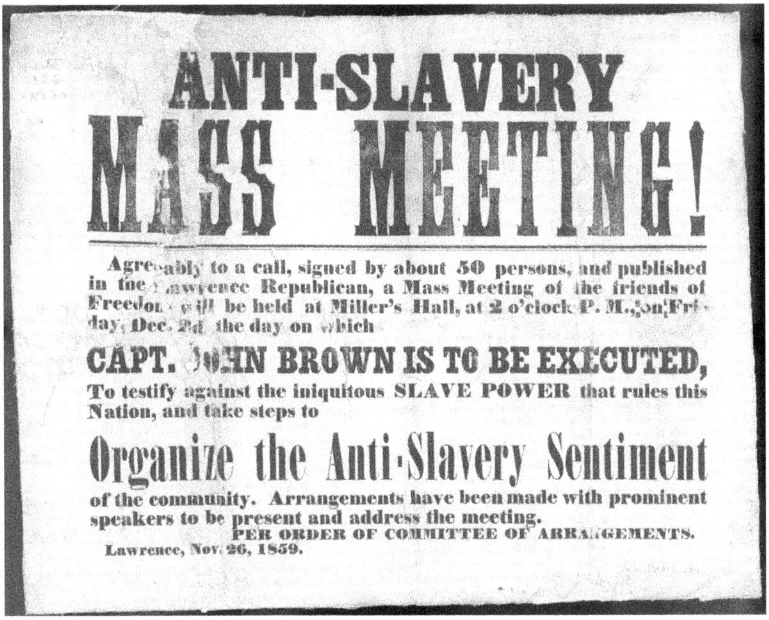

Fig. 20. Handbill calling for an "Anti-Slavery Mass Meeting" in Lawrence, Kansas, given the imminent execution of John Brown in Virginia. Kansas State Historical Society.

ern rulers," he lamented, "that it scarcely dares to say that it admires the heroic old Puritan." Yet, in ages to come, "they will read that a poor old man, with a handful of brave companions, threw themselves away in a protest against Slavery." Sentiment is already changing, he acknowledged, for "two months ago respectable papers were fain to stigmatize him, that they might haply escape the suspicion of sympathizing with him. Now, no respectable paper would like to do such a thing."[104]

While many rumors had circulated about a possible rescue attempt for John Brown, no similar plots spread about his captured comrades still in jail.[105] And yet, friends in Kansas, particularly those men who had fought alongside the Kansas men of Brown's Harpers Ferry group during previous Free-State clashes, were willing to lend a rescuing hand. When Brown's fate was being decided, Charles Lenhart—the former Davenport, Iowa, printer and early guerrilla leader in Kansas—was on his way east to help his close friend John Cook. Lenhart finagled work with the *Charles Town (WV) True Democrat* and, posing as a John Brown hater from Missouri, joined a militia company guarding the prison where Cook was being held. He arranged with Cook and his cellmate, Edwin Coppoc, to make their escape on the night of December 14, 1859, when Lenhart was going to be on guard there. An unexpected visitor led Cook to postpone the escape to the next night, but Lenhart was not on duty. The two were captured and hanged, as scheduled, two days later.[106]

Another rescue effort began in early February as Aaron Stevens and Albert Hazlett awaited hanging. Antislavery man and Kansas relief organizer Thomas Wentworth Higginson had raised funds to help set them free but found nobody in New England to break them out of jail. So through a messenger Higginson contacted James Montgomery in Kansas, and he recruited eight others willing to save the two prisoners from death by angry Virginians. All had arrived in the Harrisburg, Pennsylvania, vicinity by mid-February and were a hundred miles from where Stevens and Hazlett sat in a Charles Town jail (seven miles west of Harpers Ferry). Together Montgomery, Higginson, and the others reviewed possible difficulties to completing such a mission, including "a week's journey through a mountainous country by night, carrying arms, blankets, and provisions; attacking a building— the Charlestown [*sic*] jail—protected by a wall fourteen feet high and defended by sentinels without and within; and retreating with prisoners and wounded by daylight." Montgomery, before reaching a decision, made up his mind to scout the country to Charles Town. Higginson went to Ohio and found Charles Tidd, one of the escapees from Harpers Ferry, who advised him that while this territory "was the best guerrilla country in the world" with "all crags and laurel-bushes," such a dash in the freezing winter would be impossible. Meanwhile, Montgomery and Silas

Soule—one of John Doy's daring rescuers from jail the previous year—rode south.[107]

With Montgomery's southern Kentucky accent and Soule striking a convincingly cheerful pose as an Irishman, the two made their way to Charles Town. There Soule purposely got thrown into the jail for drunkenness and informed Stevens and Hazlett of their plans. The two men were grateful but dismissed the plan as impossible owing to the prison's constant guard of eighty men.[108]

Soule, upon his release, shared the prisoners' comments with the group at Harrisburg. Montgomery underscored the results with what he too had seen; escaping through a countryside full of alert people would be difficult. The final blow to the scheme came about when continuous heavy snows rendered any quick rescue unworkable.[109]

XI

With the Harpers Ferry debacle and John Brown disparaged in the North and South alike, the question naturally arises: how did John Brown become a legend? How did this bungler of Harpers Ferry become a martyr?

First, Brown's name persisted in arguments and southern acrimony that filled newspapers during the ensuing year and thereafter. Second, within months of Brown's death, James Redpath, the firebrand agitator and previous Kansas correspondent for the *New York Tribune*, rushed two books into print—*The Public Life of Capt. John Brown* and *Echoes of Harper's Ferry*. The first was a highly successful heroic account, and the latter contained commentary and addresses by notables at the time of Brown's trial and execution.

Then there were the words of persuasive northern intellectuals, the Transcendentalist literary figures writing in defense of John Brown and his actions. In particular, Henry David Thoreau, who delivered three lectures on "A Plea for Captain John Brown," portrayed him as the "bravest and humanist man in all the country" about to be "an angel of light." And Ralph Waldo Emerson, in a similar series of lectures during the weeks after John Brown's capture, declared that John Brown's martyrdom would "make the gallows as glorious as the cross." These statements, with the help of those by other writers, helped rescue Brown from disrepute by justifying and glorifying him and his actions.[110]

Finally there was the marching song "John Brown's Body," sung to the tune that in 1862 would become associated with Julia Ward Howe's "Battle Hymn of the Republic." Within eighteen months of Brown's death, new volunteer troops were singing about John Brown and how his spirit still lived though his "body lies a mouldering in the grave." Among the lyrics,

> He captured Harper's Ferry with his nineteen men so few,
> And he frightened "Old Virginny" till she trembled through and
>   through;
> They hung him for a traitor, themselves a traitor crew,
> But his soul is marching on; Glory, &c.[111]

Brown's passage into legend doubtless lay partly in timing. His stunning attack reignited the tinder of antislavery sentiments that northern Democrats had tried so hard to smother. But his acts did more; they made the slavery issue newly inflamed and raw, sopped with northerners' blood and emotion. His stand at Harpers Ferry struck dread in the hearts of southern slaveholders fearful of slave insurrection and stirred ultra-abolitionists' delight in his having struck a blow against the system in "slave power" territory. The attack also sent Republicans into frantic denials of being complicit in the raid as it provoked southern fury over northern applause and sympathy for Brown.

After initially deploring Brown's Harpers Ferry actions, public sympathy for Brown grew as people read stories of his conduct while awaiting trial and hanging. His firm dignity, calmness, and serenity in the face of his impending hanging inspired and added to Brown's legend. In tribute to Brown at his burial, the abolitionist orator Wendell Phillips glimpsed what the Old Captain and his men had stirred from beneath: "John Brown has loosened the roots of the slave system; it only breathes,—it does not live,—hereafter."[112]

In Iowa, abolitionist Edwin James wrote to his niece that "this mission of John Brown may awaken us" though he feared the "leprosy" of slavery's sin "has so deeply polluted the blood and destroyed the moral stamina of the white race that our restoration is impossible." Doubtless, he thought, Brown "was *God-sent* and *God-sustained* for the salvation of the most abandoned race of sinners earth ever saw—to-wit, the race of northern apologists for slavery." Judged by the kind of Republicans the people elected to office, he maintained, "there is no hope for us." And yet, conscientious antislavery men "must, it seems to me, give John Brown his highest and most unqualified praise" and at some time "rise up, go and do likewise."[113]

In Kansas memories of Brown's trial and hanging mingled with recollections from earlier years of his Pottawatomie massacre, the Battles of Black Jack and Osawatomie, and his Missouri slave liberation raid. Those who loved Brown pointed to his brave attacks against slavery, whether standing up to proslavery Missourians, raiding to liberate the enslaved from Missouri, or launching his daring foray at Harpers Ferry in hopes of inciting insurrection, which, though he failed, captured the nation's attention. Those who hated the old abolitionist pointed to his participation in killings and in using broadswords to hack apart five strongly proslavery men at Pottawatomie Creek in mid-1856.

But Free-State settlers also recalled that when proslavery men had by intimidation and force threatened to drive them out in 1856, Brown's aggressiveness made the doers think twice. They saw the situation as Joseph O. Shelby came to see it. Shelby once had a hemp plantation near Waverly, Missouri. He felt the occasional loss of runaways and in 1856 had led Missouri guerrilla bands into Kansas. During the Civil War he became a noted

Confederate cavalry commander, and, at war's end, unwilling to surrender, he had led a thousand of his troops to Mexico. But after a two-year stay, Shelby returned to Missouri. He soon outgrew the bitterness of border times and in later years discussed John Brown's place during the Kansas turbulence.

> I was in Kansas at the head of an armed force about that time. I was there to kill Free-State men. I did kill them. I am now ashamed of myself for having done so, but then times were different from what they are now, and that is what I went there for. No Missourian had any business there with arms in his hands. I ought to have been shot there, and John Brown was the only man who knew it and would have done it. I say John Brown was right. I knew the men he killed. I condemn his killing of the younger Doyles [at Pottawatomie Creek], but the others got only what they deserved. After that I had great respect for Old John Brown. Those were days when slavery was in the balance, and the violence engendered made men irresponsible.

Shelby had come to view John Brown as "the only Kansas man who had the right idea of the conditions existing there and the only man who had the courage to resist Missourians at the muzzle of the rifle. [B]rown was the bravest man who ever stood upon a scaffold."[114]

What this hard-edged admiration for Brown underscored was that the Old Captain took on proslavery belligerence at a time when the fate of the Kansans' cause was in doubt, and he showed a readiness to fight when it needed to be shown. It took the swagger out of the proslavery border Missourians, and there is no denying the resulting terror he and James Montgomery, Charles Lenhart, and others struck in the hearts of proslavery Missourians in reversing their freewheeling actions. The flow of northerners into Kansas ultimately made the difference at the ballot box, but the Free-State guerrillas' reap-what-you-sow strategy essentially turned the tables on proslavery aggression. Of course, the initiatives of guerrilla chieftains also bred Free-State divisions, for they went against the defensive-minded desires of conservative Free-State leaders who resented the radicals' uncontrolled boldness.

Yes, Brown's subsequent legend became overdrawn and the focus on him exaggerated his true place at the center of Kansas developments. The limited effectiveness of his go-it-alone manner—keeping his organization and equipment separate from those of other Free-State forces—became lost in memory's elevation of Brown as a leader in the glorious cause against slavery. Nevertheless, the events he fashioned out of personal nerve, determination, cool-headed resolve, and artful alliance with radical news writers tipped the direction of sectional conflict.

There was a cost, however, for those Iowans who joined or admired him. Looking at his struggles in Kansas and his times in Iowa, the antislavery editor of the *Davenport Gazette* wrote, "He became a monomaniac upon the subject of slavery and devoted his life to its extinguishment, without regard to the consequences either to himself or others."[115] When the situation began to go badly at Harpers Ferry, Brown made no effort to save his men. Likely with that idea in mind, George Gill, who had been with Brown from 1857 to 1859, subsequently wrote that "Brown's memory will never be as sacred a thing to me as the memory of some who fell with him."[116]

Brown's influence on Iowans did not end with his walk to the scaffold, for his times in Iowa had helped pave the way for what followed. As chapter 9 tells, by firing the hearts of other young Iowa Quakers to want to do the same, he opened the door to their deaths in Missouri one year after his own.

9

North and Back

Captors and Liberators

I

The slavery conflicts in Kansas gradually quieted down but not completely for the flow of fugitive slaves from the Kansas Territory to Iowa continued up to the Civil War. The first publicized event of early 1860 came in mid-winter.

Four young black men appeared on Friday, February 3, in Tabor, Iowa. These "finely built big men" in their early twenties had left the Choctaws in the Indian Territory of southern Kansas, where some Indian tribes enslaved blacks. Blacks also were fleeing Cherokee slavery.[1] The names of three of these runaways are known: John Martin and brothers William Thompson and John Thompson.[2] By early evening, townsmen had made ready a two-horse covered wagon, and two Tabor men, Edward T. Sheldon and Newton Woodford, drove their four passengers northeast over snow-covered ground toward Lewis, Iowa.

About sixteen miles out they approached Mud Creek, a tributary to the West Nishnabotna River. They stopped at a spring near the road to feed and water the team. Here two young men from the Mud Creek settlement of nearly all Democrats spotted them. Sensing the strangers to be rescuing blacks, the two hurried over to the nearby farm of the local justice of the peace John Cramer. Cramer issued the two a warrant, and they sped back to make an arrest, catching up to the wagon party a few miles northeast of the river crossing. Brandishing weapons, the two men took the wagon group into custody with little resistance.[3]

The captors accompanied the wagon back to Justice Cramer's place, where the two Tabor drivers, Sheldon and Woodford, were held overnight. Cramer, without evidence that the black men were runaways and unsure of what to do, held the two drivers for a hearing at his place while directing the local men to take the four wagon passengers to the jail in Glenwood, the county seat several miles west. Once there, however, the catchers learned that the sheriff was away on business until later that night. When some of their friends in town began talking up the idea of taking the captives to Missouri, the two catchers had cold feet, fearing this situation was becoming far more complicated than they had expected.[4]

So Joe Foster, one of the fellows urging a Missouri run, took the reins to convert the jail idea into a kidnapping scheme. The two original slave catchers abandoned their involvement after helping Foster escort the black men back to where they had captured them. After initially putting their captives in a barn outside town, they soon moved them to Joe Foster's place on Silver Creek, about three miles from Justice of the Peace Cramer's quarters. Meanwhile, Foster recruited five other men to help make the dash for Missouri.[5]

A local man got wind of the scheme and informed a local Congregationalist farmer near Glenwood. The farmer brought word to Tabor about the waylaid covered wagon group and of the black men's jailing in Glenwood. George Gaston quickly brought together several antislavery neighbors at his house to figure out what to do.

About midnight, responding to a knock at his door, Mills County sheriff E. B. Samson opened it to find a party of Tabor men asking if he had the black men in his jail. Being unaware of the unfolding events, Sampson replied there were none to his knowledge, but he went to the jail, where the jailor also reported that he knew nothing about them. Upon hearing this news, the Tabor party now suspected that the reported captors were in fact kidnappers transporting the four black men to Missouri, so they rode off in that direction.[6]

When their search proved fruitless, the pursuers returned to Tabor and waited. On Saturday a man arrived in town who reported that a trial concerning the two Tabor whites caught driving the black men through the area was under way at Justice Cramer's house. The man had urged Cramer to postpone the proceedings for a day, and the justice granted his request. So on Sunday at 1:15 p.m. Tabor men attended the court, and two of the men acted as counsel for the defendants. Through the afternoon and into the evening Justice Cramer listened to arguments.

While the hearing was in progress, two young Tabor men decided to return home. When they were about to leave, a local resident quietly told them the black men were at Foster's, so they went down the road in that direction. Upon arriving and seeing suspicious movements at his place, they waited out of sight nearby.[7] When darkness settled in, the two noticed men loading a four-horse wagon. The two ran back to Justice Cramer's and arrived as the proceedings were ending and Cramer had ordered the release of Sheldon and Woodford.

Hearing the kidnappers had been found and were about to escape, fifteen Taborites went to James F. Wing's place, where Wing's wife was already outside cutting hickory poles into clubs. Weapons in hand, the men climbed into two sled wagons and followed the kidnappers' wagon tracks southeast through the snow. The track proved easy to follow because one wagon wheel continuously cut into the unbroken snow. The chase ensued in the full moon night. The pursuers drove down the west side of the Nishnabotna River to the small settlement of White Cloud, where locals informed them the wagon had been seen crossing the river a short time earlier. The Taborites pressed on as the wagon trail took a line south along the east divide of the river.[8]

Their horse-drawn sleds gradually overtook the heavy wagon filled with five white and four black men at about ten miles east of Tabor and twenty miles from the Missouri line. The kidnappers' four-horse team, which had been following the lead of Joe Foster (drunk) on horseback, was nearly winded when the advance sled of the Tabor men came alongside and "ran into the leaders, swinging them about and entangling them." With three holding revolvers and the other twelve wielding their hickory stakes, all but the sled drivers jumped out to surround the wagon. The outnumbered kidnappers, despite having more guns and knives, gave in. "Not a shot was fired on either side," stated one report, "except by the blacks, who for joy, discharged two up in the air...." The four-hour chase now over, the Tabor men gathered up the weapons and escorted the kidnapper party to Tabor.[9]

At daylight they pulled up before the town hotel. Here, recalled Rev. John Todd, all went inside to get "warmed up after an all night's cold ride. Breakfast was soon ready for all the company but the pro-slavery party objected to eating with "niggers"—declared they were not used to that, and did not propose to begin now. 'Oh, well!' said the landlord, 'you needn't. You can sit down and eat, and the others can eat afterward.' They sat down to breakfast, and by the time they were through, the fugitives were well started on their way to freedom, and the kidnappers saw them no more."[10]

The four young black men were taken two miles east to L. E. Webb's place for food and rest. By evening they climbed into a sled where three Congregational church members—Origin Cummings, D. A. Woods, and L. B. Hill, "each with a double-barrel shotgun"—set out for Lewis, Iowa. Reaching L. B. Hill's farm, the group shifted to a wagon for the rest of the trip, as the team would be able to cross the frozen rivers and creeks at low bank areas. They drove northeast on the divide between Walnut Creek and the East Nishnabotna River through Montgomery, Pottawattamie, and Cass Counties. By Tuesday morning they were eating breakfast at Oliver Mill's place north of Lewis, and the black men rested up for the next stage of their flight. Rest they needed, for the previous four days had brought sleepless fear, intense excitement, and luckless travel since arriving in Tabor.[11]

Residents of Grinnell saw the four men arrive in a wagon driven by a Quaker, 150 miles from Lewis. Here their story took another turn. All four remained for a time in town, each boarding with a resident family. Two of them, however, longed to go back to the Choctaw lands in Kansas Territory and free their loved ones. One in particular was eager to retrieve his wife and children. Meanwhile, they also expressed interest in learning to read at school, and the one man was keen on being able to read road signposts to ease his escape with his wife. Encouraged by leading Grinnell abolitionists, the four enrolled at school.[12]

Months before, townsmen had registered in the school sixteen-year-old Frances Overton, a female fugitive who for the past year had lived with the family of Amos Bixby, a reform-minded lawyer. But when certain community members saw four new black men stepping forward to attend, they balked. Resistance swelled; talk was in the air that "the niggers must go" and that "their daughters should not sit with the niggers."

Gathering at the town schoolhouse on March 12, 1860, the contending parties at first danced around the issue, but then one townsman stepped up and put the matter squarely: "We want to exclude the niggers."[13] A motion to that effect brought a surge of heated, passionate debate and insults traded between abolitionists and their opponents. One cried out, "They *shall never enter those* doors unless over my dead body!"[14] When the motion to exclude them came up for a vote by a show of hands, it fell short by eight out of the fifty voting. Then calling for a written ballot, the outcome fell short again, this time by five votes.[15]

The people on the losing side, more than disgruntled, were determined to yet have their way. The next day people on both sides, now armed, carried their convictions to the schoolhouse door. Superintendent Leonard Parker himself had anticipated trouble and arrived early, carrying a "stout walking stick."[16]

The opposition leader, an old sea captain named Nathaniel Winslow Clark, stepped up into the school. He equated blacks with property and, not long before, had met a slave hunter south of town who was looking for the two runaways of Stephen Nuckolls from Nebraska City. Clark had told the slave chaser that additional money could be made by nabbing Frances Overton at nearby Grinnell. Joining Clark at the school was a town grocer, Samuel "Scotch" Cooper; both men had several daughters at the school.

The primary room teacher hurrying to find Superintendent Parker, "rushed into the upper room saying, 'What shall I do?' Clark and Cooper are threatening 'to come and to drive those colored boys out of my room.'" Before Parker could speak, "glancing down the stairway she exclaimed, 'There they are now.'" Superintendent Parker ran downstairs and later described what happened:

CITIZENS. We have come to see that the niggers don't come to school.

SUP'T. Very well, bring me a line from the directors, requesting that they shall not be admitted, and they shall not come an hour longer.

CITIZENS. We know where the directors stand, we'll not do that.

SUP'T. Then remember, gentlemen, that every pupil permitted by the directors to come to this school is under my protection on the school grounds and during school hours.

CITIZENS. You don't mean to say you'll fight for the niggers.

SUP'T. I mean to defend every pupil rightfully here who is attacked.

CITIZENS. We'll know where to find you then.

SUP'T. You certainly will.

Seeing the black students had not yet arrived, the two "withdrew to intercept them before reaching the school grounds." Word swiftly spread through the village that spring morning as a crowd gathered quickly and surrounded the four black students near the church. Although they stood their ground and a majority stood with them to let them enter the school, the four shortly consented to "return to their boarding places." And the school's directors, fearing more outbursts, ended the school term ten days early.[17]

Feelings continued to run strong. Writing to her mother a week later, Sarah Parker noted, "The town is not settled yet." Even among regular Congregational Church members, opinion was split, for several in the crowd had turned against further pressing the issue.[18]

The former sea captain, aggravating tensions further, wrote to a St. Louis newspaper and disclosed the school's contested issue and what he knew of the blacks in Grinnell. Reading it made the locals uneasy that Frances Overton's former master might show up in town, so Grinnell's antislavery leaders scouted out a new home for her. Within days Superintendent Parker arranged for someone to escort her via a nighttime ride to a Quaker settlement some fifty miles north in Hardin County.[19]

The black men soon left town for Springdale, the Quaker settlement seventy-five miles east, where they remained into the summer. In August they met Charles Ball (age twenty-three), Edwin Morrison (twenty-one) and his cousin Albert Southwick (twenty-three), and Joseph Coppoc (nineteen). The young Quakers were coming from Kansas; Coppoc was returning to his Springdale home, and the others had formerly lived there. They had been part of a three-wagon train escort for a sizable group of runaways and freedmen from Topeka. After a brief stay, Ball, Morrison, and Southwick left to return the wagon teams to Topeka and then proceed to their parents' new homes near Pardee in northeastern Kansas Territory. Shortly thereafter three of the four black men left Springdale for Kansas, and by fall they would meet the young Quakers again.

II

Pardee had a rural Quaker neighborhood south of town, where the parents of Charles Ball and Ed Morrison and several related families from Springdale had moved. Also Ransom L. Harris, a sixteen-year-old boy who recently had arrived from Springdale, was occupying a small, twelve-by-fourteen-foot log cabin on Benjamin Ball's farm.

The young Quaker men, after having seen John Brown arrive in Springdale with twelve liberated blacks and after having themselves helped bring another Iowa train of runaways from Kansas a few weeks earlier, were filled with antislavery feeling and ready to do more. They dubbed Harris's small cabin their own antislavery Blue Lodge. "In the little log cabin," wrote Ransom, "we did our own cooking and worked on nearby farms, returning to the cabin at night to sleep." No sooner had they settled in when the three black men from Indian Territory showed up and asked for their help in freeing family members who were left in Indian lands. They convinced Ball, Morrison, Southwick, and Charles "Chalkley" Lipsey, a new companion in Pardee, to join in this new adventure. What happened next would become a sad story of attempted slave liberation, betrayal, and death.

From Pardee the Quakers went to Lawrence in search of additional men to carry out their quest. They found three men to join them and turned control of the venture over to a local wagon shop operator, John Dean (originally from Allamakee County, Iowa). Bluntly radical though a gutless braggart, Dean recruited his friend William Clarke Quantrill, then going by the name Charley Hart, plus a man named John S. Jones.[20]

Harris described Quantrill, who was five feet ten inches tall and 140 pounds with "blue eyes, a Roman nose, [and] sandy complexion," as having "a reserved, insinuating and rather persuasive voice" along with "a restless glance of the eyes" and "a nervous swing" to his walk. Unknown to these Quaker idealists, Dean's friend was a transient without moral convictions.

Quantrill cunningly played a double game: satisfying proslavery men that he made acquaintance with abolitionists only to learn and undo their plans and convincing radical antislavery people in Lawrence that he stood with them as an abolitionist liberator of the enslaved.

Quantrill, however, mainly wanted money. He obtained reward money from giving away a runaway's location to slaveholders or from kidnapping and delivering runaways back to the slaveholders. If he ran into trouble with one side, he relied on the other for protection while planning another easy money scheme. He skillfully befriended Rev. John Stewart, an antislavery man, and stayed at his stockade when in hiding and became friendly with other radical antislavery men who came through the area.[21]

Charles Ball had first met Quantrill through antislavery man John Dean in an April trip to Lawrence and then again in August after returning the wagons from Springdale, Iowa. Quantrill, who boarded at the City Hotel, gradually became friendly with Ball and gained influence in his group's antislavery plans.

From Lawrence the group got as far as Osawatomie on the Kansas border before their scheme to liberate the black men's family members fell apart. Too few men had joined to carry it out adequately, too little money was available, and winter was coming on. The three black men's increasing distrust of Quantrill also helped their decision to abort the venture. Instead of splitting up and going their own ways, however, the men stayed and listened as Quantrill began promoting an alternative, a raid on the Morgan Walker farm in Missouri to free his slaves. This plan had been in Quantrill's thoughts for some time.

During the early summer Quantrill had often urged Reverend Stewart to join in such a foray on Walker's place, but the wary preacher had refused. Quantrill knew that Stewart had a price on his head in Missouri and might be delivered up to authorities if Quantrill could get him there. Eli Snyder, who had his own band of antislavery Jayhawkers and a $1,000 reward for his capture in Missouri, heard about Quantrill's scheme at Osawatomie. Snyder warned the others of trouble if they followed Quantrill. He knew him well, had absolutely no trust in him, and was aware that Quantrill had a bad reputation around Osawatomie.[22]

Quantrill, seeing a raid at Walker's place as a chance to kidnap the three Indian Territory black men as well, tried talking the three into going along and argued they could be of great help in inducing Walker's slaves to leave together. The black men and others had heard enough of Snyder's misgivings and said no. But John Dean and the young men from Springdale, Iowa, likely saw it as their chance to duplicate John Brown's liberation of enslaved blacks in his Missouri raid two years earlier. Ultimately, of the ten men who had come to Osawatomie—Quantrill, Dean, Morrison, Ball, Southwick, Lipsey, Jones, and the three runaways—only six remained after Jones and the three Indian country blacks withdrew.[23]

Morgan Walker, a settler who had come from Kentucky twenty-six years earlier, lived in Jackson County, Missouri. The farm was two miles north of the hamlet of Blue Springs (today just southeast of Independence, Missouri), and its eighteen hundred acres amounted to a mix of fields, woodland pasture, and dense timber. On it the ambitious landowner had built a spacious log house, cabin quarters for those held in slavery, and various outbuildings for his stock operation.[24]

Meanwhile, the antislavery raiders gathered blankets and camp cookware for their planned incursion in early December. For arms they took only revolvers and knives because rifles, they judged, would draw the suspicion of passersby. If asked their destination, the raiders had agreed to say they were going to work on a railroad grading project of the Missouri Pacific Railroad east of Jackson County.

Accounts of the raid vary among persons who knew parts of or supposedly participated in the venture. What follows draws on some writing of Ransom L. Harris, who remained at Benjamin Ball's cabin in Pardee during the raid, and especially on the research findings of Kansas historian William Elsey Connelley.

The first day of the two-day journey the group of young raiders spent passing through twenty miles of bottomlands from the Kansas line to Indian Creek in Missouri, where they camped for the night. The next day they made higher ground and struggled through considerable timber and brushlands. Upon coming near Morgan Walker's farm, the small party hid in a thicket of nearby woods during the afternoon.

At about one o'clock Quantrill, on the pretense of reconnoitering the farmstead, notified the farmer's son Andrew J. Walker, who lived a quarter mile from his father's place, of their presence and of the intended raid that night. As payment for revealing details of what was to happen and how to frustrate it, Quantrill was to receive a horse and gun. With Morgan Walker away that day at Independence, Andrew went to the homes of four proslavery neighbors who agreed to bring their guns to his place and help resist the raiders. Morgan Walker returned home shortly before the raid. Upon listening to his son and his wife hurriedly explain the arranged plan, Morgan initially wanted to kill them all—including Quantrill—but was talked into accepting the agreement.[25]

On that moonless night of December 10, the raiding party awaited the arrival of the wagon driven by Albert Southwick and John Dean. They finally arrived in a two-horse outfit supplied by the proprietor of a hotel at Osawatomie where Quantrill boarded much of the time. While Southwick and Dean waited with the team and horses, Charles Ball, Ed Morrison, Chalkley Lipsey, and Quantrill moved at seven o'clock toward the house, which was about a quarter mile from the road.

The large log house had "a wide passageway between two front rooms and a stairway to sleeping rooms above" and a fifty-foot porch running along the entire east side. Andrew had placed three men in a small room at the north end that his father used as a tack room for bridles and saddles. Outside this room on the porch was his mother's loom, behind which Andrew Walker and another man concealed themselves. All of the men carried shotguns loaded with buckshot.[26]

Walker's bloodhounds set up a chorus as Morrison, the party's agreed-upon spokesman, entered the farmstead and stepped onto the porch. Lipsey stood behind him and Quantrill off to one side with Ball ready to gather together the slaves. What happened in the next moments has been variously explained. One source has stated that when Morgan Walker answered the door and the men entered the house, Morrison told him they were there to free his slaves, while another has it that Ball did the talking. Other biographers of Quantrill's write that it was he who demanded Walker's slaves, horses, mules, and money. But the most reliable report of what happened was provided in an 1883 letter written by Morgan's son, Andrew:

> They told my father they were going to take his slaves, he had thirty two slaves. They told him they would take his slaves, his horses, his mules and his money. There were about 100 horses and mules. My father asked Ball if he had talked with the negroes and whether they wanted to go or not. He said he had, he told him to go and get them then, but that if there were any that did not want to go to let them stay. Quantrill said he would take care of the old folks and they could go and get the negroes.

What followed is generally agreed upon: when Ball left to find the slaves and Morrison and Lipsey stepped back outside, Quantrill remained inside. Andrew Walker's companion behind the loom fired a premature shot that prompted a volley from the others. "Morrison fell dead. Lipsey fell from the porch with a charge of balls in his thigh." Ball, unhurt and firing his revolver aimlessly, ran as Walker's men fired another volley in his general direction. But upon hearing Lipsey's cries for help, Ball ran back and carried him into the brush only to discover the wagon was no longer there. Southwick and Dean had departed, the latter having been hit in the foot evidently by a stray shot.[27]

Concluding that the raiders had escaped, Walker and his neighbors pulled Morrison's body off the porch and soon notified the county sheriff. Neighbors came to view the dead man, who had been "straightened for the grave." The next day the coroner's verdict indicated that Morrison had "come to his death by gun shot, shot out of a musket or shot gun. He was shot in the right side with twenty buck shot and seven old shot holes in the same side, and in the right arm three fresh shot and seven shot holes." By day's end they buried Morrison in a rough coffin out near the road. In the meantime, Charles Ball lay in the brush with Lipsey, caring for his wounded companion as best he could.[28]

Two days passed, and apparently Ball could not find a way to get his friend over the border into Kansas. Lipsey was in too much pain to walk, and when Ball walked to a nearby farm and made off with a horse to carry his friend, Lipsey was yet unable to ride. So for the time being Ball waited in hopes that his partner's strength might revive. The next day a slave belonging to Walker's neighbor noticed the two men. He had been hunting a hog in the woods and came upon Ball and Lipsey resting beside a small campfire with a horse tied nearby. In visiting, the two invited him to escape with them to Lawrence, Kansas, and asked him to bring a wagon and team. From Lawrence, they promised, they would see that he would be taken to free Iowa and then on to Canada. The slave listened and agreed to go with them, but upon departing he went immediately to his slaveholder and told what he had discovered.[29]

At once the neighboring slaveholder rode for Morgan Walker's place to share the slave's story. Andrew Walker, his father, his brother, and Quantrill readied their arms and went out to the site. As they drew close Ball stood up and Lipsey, badly wounded, was on his elbows; both men had revolvers in hand. At that moment

Fig. 21. A Quaker from Springdale, Iowa, who had accompanied his family to the Kansas Territory, Charles Ball participated in a slave liberation raid on the Morgan Walker farm, where he lost his life. From Lutz, "Quantrell, the Guerilla Chief," 511.

Fig. 22. Eighteen-year-old Charles "Chalkley" Lipsey joined Charles Ball and Ed Morrison in carrying out a raid to free slaves at the Morgan Walker farm, and all three lost their lives in the attempt. From Lutz, "Quantrell, the Guerilla Chief," 512.

Morgan and Andrew fired, killing them both. Within hours, as neighbors watched, slave-dug graves were readied at the site where Ball and Lipsey died, and the two were buried without coffins. Within a day, as so often happened in the nineteenth century, the graves were desecrated when physicians in the area learned of the burial, dug up the bodies, and carried them off for dissection.[30]

The Morgan Walker raid brought home the dangers of slave liberation attempts. In their effort to help up to twenty-five enslaved people escape, the young Quaker men's antislavery idealism had failed to overcome the facts of having too few men and equipment, of having selected poor leaders, of suffering abandonment at the scene by wagon mates, and of being betrayed by a presumed friend.

The three black men from the Indian Territory who did not join the venture stayed in Osawatomie and subsequently became Union teamsters in the Civil War. The fourth member who had remained in Iowa returned briefly to Grinnell in 1861.[31]

III
Another wagon train from Kansas to Iowa took shape in midsummer of 1860. In Wakarusa, Kansas Territory, a group of men prepared a large black refugee expedition to reach Iowa, one later known in Kansas as "The Last Train."

Rev. John Stewart arranged for a dozen or so men to meet at Wakarusa. All volunteers committed several weeks of their time beginning June 13, 1860, to help assemble a group of refugee black people for a trip from Kansas Territory north to freedom. Joining the Methodist pastor to chaperone the group to and across Iowa was Charles Leonhardt, a Free-State fighter who had come to Kansas in one of the trains of the New England Emigrant Aid Company's effort.[32] Among Stewart's volunteers also was Joseph Coppoc, whose Iowa brothers, Edwin and Barclay, had joined John Brown's raid on Harpers Ferry, Virginia.

Stewart, known as "the fighting preacher," was a radical abolitionist with little money. He lived with his wife and child in a timbered area of his claim on a horseshoe bend of Wakarusa Creek south of Lawrence. From his stockade-fortified residence he occasionally preached, raised some cattle, and sometimes trafficked in horses and cattle stolen from proslavery farms, a practice that his antislavery friends winked at as for "the cause." He also dedicated himself to helping manage Underground Railroad traffic. After helping rescue Dr. John Doy (convicted for abducting slaves) from a jail at St. Joseph, Missouri, in September 1859, Stewart spent the next three months making night trips into Missouri while disguised as a peddler and enabled the escape of a total fourteen enslaved persons.

Now in late December, having recently returned from an eight-day journey freeing "two of my black brethren" and suffering from frostbite, Stewart wrote Thaddeus Hyatt (president of the National Kansas Committee) and asked for help. His horse had died on the trip, and he faced the difficulties of paying traveling expenses and of determining "what to do with the slaves when we get them." Stewart explained, "There is something wrong in Nebraska & Iowa I am fearful that some have been captured there and sent back. Is there any organizations that can be brought to bear so as to take charge of fugitives, Please write me all the information you can on this point as soon as possible. . . ." Limited time and expenses had produced a log jam of enslaved people who were vulnerable to recapture, a problem that would not be resolved until June the next year when Stewart and friends pulled together enough provisions to make their journey north.[33]

Getting to Iowa was dangerous business, as Stewart well knew from Doy's failed attempt the previous year. Indeed, Stewart's situation resembled that of Dr. Doy. Both men were trying to deal with rising incidents of black men and women—slave and free alike—being snatched away by professional kidnappers and slave hunters in Douglas County. Both men also relied on antislavery friends to help pull together what was needed—wagons, teams, supplies, and money—for their trips. And both were attempting to transport not simply one or two persons but a dozen or more at a time.

The danger of recapture and kidnapping increased the risks for runaway black people who had to stay long in Kansas Territory. Since the winter of 1858–59 gangs had turned kidnapping into a thriving business around Lawrence. And to the east at Wyandotte, officials were abetting it as "pimps" of the enterprise. "We can scarcely take up a Territorial newspaper," wrote the *Lawrence Republican* editor, "without finding an account of one of these nefarious attempts."[34] Unable to protect the black people there, exasperated antislavery men looked to removing willing persons to Iowa, as reflected in Doy's and Stewart's efforts.

Mere weeks before Stewart's group left for Iowa, proslavery slave hunters had skirmished with runaways and others at Stewart's cabin stockade. On an early May day Stewart was in Lawrence visiting a friend when "a runner came in with word that his place had been attacked and one man taken and one wounded." A number of runaways were at his place, and some slaveholders had hired several men, including the notorious Jake Hurd, to retrieve them. The slave catchers rode up to Stewart's place and found some runaways plowing a field. Stewart had armed the workers with revolvers, and they fought back. After exchanging some twenty shots, their pursuers wounded one in the hip and then withdrew with one captive, a free boy who had been living there for two years.

Learning of the fight in progress, Stewart's friend reported: "We started off as quick as possible, but could only raise four horsemen, and by the time we got our arms they were off a good way. We followed them about six miles, but found that they all had good horses and were so far ahead that we could not overtake them."[35]

Stewart rushed to get the Iowa expedition ready and by mid-June 1860 had rounded up three wagons and teams, supplies, and men. Many details were still unknown: the roads, trails, and people along the route. What Stewart did have, however, were four young Iowa Quakers—Joseph Coppoc, Charles Ball, Edwin Morrison, and Albert Southwick—who knew the way north and across Iowa to their families at Springdale.

The train, better armed and manned than Doy's had been, gradually moved northward and avoided notice as much as possible. On the now-established trail the wagons crossed the broad swells of grassland toward Nebraska City. They met no interference, but sensing danger as they neared Nebraska City—perhaps down at the ferry owned by proslavery man Stephen Nuckolls—they instead went upriver to Wyoming. Wagon train members stayed the night at a storehouse of the local Republican paper, and the next day a Wyoming ferry owner, a Free-State man, gave them safe passage across the Missouri.[36]

Going ashore they drove to the hamlet of Civil Bend and then Tabor. "Of the generous reception we obtained at the hospitable homes," remembered train member Charles Leonhardt, "I need not say a word. Language is inadequate. It is the Iowa 'Oberlin.'" Here the black people were "amazed when they found themselves recognized as human beings." These antislavery settlements had known of their coming and arranged to house them. "Willingly we remained here several days to revive our horses," while the people also cleaned up and recuperated.[37]

Leaving Tabor they split into two separate bodies to call less attention to their presence. The larger group, with two wagons, moved northeasterly "to Indian Creek in Mills County, thence through Grove Township, Pottawattamie Co., to Lewis, to Grove City, Dalmanutha, West Milton to Des Moines." Undetected on this leg of their journey, they met with "very pleasant" treatment as "welcome guests" at each stop. Further, before leaving for the next station, a local resident checked out the line ahead to ensure it was safe.[38]

The third wagonload and its accompanying squad of men took a more southerly route, passing around the southern and eastern outskirts of Des Moines to Rev. Demas Robinson's place. The two bands would rejoin at Grinnell.

As the larger two-wagon train worked its way toward Newton without a guide, "we came very near," wrote Leonhardt, "to get[ting] ourselves into equal trouble as those we had evaded in Nebraska City." The problem began when they halted a mile west of Newton in some hazel brush. Leonhardt noted that "[we] somewhat relaxed our former precaution and care in disguising the real character of our train," thus some "passers by [sic] had seen enough to tell a good deal more about us." And, as Leonhardt put it, "stories never lose by traveling, and we found it so," upon entering the Newton settlement on Monday, August 13.[39]

At the public square with the wagon covers hanging loosely over the tops to prevent an "unnecessary display of arms," the passengers and their escorts began preparing lunch. Before long an elderly woman arrived with milk for the runaway women and children. A crowd gathered round on the wooden sidewalks, and while some gave friendly cheers, others, in particular the older ones, began yelling epithets of "Nigger thieves" and calls to hang them. Then "at last, shouts after shouts came ringing through the air" from supporters defying the train's detractors: "Why don't you take them, now is your only chance, you Negro driving Democrats."[40]

Uneasy amid the shouting, the train's escorts decided upon a show of strength and determination, unfurling the wagon covers so all could see the Sharps rifles—also called Henry Ward Beecher's Bibles—that both the escorts and fugitives carried. Upon seeing the exposed arms held and ready, the hecklers decided they were "hard customers" and departed, leaving the train's operators "to enjoy many hearty shakes of the hand from true friends of the Cause."[41]

Within three days Newton's *Jasper Free Press* disclosed the group's presence in Iowa:

> On Monday last, about noon, two covered wagons passed through Newton, containing fifteen negroes from Missouri and Kansas, who were making their way toward the north star. The wagons were accompanied by some 12 or 15 white men on horseback, who appeared to have charge of the cargo of "human chattels." The negroes and the whites were heavily armed, and presented quite a warlike and very daring appearance. They said that when they started there was a large company of whites and one hundred slaves, taken from Missouri and of the Waukarusa, in Kansas and that they separated on coming to Iowa into different companies. A squad of 19 passed a few miles South of this on Monday. They camped a short distance from town for several hours, and then proceeded on their journey.

The news story (with its exaggerated numbers) attracted public interest, and other state newspapers picked up and repeated the story.[42] An anti-abolitionist editor saw the wagon group as evidence that, instead of learning the lesson of failure at Harpers Ferry, "nothing less than an open war against the constitutional rights of the South, suits their purpose." Such men in their temerity "have no claims upon the sympathy of patriotic, law-abiding men." Another pointed out how these "negro thieves" furnish "material aid and means to convey them to Canada—where, during the long winter, they may learn to steal, starve and freeze."[43]

After a brief rest immediately east of Newton, the train continued another sixteen miles toward Grinnell, arriving in late afternoon. At a hastily organized town meeting and rally at the schoolhouse that evening, the visitors, though weary from the long Monday travel, enjoyed hearing the greatest praise yet. Josiah B. Grinnell welcomed them all with a jocular reference to these travelers as "Southern gentlemen traveling north for the benefit of their health." The tired travelers, he pleaded, could use clothing and supplies. Grinnell's remarks contained no reference to the color of the strangers, impressing Leonhardt. At the end of the meeting all visitors were called upon to stand, and a motion carried that "those who have room to spare should take some of us home, [and] that all assistance otherwise [given] would be thankfully received at the residence of the Hon. J. B. Grinnell."[44]

The travelers stayed in Grinnell until Wednesday morning, the fifteenth, when Amos Bixby, lawyer and Republican candidate for district clerk of Poweshiek County, guided the rested party to Brooklyn, sixteen miles east, and then twenty miles farther to Marengo, camping half a mile east of the settlement. Grinnell sent on a note ahead to William Penn Clarke that "tomorrow or next day there will be a company of 20 odd persons well armed passing on to Springdale. If they are to be troubled I trust they may have a fair warning."[45]

Democrats took full advantage of the news in this election year. They linked Josiah Grinnell—a Republican state senator, a delegate to the Chicago national convention, and an influential man in Republican politics—to the "lawbreakers," whom he "entertained at his house" and found shelter for others "in the houses of friends." Further, by confusing Joseph Coppoc on the rescue train with his brother Barclay of Harpers Ferry fame, the Democrats charged Grinnell with raising money for "an escaped murderer, . . . who now, in open day, braves the law he has foully outraged."[46]

As for Bixby, the opposition press decried how he, "in open day, on one of the public highways," was the "chaperon [*sic*] of a band of negroes, stolen from their masters in Missouri, and furnished material aid and means to convey them to Canada." An angry editor of the *Cedar Democrat* decried their actions, asking, "Why is it that these nigger stealers are allowed to pass unmolested through Iowa with their plunder?—it seems to us that the State has been disgraced long enough."[47]

Jabbing back, the editor of the *Iowa State Register* challenged: "If these devoted allies of the slave-breeders feel aggrieved, why don't they strip off their coats and boots, and make tracks after the fugitives?" No, the editor pointed out, "they sit in their easy chairs and make wry faces, instead of arresting the fugitives and taking them back to their alleged owners."[48]

Unaware of the political hullabaloo, the wagon train left the overnight camp east of Marengo and moved toward its destination at Springdale. That evening the train reached the west bank of the Iowa River, within sight of Iowa City, and the people camped unobtrusively on the large farm of Gilman Folsom, a noted "stormy" lawyer and rabid Democrat. From Folsom's place—close by the bend at the narrowest place on the river—Ed Morrison and Joe Coppoc went on ahead to West Branch and Springdale (ten miles east) so their community and their families could prepare to receive and shelter the incoming passengers and escorts.[49]

On Friday morning, August 17, before sunrise, the three-wagon train crossed the Iowa River and made it to West Branch for breakfast. The Springdale Quakers took over the passengers' care upon their arrival, though Leonhardt noticed some were more willing than others to be actively involved. Perhaps several feared public notoriety similar to what arose the year before from John Brown's association with Springdale. Leonhardt came away especially impressed by William Maxson, who lived a few miles from Springdale. "Maxson was a great enthusiast, a tower of strength in the Cause, we had heard," and on his parlor walls hung oil paintings and ambrotypes of John Brown and his men. His house "proved to be a well regulated free boarding place" for Kansas escorts and passengers alike ". . . til the former could return to Kansas and the latter had found places to work."[50]

Of the passengers, Nancy and a man called Black Jack soon married and settled as renters on the farm of the Coppoc brothers' stepfather, Joseph Raley. When the Civil War began and Iowa called for colored troops, Black Jack enlisted and died at the Battle of Shiloh. Johny, who added Clark to his name for the kindness of Sidney Clarke, also joined up with the colored unit, served through the war, and upon discharge died of pneumonia at Davenport. A man called My George married and remained in Cedar County while yet another called Our George entered service in the army. He married and lived in Oskaloosa, Iowa. A woman named Kate, whom John Stewart and Sidney Clarke accompanied to Boston, Massachusetts, eventually went back to Kansas and married a man in Leavenworth.[51]

Their escorts on the train, upon resting after their nearly two-month journey, went their own ways. Sidney Clarke returned to Kansas, fought in the Union army during the war, and then served three terms in Congress. At Iowa City on October 13, 1860, Charles Leonhardt met one last time with John Stewart, who stopped there on his way back to Kansas from Boston. Leonhardt never saw him again and remained in Springdale for several years. He met and fell in love with Esther, the eldest daughter of Springdale Underground Railroad operator Griffith Lewis, and within eight months they married. Charles had graduated in law at Cincinnati that spring and began a legal career. Joe Coppoc stayed in Iowa, served as a major in a colored infantry regiment, married, and became a Baptist minister. Morris Walton, one of the coachmen, from Auburn, and Warren Bassett returned to Kansas. Walton farmed southwest of Topeka, but Bassett eventually moved to Ohio.[52]

Finally, although Joe Coppoc stayed behind, the other three Springdale comrades—Charles Ball, Ed Morrison, and Albert Southwick—drove the wagon teams back to their owners in Lawrence. As mentioned in section 2 of this chapter, they accompanied Ball to his parents' new farm at Pardee, Kansas, where they launched another slave liberation attempt that was marked by calamity.

IV

Kidnappers of free and runaway blacks operated mainly out of two proslavery towns—Lecompton, which was a dozen miles northwest of Lawrence, and Wyandotte, some thirty miles east near Kansas City. In 1860, with slaves bringing high prices and with federal officials in the territory being reluctant to punish those who either captured and returned runaways for money or sold free blacks into slavery, the gangs acted with impunity.

"This kidnapping business must stop," warned the editor of the *Lawrence Republican* in mid-August. "The freemen of Kansas owe it to themselves to stop it." Indeed, he continued, "if there is any crime which stands out in unrelieved devilishness, which deserves universal outlawry and prompt punishment by death, it is this infernal business of kidnapping men and women to sell them into a terrible and life-long bondage."[53]

Of the kidnappers, the most notoriously active was Jacob Hurd. Though he was a northerner from Pennsylvania who lived northwest of Lawrence within four miles of Lecompton, he held firm proslavery views and made money recapturing or stealing black people from slavery and selling them back. Wrote Kansas historian William Connelley, Hurd was "the right-arm of the rough element, the 'terror-raiser' of the pro-slavery party in Kansas," and, "possibly the most daring border-ruffian that ever lived in Kansas." Loudmouthed, violent, and fearless, he "gloried in the name 'Jake Herd, the Border-Ruffian.'"[54]

His most memorable proslavery triumph had come in leading a band of twenty men on January 25, 1859, to intercept Dr. John Doy's small Iowa-bound wagon train with its three whites and thirteen blacks. Taken to Missouri, the captives endured rough treatment and cursing crowds as they passed through towns. In jail the white detainees were jeered, but some arrested blacks faced torture. The black prisoners were either "taken away forcibly or prevailed on to choose masters" or, in the case of their wives, "carried to Kansas city and other places, probably to be sold down South." Two in particular who claimed they were free and not enslaved suffered cruelty. Doy watched through the grates of his cell door as Jake Hurd came to the jail. He "made them put on their coats, handcuffed them, and chained them together, and whipped them most unmercifully to make them confess they were slaves, but they persisted in asserting that they were freemen."[55]

Such bald-faced efforts, despite the praise they won in proslavery border towns, hardened Free-State attitudes. Perhaps by 1860 the easy pickings around Lawrence were gone, and Hurd decided better thievery lay northward in Nebraska Territory and Iowa. On September 20, 1860, Hurd and two cronies, N. H. Beck and Joel Wildey, were on a western Iowa road some six miles south of Council Bluffs when opportunity called.

Below the "Willow Slough" bridge the men came upon three free blacks, two young men and a girl, going north. Quickly they were "waylaid, forced to turn out into the bushes, gagged and carried off." No one knew anything about it until three days later when a man living a few miles south of Council Bluffs brought to town a horse that had showed up at his farm. It turned out that a farmer south at Civil Bend had lent it to the black travelers.

The incident at once became the talk of Council Bluffs, and then on the next night, September 25, a letter arrived from John Williamson, one of the captives, notifying friends of his situation. Williamson wrote that he had escaped his captors near Oregon (above St. Joseph), Missouri, but on his way back toward Iowa he had been arrested as a vagrant and put into a jail in Rock Port. He did not know what had happened to his two in-laws. The letter brought even greater public excitement in Council Bluffs, and its citizens quickly raised $50 for Sheriff Craig and City Marshal Smith to travel there and obtain Williamson's release. It also prompted considerable local gossip about possible perpetrators, with suspicions pointing "to several men in this vicinity as engaged in the accursed job."[56]

John Williamson, it turns out, was the man who had engineered the escape of Stephen Nuckolls's two slave servants Eliza and Celia Grayson at Nebraska City and then evaded Nuckolls's grasp during December 1858. Having become too risky to work back and forth from Civil Bend to Nebraska City, the twenty-five-year-old Williamson went in a new direction. On March 1, 1859, Reverend John Todd of Tabor married John and twenty-year-old Betsy Ellen Garner (sister of the two boys who earlier had been beaten by the mob of Nuckolls's men chasing runaways Eliza and Celia). The couple moved to the second ward of Council Bluffs, where John found employment as a laborer. Twenty-one-year-old Henry Garner (having received in June $6,000 from Nuckolls for the mob beating he had suffered) joined them and also found work as a laborer. Then, in September 1860 Betsy had fallen ill, and John and Henry traveled to Civil Bend to bring back her sister, Maria (age seventeen). As they neared Council Bluffs, Jake Hurd and his partners caught and kidnapped them.[57]

Upon his release from the Rock Port jail, John Williamson returned to Council Bluffs and, being well greeted, "exultingly swung his hat in the streets of Council Bluffs." Meanwhile, Ira Blanchard, the Garners' guardian in Civil Bend, at once had dropped everything and along with George Gaston from Tabor took up the search for Henry and Maria. The men spent several days scouting northwest Missouri, traveling all the way to St. Joseph. They learned enough there to conclude that the kidnappers had taken the Garners to St. Joseph and then on to St. Louis for sale. Gaston returned home, and Blanchard hurriedly prepared to catch a steamboat for St. Louis. Blanchard took one more important step as well: he sent a telegraph dispatch, which "arrived just in time to save them from slavery, and secure the arrest of the kidnappers."[58]

When Blanchard stepped off the boat at St. Louis, he immediately walked to the slave market section and slave pens. Finding the keeper, he told him of two persons brought in for sale who actually were free blacks. Unwilling to hand over the two people on only Blanchard's say so, the skeptical keeper took him to see how the two captives would respond upon seeing Blanchard.

Rev. John Todd described what happened next: "When Dr. Blanchard entered, Henry, suffering severely yet from the blow he had received, and apparently in utter despair of any relief in the future, did not look up. But Maria no sooner looked up than she jumped up and ran and threw her arms around him, exclaiming, 'Oh! Dr. Blanchard! Where did you come from?' The testimony was indisputable."[59]

V

The keeper released the Garners to Blanchard. They were not in the best shape, as Henry had been severely beaten (this insult on top of the Nuckolls's mob beating two years earlier) and Wildey had sexually violated Maria on the journey to St. Louis. By October 4—two days after Hurd, Beck, and Wildey were arrested for kidnapping—Blanchard had made arrangements for Police Officers Woodworth, Brooke, and Henly to transport the prisoners to Iowa for trial.[60]

All boarded the steamer *Warsaw* the evening of October 4 and embarked. But what a journey it became. Though all three kidnappers were heavily manacled with their ankles shackled, soon Jake Hurd became highly "restive and reckless." He began not only "demanding his revolver" but also sneering between curses "that he could never be taken to Iowa, where he was certain he would be lynched as soon as he arrived." To quiet him down they allowed him to think he might be taken to St. Joseph for trial, and he fell into a more tolerable "sullenly quiet" state until the steamboat arrived at seven the next morning.

Then upon seeing a public carriage waiting for them, Hurd spouted anew, demanding to know where the bus was going to take him. "Swearing he would not leave St. Joseph as a prisoner alive," Hurd's "torrent of invectives" defied the police to take him elsewhere, but with tough work they muscled him into the bus and were on their way. Still, no sooner did the horse team pull the bus up to the gangplank of the steamer *The Spread Eagle*, then Hurd let all hell loose again. Forty to fifty of his friends had been present when he was pressed into the bus, and all of them had followed it to *The Spread Eagle*. They noisily gathered about the gangplank at dockside, and Hurd made the most of it as he "flung himself upon the ground, and made it necessary for the officers to drag him by main strength on board." All the while he gave "violent resistance" and spewed profane abuse on the police. He hoped his sympathizers would step in to help, but they did not interfere with the officers. Nevertheless, Hurd "raved and cursed," especially at Woodworth—the main officer—and threatened him with "the most excruciating of deaths" if not by his own hand then by his avenging friends. His wild screams persisted until shortly after the vessel pulled away.

Then the mood aboard ship began to turn. Though Hurd's violent conduct upset numerous passengers, others wanted to know who had had him arrested. The mere mention of Dr. Blanchard's name brought denunciations from those who knew him "as a notorious and rank abolitionist, well known as a runner off of slaves, and one who ought long since to have been hung." No violence erupted, however, for Hurd's onboard sympathizers faced the policemen's determination to deliver the prisoners, the captain's determination to keep order, and the willingness of many westbound settlers to join in protecting the officers. But forbearance toward Blanchard frayed as the steamer reached larger upriver towns where Hurd's situation had been telegraphed.

Indeed, reaching the next night's stop above St. Joseph at a town on the Kansas side of the river, who should come on board but the brother of Stephen F. Nuckolls. Described as a gentleman "of wealth and high standing in the community," he and some friends had come to exact revenge on Blanchard by riling up the crowd against him. To the officers and passengers he grumbled how "two negroes of his brother had been run off by this Blanchard; Blanchard himself rowed them across the river, took them to and sheltered them at his house, and thence sent them off northward." Not only that, Nuckolls claimed that Blanchard then sued his brother for $8,000 for having maltreated Henry, with "the negro himself being [allowed to give evidence as] the witness on whose testimony the verdict was given."

Then, turning directly to Blanchard, Nuckolls called him "a 'nigger thief,' 'penitentiary bird,' 'fit only for the gallows'" and, "to make very fine mince meat of Blanchard," turned to those around and "offered a reward of one hundred dollars to any one who would put the reprobate over the vessel's rail and on the gang plank." Blanchard asked for and received the support of the boat's captain and the police. The captain declared he would not interfere with what the people did onshore, but on his boat he would do all he could to make sure his passengers were protected and unmolested. Nuckolls then departed with his friends. When the captain saw the crowd onshore growing larger and more menacing, he withdrew the gangplank and, to Blanchard's relief and Hurd's dismay, proceeded upriver.

All this disturbance left many onlookers with the impression that "though Jacob Hurd was certainly a big rascal, 'old Blanchard was a bigger one.'" And then, when officers learned at a landing above the town of Brownville that "their approach had been telegraphed from Brownsville [sic] to Nebraska City" and that a large crowd awaited them, the captain warned that "it would not be safe to convey the party" there and "he had better land them at some point in Missouri." They decided to go ashore at the landing for Hamburg, Iowa, a mile away from the Iowa line. While Blanchard went to a justice of the peace to obtain a warrant for Iowan officers to come, rearrest, and receive the kidnappers at the border from the St. Louis officers, the party walked to "within a few rods of the State line" and stopped at a farmer's house.

Meanwhile, word of the development had reached Nebraska City, and soon "three men on horseback, and eight or ten men in a wagon, drove up" to declare "that the prisoners should not be taken out of Missouri." By the time Blanchard returned with three Iowa officers and authorization to act for the state of Iowa, "at least fifty men had gathered" who opposed removing the prisoners from Missouri. Their leader—a man by the name of Durst—proceeded to rail against Blanchard and his history and of the group's intensely felt low estimate of him.

When the St. Louis officers directed Hurd to get into their wagon, he refused but was willing to walk to the Missouri border. His two fellow kidnappers "made no objection, but rode forward willingly." At this critical spot,

> Woodworth said to the Iowa officers, "Gentlemen, here is your prisoner; take him." The crowd menacingly closed up, and defied them to lay a finger upon him. Blanchard stood with his pistol drawn and holding the warrant and his brother constables were also armed, but none dared to touch Hurd. There was no strife about Beck or Wildey. They stated their willingness to go anywhere with Woodworth, but declined to go with Blanchard. Hurd said he would go anywhere with Woodworth, except into Iowa. Some were so incensed against Blanchard that they proposed to yield up Hurd on the condition that Blanchard should be handed over to them. The Iowa officers at first showed a strong determination, but finally failed to act.

Feeling the heat rising and growing hotter by the minute, Blanchard "turned his horse's head and drove off, telling Woodworth to keep the prisoners, that he would see him again."[61]

The three St. Louis officers took the prisoners by wagon twenty-one miles to Rock Port and arrived at midnight only to find out it had no jail. Within half an hour a crowd sympathetic to Hurd filled the hotel lobby. In their hotel room the officers chained themselves to the prisoners and put a bedstead up against the door. The next morning the situation was no better; indeed, they saw a growing crowd "much excited against Blanchard, many proposing and some fiercely threatening a rescue of Hurd."

Later that afternoon came J. A. Harvey, an attorney from Sidney (the county seat of Fremont County, Iowa). He "asked Woodworth to hold on to the prisoners, stating that the necessary force to take them would soon be down." But witnessing the impassioned crowd, Woodworth concluded he must do something, so he "got his party into a stage, and started for Savanna." Members of the crowd followed them some four to five miles when Woodworth ordered them to stop. The officers and their prisoners pressed on their way, arrived the next morning, "and thence took the cars to St. Joseph." The sheriff put Woodworth in contact with the state's attorney, "who said there were four indictments there against Hurd" ready to be filed in case a habeas corpus writ were served. Woodworth considered returning Hurd to St. Louis while "leaving Wildey and Beck, with whom little could be done, at large." But after hearing that someone along his route intended to file a writ of habeas corpus, he decided instead "to surrender Hurd instantly to the officers of St. Joseph on the warrant they held," and "the relieved officers returned to St. Louis."[62]

Ultimately, by mid-November Missouri governor Robert Stewart received a requisition for Hurd from Governor Samuel Kirkwood of Iowa, and Stewart ordered the St. Joseph authorities to deliver him up to the Pottawattamie County sheriff in Council Bluffs. The county sheriff brought him before a justice of the peace for kidnapping charges, and "in default of $800 bail, he was committed to prison" while awaiting trial. But then, assisted by others on the outside, "he made his escape during the delay, and none of the parties were ever brought justice for the offense." Within two years, however, Hurd was reported to have met his end in Kansas, where he was hanged for horse stealing.[63]

The kidnapping of three black people from Iowa invariably entered state politics during that presidential campaign year when slavery and secession issues so intensified public feeling. Weeks before the November 6 election, the *Des Moines Iowa State Register* linked the Garner kidnappings to Iowa Democrats and remarked on how so "much is said by the pro-slavery Democracy about the great wrong inflicted by abolitionists in abducting slaves and hurrying them through to Canada; but little is said in condemnation by the same party, when free citizens of the State of Iowa, are attacked by pro-slavery ruffians, bound hand and foot, separated from their families, and given over to the 'everlasting curse of bondage.'"[64]

In a similar vein the editor of the *Muscatine (IA) Weekly Journal* wrote: "If these negroes had been kidnapped *out* of slavery instead of *into* it, the Democratic papers would have set up a tremendous howl over the violation of law. Now, they are as still as mice, having no condemnation to utter."[65]

Epilogue

The Kansas Territory imbroglio kindled Iowa's involvement in the Free-State cause. The state provided settlers and arms secretly taken from the state arsenal, aided Free-State wagon trains on their way across the state, offered sanctuary to free-Kansas fighters, and its antislavery settlements enabled John Brown to train and prepare his compatriots for their raid on Harpers Ferry. Furthermore, the state's citizens, especially those of evangelical faith, assisted runaways from slavery on their escape trek from Kansas north to and across Iowa. These eventful actions in the Kansas cause contributed to the pivotal lead-up to Civil War.

In the Bleeding Kansas story tradition, concentrated as it is on political and violent events within the territory itself, the parts that nearby states played in shaping the record have been little told. Popular portrayals treated the closest slave state, Missouri, as simply a nemesis, wholly proslavery and southern, and its closest Free State, Iowa, as a forgotten friend and hence inconsequential.

The true historical narrative of these states, however, is far more complicated, with the Kansas story enhanced when placed in the framework of nearby western states involved in the territory's developments. Neither Missouri nor Iowa were solid in their proslavery or antislavery outlook, but the slavery issue in Kansas moved its neighbors toward one side or the other, stiffening southern identity in Missouri and strengthening northern proclivities of Iowa. Similarly, the involvements of Missouri and Iowa in the Kansas Territory influenced what happened there.[1]

In the years prior to the organization of the Kansas and Nebraska Territories, the people of both Missouri and Iowa viewed themselves more as westerners than as southern or northern in character, and they resided in states also dominated by the Democratic Party. Westerners, though they did not want black people settling in their midst, held mixed attitudes about slavery. Many readily accepted the institution without interference, others accepted slavery where it existed but opposed its expansion westward as a threat to the interests of freeholder whites, and a relative few opposed slavery outright on any terms. Shifting the course of public opinion were national slavery debates over Texas, Mexican cessions, Free-Soil movements, and abolitionist arguments.[2]

Also in flux were the populations of the two frontier states. The early generation of mostly upland southern people in Missouri and southern Iowa were accommodating an onrush of foreign-born immigrants (especially German) and freeholders who were less sympathetic to slavery. The presence of these new settlers tested ruling social and political attitudes and politics. In Missouri, Democrats fractured into a strong proslavery wing championed by Senator David Atchison and a wing that leaned toward the Free-Soilers under former senator Thomas Hart Benton. Similarly in Iowa, the new arrivals to the east-central and northeastern counties diluted the political influence of older, settled southern counties where southern sympathies thrived. By 1854, in a state where Democrats had always managed to win, Iowa's Democratic Party collapsed in the political inferno sparked by the Kansas-Nebraska Act. And yet, with the new immigration to Iowa leaving southern counties unaffected and their political sympathies intact, when a quicker but more southerly route was established across Iowa from Mount Pleasant to Tabor, many wary

Kansas-bound settlers avoided these southern friendly counties near the Missouri line and instead took the more northerly route departing from Iowa City.

The preceding chapters have addressed Iowa's interest and involvement in the Free-State cause, but the state's support was hardly unanimous. Several among Iowa's Democratic press seemed to think as did one proslavery man, who wrote that the arriving Free Staters will "dictate to us a government to preach Abolitionism and dig underground Rail Roads."[3] And so the papers editorialized, published letters opposing the Free-State position, and liberally quoted stories from western Missouri's proslavery newspapers. Looking to add to its complaints about Free Staters in the upcoming 1856 presidential contest, the Democratic editor of Iowa City's *Daily Evening Reporter* charged that "the Republican party do[es] not wish peace in Kansas.—Their success in this election depends upon fostering civil war in that territory, and in keeping the public mind excited by exaggerated and false reports of Kansas outrages." Indeed, he continued, "anarchy and civil war has followed the treasonable plottings of treasonable men." Similarly, in Bloomfield, Iowa, the Democratic editor printed, "Let no quarters be given, but let the entire abolition horde be swept from the Territory." Furthermore, he complained, "the false misstatements of the Abolition presses, in regard to the outrages committed in Kansas [have been made] purposely to create prejudice against Democracy, and secure sympathy in favor of the real aggressors in Kansas." But despite the work of Democratic editors to depict western Missourians as victims of northern aggression by organized Free-State colonization, the tide of Iowa opinion was running against them, and they knew it.[4]

Dennis Mahony's highly partisan Democratic paper in Dubuque foresaw the effects to come for his state's party by late 1855: "[N]o candid judge [can reach] any other conclusion, than that the late defeat of the party was caused by what is called 'the Kansas-

Nebraska measure'—or, to state the matter more pointedly, the breaking up of the Missouri Compromise." All should know that "the public sentiment of the free States against slavery is so deep as to be almost instinctive." Thus, the paper counseled readers not to approach the subject "save under unavoidable necessity, and then only as you would enter a magazine of powder, with a lighted candle. . . ." Despite this caution, however, "the subject was approached, in the Kansas and Nebraska bill, in a sudden unexpected manner," and it produced "recoil in the public mind of the free States." One can only hope that "the party may retrace its steps."[5]

It was not to be. Though some Democratic newspapers in Iowa regretted or opposed ending the Missouri Compromise, they continued to drum up racial intolerance over any fresh arrival of runaways via the Underground Railroad or those termed "contrabands" during the ensuing Civil War. In response the Republican Party leaders, though not without internal consternation, stood up to and combated the attacks, passing measures for black equality. They successfully trounced Democrats in subsequent state elections, leaving them reduced to minority party status.[6]

II

Kansas "was where the war started, not Fort Sumter," wrote a recent commentator, "and everyone involved knew exactly what the killing was about."[7] This statement, however, exaggerates the situation in the territory. For most families settling Kansas, they simply wanted to make a new home for themselves in the cheap abundant lands that had been recently opened and to become part of sweeping westward expansion.

Both proslavery and Free-State backers had to do more than convince committed partisans to come; they also had to win the sentiments of the unconcerned, those numerous "westerner" pioneers flowing into the new territories with no conscious stand on the slavery question. Tough-minded partisans on both sides tried persuasion, propaganda, legal and illegal maneuvers, and intimidation to bring enough settlers into Kansas to vote their way. Stirring voting allegiance from individuals and families absorbed in their everyday, ordinary concerns to improve their lives was no easy matter. Even though most newcomers "knew what the killing was about," they wanted to stay out of it. They were there to settle farms, not to fight.

Proslavery forces' heavy-handed methods in 1855–56 were what made those who had been previously indifferent into staunch Free Staters. "Many of them, when they came to the territory," wrote one observer there, "cared little about the question; but, being free-state men, and thus suffering from slavery-extension aggression, they soon learned to hate, not only the oppressors, but the system of slavery, from the violent extension of which they suffered."[8] Those angry enough to take action likely resembled settler and fighter Samuel Walker, a neighbor of Judge John Wakefield's (noted in chapter 3). One night in December 1855 Walker and his family stood outside their home as a proslavery band burned everything they owned, including their crops, grain in storage, and haystacks. With work impossible to find that winter, Walker recalled, "I made up my mind that, from that day forward, until either the border ruffians or ourselves were driven from Kansas, I would live at their expense." His efforts achieved mixed results but enabled him and his family to survive.[9]

Consider the settlers from Maquoketa in eastern Iowa. Several families from the area boarded three wagons and proceeded west for Kansas Territory in June 1856. They soon joined up with some settlers from McLean County, Illinois, and the total party amounted to sixty-one persons, fifteen of them men. Contemporary newspaper accounts reported that "they intended settling as agriculturalists in Kansas, and had not the remotest idea of engaging in any of the disturbances of that territory."[10]

Then, on their way from Platte City, Missouri, to cross the Missouri River at Fort Leavenworth, a body of 150 armed Missourians stopped them, ostensibly looking for Sharps rifles. Though they could see the settlers had only "ordinary" arms, the Missourians "unloaded the wagons, searched every kind of box and package," and then allowed the settlers to reload their wagons. They took the emigrants' guns and ammunition and handed them a receipt stating they would "be returned at the close of the war and by the Clerk of Platte county." They told the settlers that they must go back, and, to make sure, ten armed Missourians escorted them the first twenty-seven miles back to Liberty in Clay County. The victimized Maquoketa and McLean County group lost all the goods in their wagons and most of their money.[11]

Such events understandably changed the thinking of many people who previously had not cared one way or the other about the slavery issue, let alone joining in to decide it. Hardly becoming abolitionists, they became Free-State voters and cast their ticket to keep slavery out of Kansas and to not interfere with white, free-labor settlement.

In the turbulence, numerous black people seized the chance for a life outside Missouri slavery and escaped first into Kansas Territory and then to Iowa. Though their fate was but a secondary concern to most white settlers, a number of whites could be relied upon to help a fugitive slave. A few of the more courageous white settlers stood at hand to risk taking them northbound on the Underground Railroad.

III

These storied outcomes depended much on the neighbors of Kansas and Missouri. As frantic western Missourians pressed their proslavery goals by cutting off river migration, Iowans grew busy in supporting the Free-State cause. The prairie crossing they generously offered proved tedious and difficult, but this alternative route made Free-State success achievable to settlers at a time when they most needed the help. In this way antislavery pioneers reached their territorial destination and remain true to their desire, as Quaker poet John Greenleaf Whittier wrote in 1856, of bringing on an overwhelming majority to settle the conflict:[12]

> We go to rear a wall of men
> On Freedom's southern line,
> And plant beside the cotton-tree
> The rugged Northern pine!

APPENDIX

John Brown's Men at Three Events, 1856–59

Name of Recruit	Battle of Black Jack June 2, 1856	Winter at Springdale December 10, 1857–April 1858	Harpers Ferry Raid October 16, 1859
Frederick Brown	X		
Jason Brown	X		
Owen Brown	X	X	X
Oliver Brown	X		X
Salmon Brown	X		
Watson Brown			X
August Bondi	X		
O. A. Carpenter	X		
Benjamin Cochran	X		
Charles Kaiser	X		
Luke F. Parsons	X	X	
Henry Thompson	X		
John E. Cook		X	X
George B. Gill		X	
John Kagi		X	X
William H. Leeman		X	X
Charles W. Moffett		X	
Richard Realf		X	
Richard Richardson		X	
Aaron Dwight Stevens		X	X
Stewart Taylor		X	X
Charles Plummer Tidd		X	X
Jeremiah G. Anderson			X
Osborne P. Anderson			X
Barclay Coppoc			X
Edwin Coppoc			X

Name of Recruit	Battle of Black Jack June 2, 1856	Winter at Springdale December 10, 1857–April 1858	Harpers Ferry Raid October 16, 1859
John A. Copeland Jr.			X
Shields Green			X
Albert Hazlett			X
Lewis Sheridan Leary			X
Francis J. Meriam			X
Dangerfield Newby			X
Dauphin A. Thompson			X
William Thompson			X

NOTES

Preface

1. Howe, "Evangelical Movement," 1216-39. For the political effects on the Whig Party, see Howe, *Political Culture*, 150-80. With respect to the westward spread of the churches in the context of the Second Great Awakening, see Sweet, *Story of Religion*, 221-42. On the antislavery role of such Christian evangelicals in Kansas, see SenGupta, "Servants for Freedom," 200-213; and Wilson, "Congregationalist Richard Cordley," 185-200.

1. Uncertainty Rising

1. See McKivigan, *War against Proslavery Religion*; McKivigan and Snay, *Religion and the Antebellum*; Howe, "Evangelical Movement," 1217-22, 1224-34; Woodworth, *Manifest Destinies*, 40-54; and SenGupta, "Servants for Freedom," 200-206.

2. Silbey and McSeveney, *Voters, Parties, and Elections*, 57-59.

3. The compromise admitted California as a state, organized two territories (New Mexico and Utah), settled Texas's boundary and assumed its debts, abolished slave trade activity in the District of Columbia, and created a new, stiffened Fugitive Slave Act.

4. Harrold, *Border War*, 138-58.

5. "Fugitive Slave Bill," *Fort Madison Iowa Statesman*, October 26, 1850; and Tappan, *Fugitive Slave Bill*, 11-12. One source indicating that Senator Sturgeon of Pennsylvania also voted for it is the "Speech of Mr. Dodge, of Iowa, in the Senate, Feb. 25, 1854," *Keosauqua (IA) Democratic Union*, April 1, 1854.

6. "Fugitive Slave Bill."

7. "Opposition to the Fugitive Slave Law," *Burlington (IA) Hawk-Eye*, October 31, 1850.

8. "Denmark Congregational Association," *Burlington (IA) Hawk-Eye*, May 13, 1851.

9. "Free Soilism in Iowa," *Fort Madison Iowa Statesman*, November 16, 1850. The short-lived Free-Soil Party (1848–54) not only demanded that slavery be prohibited in the territories, but it also wanted the territories to be kept free of competition from slave or free-black labor.

10. "Free Soilism in Iowa," reprinted from the *Burlington (IA) Telegraph* in the *Fort Madison Iowa Statesman*, November 16, 1850.

11. For discussion of principal issues surrounding the introduction, debate, and passage of the Kansas-Nebraska Act, see Fehrenbacher, *Dred Scott Case*, 181–87; Freehling, *Road to Disunion*, 1:536–65; and Etcheson, *Bleeding Kansas*, 9–27. Concerning historians' past approaches to interpreting these events, see Nichols, "Kansas-Nebraska Act," 187–212; and SenGupta, "Bleeding Kansas," 318–41.

12. See Malin, *Nebraska Question*, 220–38, 450–51. For a Nebraska perspective on Iowa's involvement in pushing for the Nebraska Territory, see Morton, *Illustrated History of Nebraska*, 1:147–50. An Iowa perspective is Rosenberg, *Iowa on the Eve of the Civil War*, 79–83. See also Etcheson, "Where Popular Sovereignty Worked," in Wunder and Ross, *Nebraska-Kansas Act of 1854*, 161–62, 167–68.

13. On the character and politics of this central figure in pre–Civil War issues, see Johannsen, *Stephen A. Douglas*.

14. People did not worry when popular sovereignty was previously adopted for New Mexico and Utah Territories, where slavery was not thought workable, but Nebraska, in land from the Louisiana Purchase, was entirely another matter. See Rawley, "Stephen A. Douglas," in Wunder and Ross, *Nebraska-Kansas Act of 1854*, 67–92.

15. Freehling, *Road to Disunion*, 1:550–52; and Ray, *Repeal of the Missouri Compromise*, 207–18.

16. Russel, "Issues in the Congressional Struggle," 196–97, 206–7.

17. Quoted in Hale, *Horace Greeley*, 161. The day after Douglas's new bill came forth, antislavery partisans sought to rally those who had yet to take sides on the issue. Going beyond their Senate doors, several senators issued an open public manifesto titled "Appeal of the Independent Democrats in Congress to the People of the United States." It appeared first in the *Washington DC National Era*, an antislavery newspaper, and several newspapers reprinted it. Signed by six noted Democratic and Free-Soil senators, they pledged to resist by speech and vote this bill "as a gross violation of a sacred pledge." Missouri could never have been accepted as a slave state, they stated, without the "solemn compact against the extension of slavery" in a future territory north of its southern border. "For more than thirty years—during more than half our national existence under our present Constitution—this compact has been universally regarded and acted upon as inviolable American law. In conformity with it, Iowa was admitted as a free State and Minnesota has been organized as a free Territory." See it described as "Address

to the People" in *New York Daily Times*, January 24, 1854. See also Gienapp, *Origins of the Republican Party*, 71–72. While the "Appeal of the Independent Democrats" has been often cited as significant in the propaganda fight, "the *Appeal* exercised less immediate influence than has been believed," according to Mark E. Neely Jr. See his "Kansas-Nebraska Act," in Wunder and Ross, *Nebraska-Kansas Act of 1854*, 23–42.

18. "Slavery's Use of Nebraska," *New York Tribune*, February 24, 1854, reprinted online at Lloyd Benson, Secession Era Editorials Project, Furman University, http://history.furman.edu/benson/docs/knmenu.htm (editorials are listed chronologically).

19. Hale, *Horace Greeley*, 164.

20. "Speech of Mr. Dodge."

21. "The Nebraska Bill," *Muscatine Iowa Democratic Enquirer*, February 9, 1854. See also comments on "The Douglas Speech," *Muscatine Iowa Democratic Enquirer*, February 23, 1854.

22. The Burlington (IA) *Telegraph*'s editor shared his ominous tally that "the democratic papers which favor the Douglas Bill, with all its 'superseding' and repealing clauses, are the *Miner's Express* (Dubuque), the Fairfield *Sentinel*, the Keokuk *Dispatch*, and the State *Gazette*, of this city—four in all. The democratic journals which 'regret' the introduction and 'oppose' the passage of the bill, are the Davenport *Banner*, the Muscatine *Enquirer*, the Cedar Rapids *Progressive Era*, and the Lee County *Plaindealer*—five [*sic*] in all—the Council Bluffs *Bugle*, the Fort Des Moines *Star*, and the Keosauqua *Union* to be heard from." Printed in "The Iowa Press on the Nebraska Question," *Iowa Republican* (Iowa City), March 1, 1854.

23. "Mr. Douglass' Nebraska Bill," *Demoines Courier* (Ottumwa IA), February 16, 1854; and "The Nebraska Bill—Whig and Abolitionist," *Keosauqua (IA) Democratic Union*, March 4, 1854.

24. Rosenberg, *Iowa on the Eve of the Civil War*, 75–78.

25. On the relationship between promotion of a transcontinental railroad and passage of the Kansas-Nebraska Act, see Potter, *Impending Crisis*, 145–76.

2. The Morning Star

1. Salter, *Life of James W. Grimes*, 47–48.

2. "James W. Grimes," *Fort Des Moines (IA) Star*, June 15, 1854.

3. Salter, *Life of James W. Grimes*, 47–48.

4. Salter, *Life of James W. Grimes*, 52.

5. See "Another Nebraska Meeting," "The Nebraska Meeting," and "Signs of Public Opinion," in *Muscatine Iowa Democratic Enquirer*, March 23, 1854; and "Nebraska Resolutions," *Muscatine Iowa Democratic Enquirer*, March 30, 1854. Other Iowa towns holding anti-Nebraska meetings included Oskaloosa in Mahaska County on March 3; Davenport in Scott County on March 7; Marion in

Linn County on March 10; West Liberty in Muscatine County, Mount Pleasant in Henry County, and Knoxville in Marion County on April 5; Kossuth in Des Moines County on April 10; Ottumwa in Warren County on July 8; Elkader in Clayton County on July 15; and Burlington in Des Moines County on July 15. See "Iowa Matters," *Eddyville (IA) Free Press*, April 6 and 13, 1854; "Mass Meeting [at Kossuth]" and "Anti-Nebraska Meeting," *Wapello Intelligencer* (Ottumwa IA), April 18, 1854; "Anti-Nebraska Convention," *Clayton County Herald* (Garnavillo IA), July 21, 1854; "People's Meeting," *Burlington (IA) Telegraph*, reprinted in the *Demoines Courier* (Ottumwa IA), July 27, 1854; and "Anti-Nebraska Meeting in Warren County," *Demoines Courier* (Ottumwa IA), August 24, 1854.

6. "Session of the Congregational Association of Iowa," *Dubuque (IA) Miner's Express*, reprinted in the *Keosauqua (IA) Iowa Democratic Union*, July 8, 1854.

7. "Abolition One Idea-ism and Abolition Sympathy," *Keosauqua (IA) Iowa Democratic Union*, July 29, 1854.

8. Salter, *Life of James W. Grimes*, 54.

9. Salter, *Life of James W. Grimes*, 53.

10. A Clergyman, *In Perils by Mine Own Countrymen*, 138; and Ray, *Repeal of the Missouri Compromise*, 29. On the life of Atchison, see Parrish, *David Rice Atchison*.

11. "Speech of Mr. Dodge." It is also quoted in Craik, "Southern Interest in Territorial Kansas," 15:336.

12. Stringfellow's proslavery activity is detailed in Baltimore, "Benjamin Stringfellow," 14–29.

13. A Clergyman, *In Perils by Mine Own Countrymen*, 136–41.

14. *St. Louis (MO) Evening Post*, May 16, 1855, quoted in Craik, "Southern Interest in Territorial Kansas," 15:341.

15. On slavery-related issues and events during the territorial period of Kansas history, see Etcheson, *Bleeding Kansas*; SenGupta, *For God and Mammon*; and Connelley, *Standard History of Kansas*.

16. There were numerous other emigrant aid societies formed, including the Emigrant Aid Society of New York, the New York Kansas League, the American Settlement Company, and the Kansas Emigrant Aid Society of Northern Ohio in Oberlin. On this development, see Harlow, "Kansas Aid Movement," 1–4; and Johnson, "Emigrant Aid Company," 21–33. On the influence exercised by sources of population movement to Kansas, see two articles by Lynch: "Popular Sovereignty and the Colonization," 383; and "Population Movements," 381–404.

17. For the western Missouri proslavery perspective, see "Manifesto of the Border Ruffians: An Appeal from the People of Kansas Territory to the People of the Union," *Kansas City Enterprise, Extra*, August 28, 1856, reprinted in the *Columbus Ohio State Journal*, August 27, 1856, and clipping in *Webb Scrapbooks*, vol. 16, microfilm roll 4 of LM 92, 165.

18. When slavery was not at issue, westerners commonly saw themselves pitted against easterners over national development concerns. For two excel-

lent discussions by Bill Cecil-Fronsman about how proslavery Missourian and Free-State residents viewed themselves and their adversaries, see his "'Death to All Yankees,'" 22–33; and "'Advocate the Freedom of White Men,'" 102–15. On attitudes of easterners and westerners in Kansas, see Malin, "Housing Experiments," 95–121.

19. See Cecil-Fronsman, "'Death to All Yankees,'" 24–33.

20. *Squatter Sovereign*, February 20, 1855, as quoted in Phillips, "'Crime against Missouri,'" 76–77.

21. The target was clearly seen in the resolution of the proslavery meeting at Buchanan. It stipulated that "the fanatical abolitionists at the North have banded themselves together in social circles, church assemblies, and different political organizations, in order more effectually to make a successful crusade against the domestic institutions of the South," and "there is great and imminent danger" from "this blind and bigoted fanaticism." See "Pro-Slavery Meeting," *St. Joseph (MO) Commercial Cycle*, July 13, 1855.

22. Johnson, "Emigrant Aid Company," 23.

23. Indeed, a largely attended local meeting resolved to trade freely and deplored the association's anti-Union spirit. See Baltimore, "Benjamin Stringfellow," 18–19. Stringfellow's organization steadily lost ground. By mid-March 1856 the famous proslavery Self-Defensive Association had dissolved, or, in the words of one editor, "the age of folly has passed, and that the day of good hard practical sense is inaugurated in Weston and Platte counties." See "Kansas Affairs," *Clinton (IA) Mirror*, March 19, 1856.

24. Connelley, *Standard History of Kansas*.

25. "Missouri on Kansas," *New York (NY) National Anti-Slavery Standard*, September 30, 1854, quoting the *St. Joseph (MO) Gazette*, a Democratic paper.

26. Letter quoted from *Worster (MA) Spy* in the *Daily Davenport (IA) Gazette*, October 26, 1854. The letter is likely written by Samuel C. Pomeroy to Amos Lawrence, September 22, 1854, which is quoted in Etcheson, "Great Principle of Self-Government," 18.

27. Gleed, "Samuel Walker," 6:252.

28. "Kansas," *Clay County Tribune* (Liberty MO), reprinted in the *Pella (IA) Gazette*, February 22, 1855.

29. Parrish, *David Rice Atchison*, 170.

30. On John Stringfellow and Robert Kelley's newspaper, see Cecil-Fronsman, "'Death to All Yankees,'" 22–33. On Robert S. Kelley's proslavery extremism and his past work in Missouri, see Malin, *Nebraska Question*, 260–61, 343, 353, 381–87, 399–400; and A Clergyman, *In Perils by Mine Own Countrymen*, 204, 212.

31. Kansas Territorial Legislature, "An Act to Punish Offences."

32. Sumner, "Speech of Hon. C. Sumner of Massachusetts."

33. Quoted in Etcheson, *Bleeding Kansas*, 64.

34. Etcheson, *Bleeding Kansas*, 200-201.

35. Cited in "Missouri and Kansas," *Keokuk (IA) Daily Gate City*, May 28, 1855.

36. "Missouri and Kansas," *Keokuk (IA) Daily Gate City*, May 28, 1855; and "The Kansas Outrage," *Daily Davenport (IA) Gazette*, May 7, 1855.

37. Fanning the qualms were "stories of insults and outrages committed by Missourians circulating in the newspapers all through the Free States." See "The Bitter Fruits—the Suicide of Slavery," *St. Louis Intelligencer*, reprinted in *Vinton (IA) Eagle*, October 3, 1855.

38. "The Bitter Fruits." On the growing disgust of businessmen hurt by the troubles in western Missouri border towns, see "Getting Tired of It," *Chicago Tribune*, reprinted in *Montezuma (IA) Republican*, September 7, 1856.

39. *Windsor Vermont Journal*, April 27, 1855, quoted in Lynch, "Popular Movements," 389-91.

40. Lynch, "Popular Movements," 389-91.

41. Proof of the southern threat to southern Nebraska was seen in the recent sale of lots in Kearney City, Nebraska Territory, south of the Platte River where "a very decided majority [of the crowd] were in favor of having a Southern and Slave State" for hemp, wheat, and Indian corn production. In July the *Nebraska City News* had also advertised "Negroes for Sale." See "Slavery in Nebraska," *Council Bluffs (IA) Chronotype*, reprinted in other Iowa newspapers, including *Burlington (IA) Daily Hawk-Eye & Telegraph*, July 25, 1855, and *Demoines Courier* (Ottumwa IA), July 26, 1855. The Nebraska City reference to Negroes for sale appeared in the *Clinton (IA) Mirror*, August 8, 1855, and in the *New York (NY) National Anti-Slavery Standard*, July 28, 1855.

42. Lynch, "Popular Sovereignty and the Colonization," 387, 389-91.

43. See, in particular, two studies of settlement trends by Lynch: "Popular Sovereignty and the Colonization," 380-92; and "Population Movements," 381-404. See also Wilder, "The Story of Kansas," 6: 336. The regional origins of Kansas, as of 1860, showed that the western states (Ohio, Indiana, Illinois, Iowa) led in 1850 with 34,437 people, followed by slaveholding states at 27,440, Middle Atlantic states (New York, Pennsylvania, New Jersey) at 13,293, and New England states (Massachusetts, Vermont, Maine, Connecticut, New Hampshire, and Rhode Island) at 4,208.

44. Untitled item about dissatisfied eastern emigrants moving to Iowa published in *Keokuk (IA) Daily Gate City*, June 4, 1855. See also William G. Brown's editorial in his *Lawrence (Kansas Territory) Herald of Freedom*, May 12, 1856, quoted in Lynch, "Population Movements," 393.

45. Brown editorial in Lynch, "Population Movements," 393.

46. W. W. Boyce, M. C., in *Winnsboro (SC) Register*, reprinted in *Lawrence (Kansas Territory) Herald of Freedom*, March 29, 1856, and quoted in Craik, "Southern Interest in Territorial Kansas," 342.

47. On the general character of southern involvement, see Craik, "Southern Interest in Territorial Kansas," 334–450.

48. See *Mobile (AL) Advertiser* clipping in *Webb Scrapbooks*, 1:93, as quoted in Lynch, "Population Movements," 395.

49. *St. Louis (MO) Intelligencer*, reprinted in the *Terre Haute (IN) Wabash Courier*, September 1, 1855, as quoted in Lynch, "Population Movements," 397–98.

50. B. F. Stringfellow, "The South and Kansas," *St. Joseph (MO) Commercial Cycle*, December 21, 1855.

51. Excerpts from Atchison's letter and editor's comments in "Alarming State of the Nation—Danger of Civil War," *Burlington (IA) Weekly Hawk-Eye and Telegraph*, February 6, 1855.

52. "Alarming State of the Nation."

3. Prairie, Dust, and Wind

1. Pierce, "Special Message." The initial Free-State fears about U.S. troops working hand in glove with proslavery western Missourians, Douglas County sheriff Samuel Jones, or U.S. Marshal I. B. Donaldson in Lecompton to destroy them proved exaggerated. Indeed, commanders of troops on the ground became sympathetic to Free-State men (e.g., Col. Edwin Sumner, Col. P. St. George Cooke, Lieutenant Colonel Johnson, and Major Sedgwick), and their unwillingness to act on much beyond formal orders exasperated proslavery officials and territorial politicians, who lost confidence that troops would come down hard on their antislavery foes and settlers coming from Iowa. Samuel Walker, a settler and Free-State militia leader, recalled that in readying his attack on Fort Titus, Major Sedgwick, whose camp rested a mile from Titus's fort, informed him that "if we could attack and capture Titus before the governor sent orders to him [from Lecompton two miles away] that he would not interfere, but that if he got the orders he would be compelled to stop us." On the day of the attack, Walker made sure to arrest every messenger traveling to the troops from Lecompton and won the day without interference. And he remembered how, "many a night, after being hounded all day by the United States soldiers under the marshal or governor, I have walked into their camp and received the treatment of a prince—food and ammunition, more than I could carry away. Colonel Sumner called me to one side [just prior before his troops arrived at Topeka to disband the Free-State legislature] and said: 'Walker, I don't want to hurt any one; you are all right, and have my sympathies; but the government is against you, and I must obey the government. If the members will disperse quietly, there need be no trouble.'" See Gleed, "Samuel Walker," 264–65, 270–71.

2. Staff editorial, "David R. Atchison and Kansas," *Philadelphia (PA) American and Gazette*, November 6, 1855, clipping in *Webb Scrapbooks*, vol. 6, microfilm roll 2 of LM 90.

3. "The Kansas Meeting," *Keokuk (IA) Daily Gate City*, February 14, 1956; SIGMA, letter to the editor, *Muscatine Iowa Democratic Enquirer*, February 14, 1856; "Large and Enthusiastic Kansas Meeting at Marion Hall [in Burlington]," *Davenport Daily Iowa State Democrat*, February 15, 1856; "Aid for Kansas," *Davenport Daily Iowa State Democrat*, February 20, 1856; and "Kansas," *Davenport (IA) Daily Gazette*, February 22, 1856.

4. "Border Ruffianism—Its Effect on Missouri and Iowa," *Clinton (IA) Mirror*, April 16, 1856.

5. "A Trip to Nebraska," *Muscatine (IA) Democratic Enquirer*, May 24, 1855.

6. See "Route to Kansas" and an accompanying article by Editor G. W. Brown, "The Commercial Question: Steamers between Alton and Kansas," *Lawrence (Kansas Territory) Herald of Freedom*, May 3, 1856.

7. The western counties were yet largely empty of settlers although a few from Iowa had lived for a time in Nebraska and Kansas during pre-territorial years. For example, along with his family and fellow workers Charles and Sylvia Tolles, Ira Blanchard had worked for years at the Baptist Delaware Indian Mission in Kansas until moving to southwest Iowa in 1848. Also George and Maria Gaston—followed by Elvira Gaston Platt (George's sister) and her husband, Lester Platt—had worked at a Pawnee mission in Nebraska until 1848 and then moved into Fremont County near the Blanchards' place. All of them became staunchly antislavery and vital participants in Underground Railroad operations from Kansas that reached into western Iowa.

8. Statement of William E. Connelley, Topeka, Kansas, dated June 7, 1907, about a conversation with John Armstrong in 1906. A photocopy is in the John Brown/Boyd B. Stutler Collection Database, West Virginia Memory Project.

9. John; his wife, Eliza; and those of their more than eight children who were still at home had lived on a farm just west of Waukon in northeast Iowa since 1851. In 1818, when at age twenty-one he was admitted to the bar and married Eliza, the couple had lived in Illinois. In the late 1840s they moved to Wisconsin; then to St. Paul, Minnesota, where he was elected its first justice of the peace; and on to Iowa. His military involvements began as a sixteen-year-old scout soldiering in the War of 1812, and he later showed his aptitude as a scout again during the Bl231ack Hawk War of 1832, which saw him promoted to major. Wakefield afterward wrote an insightful history of the conflict. See Stevens, "Introduction," in Wakefield, *Wakefield's History*. For information on his years in Allamakee County, Iowa, see D. B. Raymond's reminiscences, which were contributed to the *Waukon (IA) Standard* in 1877 and reprinted in Alexander, *History of Winneshiek*. See also Allamakee County IA Archives Military Records, "Some Military Land Grants"; Leo V. Ryan, "Waukon's Battle to Become the County Seat: 1853-1857," *Allamakee County Standard* (Waukon IA), August 16, 2005, http://www.waukonstandard.com/main.asp

?Search=1&ArticleID=33120&SectionID=24&SubSectionID=36&S=1; and Ryan, "Brother Leo V."

10. As a young Illinois lawyer, Wakefield had entered politics after the state legislature in 1823 passed a resolution to assemble a convention that would likely permit slavery in the state. He threw himself into the anti-convention campaign, writing and delivering speeches in the state that helped defeat the slavery initiative.

11. Phillips, *Conquest of Kansas*, 41.

12. Wulfkuhle, "Kanwaka," 3.

13. Wulfkuhle, "Kanwaka," 3.

14. Phillips, *Conquest of Kansas*, 41–43, 53; and Connelley, *Standard History of Kansas*, 1:77–84.

15. Cordley, *History of Lawrence, Kansas*, 22; Phillips, *Conquest of Kansas*, 41; and Connelley, *Standard History of Kansas*, 1:384.

16. Sanborn, *Life and Letters of John Brown*, 173–74; and House of Representatives, *Report of the Special Committee*, 414–16. Clairborne Jackson's view that no residency was required was commonly held. A Clinton, Iowa, editor commented that "Southern Slavery propagandists, and Northern apologists for their worst aggressions, tell us the Missourians' claim to the elective franchise is equally valid as the settlers, who have been sent for the express purpose of establishing free institutions. This position is manifestly absurd." *Clinton (IA) Mirror*, May 30, 1855.

17. Sanborn, *Life and Letters of John Brown*, 174.

18. McKivigan, *Roving Editor*, 269, 280n; Phillips, *Conquest of Kansas*, 323; and Wakefield, *Wakefield Memorial*, 241.

19. "A Letter from Kansas," dated July 12, *Burlington (IA) Daily Hawkeye and Telegraph*, August 2, 1856.

20. Transcriptions of letters, George W. Cosley, Lawrence, Kansas Territory, to his brother, September 1, 1856, and daughter Ann Eliza Cosley, to her aunt Matilda Barber, September 2, 1856, are available at the Wakarusa River Valley Heritage Museum; and Strickler, "Report of H. J. Strickler."

21. Lenhart's physical appearance is mentioned in Hawes, "In Kansas with John Brown," 73.

22. Brown, *Reminiscences of Old John Brown*, 9. Lenhart's activities during the Bleeding Kansas era are reviewed in Midfelt, *Secret Danites*, 88–98.

23. Brown, *Reminiscences of Old John Brown*, 9.

24. Phillips, *Conquest of Kansas*, 357–58.

25. Root, "First Day's Battle," 43–44.

26. Phillips, *Conquest of Kansas*, 358.

27. Villard, *John Brown*, 215–16.

28. A twenty-year-old Illinois man named John Jones was on his way home with some flour bought at Blanton's store, which was located next to the store-

keeper's toll bridge, where the road toward Hickory Point crossed the Wakarusa River. Into the store walked two young proslavery men who accosted Jones. A person had handed him a pistol, but when the men raised their muskets and warned they would shoot unless he handed it over, Jones instead gave it back to the pistol's owner and departed on his horse. Not about to let the matter drop, the two men followed the accused abolitionist and near the bridge shot Jones in the back. The mortal wound soon took his life, and news of it reached Lawrence about noon. See Phillips, *Conquest of Kansas*, 286.

29. In a proslavery Missouri newspaper, it is reported that "Messrs. Cosgrove and Dr. Brannon were on their way to Franklin, K.T., from Lecompton." See "The War in Kansas Commenced!: Dr. Brannon Shot! Two Abolitionists Killed!!," *Westport (MO) Border Times*, reprinted in the *Liberty (MO) Tribune*, May 22, 1856.

30. "Three Free State Victories, Civil War Raging in Kansas," letter to editor sent June 4, 1856, from Lawrence, Kansas Territory, *Chicago Tribune*, and reprinted in *Iowa City Republican*, June 12, 1856; and Phillips, *Conquest of Kansas*, 314.

31. *Davenport (IA) Daily Gazette*, August 1, 1856.

32. Root, "First Day's Battle," 43–44.

33. On Lenhart's run-in with the store owner, Pat Laughlin and on Lenhart's propensity to drink during lulls, see Mildfelt, *Secret Danites*, 96, 98. The shooting of Lenhart at Geary is noted in varying inconsistent accounts: "Shooting Affray in Geary City," *Atchison (Kansas Territory) Freedom's Champion*, reprinted in *Quindaro (Kansas Territory) Chindowan*, March 27, 1858; and Gray, *Gray's Doniphan County History*, 20.

34. Villard, *John Brown*, 571–72.

35. Villard, *John Brown*, 655n46.

36. Lekwa and Bennett Community Club, "Those Who Left, Part I (Chapter 10)," in *Bennett, Iowa, and Inland Township*, 28–30; Butler, *Personal Recollections*; and "Another Kansas Outrage," *Davenport (IA) Daily Gazette*, May 20, 1856.

37. For Butler's most complete description of the mid-August 1855 event, see Butler, *Personal Recollections*, 48, 66–72.

38. Butler, *Personal Recollections*.

39. Butler, *Personal Recollections*.

40. Butler, *Personal Recollections*.

41. The incident, as reported from the proslavery view in the *Squatter Sovereign*, is reprinted in Wilder, *Annals of Kansas*, 55. For Rev. Pardee Butler's memory of it, see chapter 7 of his *Personal Recollections* and his deposition in the House of Representatives, *Report of the Special Committee*, 960–63.

42. "Rev. Pardee Butler," *Lawrence (Kansas Territory) Herald of Freedom*, May 10, 1856; and "Letter from Rev. Pardee Butler, for the *Herald of Freedom*," *Herald of Freedom*, May 17, 1856.

43. "Letter from Rev. Pardee Butler."

44. "Letter from Rev. Pardee Butler."

45. Kelley wrote to a friend that day, "As the steamer Aubrey leaves we have just finished 'tar and feathering' the Rev. Pardee Butler, who was shipped on a raft from this place in August last. He escaped hanging by only one vote. Butler, you know, is a rank abolitionist, and was promised this treatment should he visit our town. In the event of his return, he will be hung." Letter excerpt reprinted in Martin, "First Two Years of Kansas," 137.

46. While Butler did not detail the tar and feather experience, six weeks later—as reported in the *Burlington (IA) Weekly Hawk-Eye and Telegraph*, September 3, 1856, and the *Davenport Daily Iowa State Democrat*, September 3, 1856—another Iowa preacher from Anamosa, Rev. W. Sellers, did describe the tar and feathering of himself. In mid-June he went to Rochester in northwestern Missouri for a series of sermons, but upon arriving in town, he was met by persons who declared, "This North Methodist preaching would not be tolerated longer in the country." Members of the mob carried the minister to the middle of the street and shot and killed an old church member at the scene. After Sellers heard threats to cut his throat or shoot him, Sellers recalled that mob members ultimately "carried me across the street, between another store and warehouse, to a tar barrel which was sunk in the ground, and throwing me down on my back with considerable force, held me there, while they consulted as to the manner in which the tar was to be applied. Some said put him in head foremost; others were for stripping me. At last they concluded to do the work without stripping me. [T]hey commenced putting on the tar with a broad paddle. After completely saturating my hair, they gave my eyes, ears, face and neck each a plastering. I had on a black coat, satin vest and black cloth pants. They tarred my cravat, shirt bosom, and my clothes, down to my feet. They then let me up.

"I was so sore I could scarcely stand on my feet, but oh the agony of my eyes. They appeared like balls of fire, and I thought they would burst out of my head. Although it was noon, and the sun was beaming upon my head, I groped my way as at midnight. I groped my way into the street, they following me with their revolvers cocked, telling me to step faster, at the peril of my life. I was in so much misery, I knew not where I was going. I could see objects, but could not distinguish one from another. By the time I got across the street . . . the tar had melted some, and I could distinguish between males and females." While some female members of his flock "ventured out in the midst of this mob to rescue their pastor from the bloody clutches," others had fainted or "were crying and wringing their hands in excessive grief." He continued, "I found my horse in the yard with the bridle on, and with the assistance of one of the mob, I got the saddle on, and started to go to some place on my road as quickly as possible to get the tar washed out of my eyes. The mob followed me, however, turned me back, and made me go towards Savannah."

47. "A Preacher 'Tarred and Feathered' in Kansas," *Montezuma (IA) Republican*, June 7, 1856; and Pardee Butler's "Kansas Letter" to the editor, *Tipton (IA) Advertiser*, May 29, 1858.

4. "Do Come and Help Us"

Chapter title: From Julia Louisa Lovejoy's letter to the *Concord (NH) Independent Democrat* and *New York Evening Post*, August 25, 1856, that was published in Pierson, "'A War of Extermination,'" 122. Julia had come to Lawrence, Kansas Territory, in 1855 with her Methodist minister husband, Rev. C. H. Lovejoy.

1. Parrish, *David Rice Atchison*, 191; "Slaves for Kansas," *Atchison (KS) Squatter Sovereign*, April 8, 1856; and "Slaves in Kansas," *Atchison (KS) Squatter Sovereign*, July 8, 1856. The latter issue sought to assure slaveholders of the safety of their property if brought to Kansas. The *St. Louis Democrat* wrote of spotting a group of "twenty young men" from Charleston, South Carolina, and "a party of fifteen Tennesseans accompanied by 25 slaves," and of how "a band of some 500 Georgians, well armed, is on the way." The article was reprinted in *Keokuk (IA) Daily Gate City*, March 24, 1856.

2. Quoted in "Southern Emigration to Kansas," *New York (NY) National Anti-Slavery Standard*, March 22, 1856.

3. "A Waste of Toadyism," *Keokuk (IA) Daily Gate City*, April 29, 1856. The sale of some of his slaves to fund the expedition is described in "Selling Negroes to Make Kansas a Slave State," *Montgomery (AL) Advertiser*, reprinted in *Davenport (IA) Daily Gazette*, January 29, 1856. For a broader treatment of Buford's initiative, see Walter L. Fleming, "The Buford Expedition to Kansas," *American Historical Review* 6, no. 1 (October 1900): 38–48. The disparaging comment toward some of Buford's men is given in Axalla John Hoole's letter from Kansas City, Missouri, June 22, 1856, to his South Carolina sister, Elizabeth Euphrasia Hoole, in Hoole, "A Southerner's Viewpoint," 56.

4. See sketch of Samuel D. Lecompte in *Kansas: A Cyclopedia of State History*, 2:128. Concerning questions of Judge Lecompte's actual legal part in events surrounding the sacking of Lawrence, see Malin, "Judge Lecompte," 465–94.

5. On the gathering of proslavery units as a posse to surround Lawrence, see Phillips, *Conquest of Kansas*, 265–66, 269, 280, 284–85, 289–91. For the difficulties of a recruit in one of the volunteer proslavery units, see an unidentified Leavenworth sergeant's humorous diary notes in "Notes on the Proslavery March," 45–64.

6. Phillips, *Conquest of Kansas*, 278–80; and Connelley, *Standard History of Kansas*, 548–50.

7. Phillips, *Conquest of Kansas*, 291–93; and Connelley, *Standard History of Kansas*, 549–50. For another view of the reporting of that day's events at Lawrence, see Malin, "Judge Lecompte," 465–94.

8. Phillips, *Conquest of Kansas*, 294–301; and Connelley, *Standard History of Kansas and Kansans*, 550–53. For another view of the reporting of that day's events at Lawrence, see Malin, "Judge Lecompte," 465–94.

9. As a propaganda victory for the North, see Etcheson, *Bleeding Kansas*, 105.

10. "Are the People of Iowa in Favor of Ruffianism?," *Burlington (IA) Daily Hawk-Eye & Telegraph*, July 23, 1856.

11. Oates, *To Purge This Land*, 126–37, 151–57. On various interpretations over the years about the motives behind, and the results of, the Pottawatomie killings, see Peterson, *John Brown*, 62–69, 91–92, 124, 156–58.

12. Gleed, "Samuel Walker," 262.

13. "The Reign of Blood in Kansas," *Chicago Press*, reprinted in the *Davenport (IA) Daily Gazette*, May 28, 1856.

14. Andreas, *History of the State of Kansas*, 136.

15. Quotation printed in Martin, "The First Two years of Kansas," 136.

16. On aspects of the Sharps rifle's history in Kansas, see Isely, "Sharps Rifle Episode," 546–66; "Sharpe's [sic] Rifle," *Alton (IL) Courier,* reprinted in *Dubuque Daily Republican*, December 22, 1855; "Sharp's [sic] Rifle," *Boston Daily Courier*, December 21, 1855, with clipping in *Webb Scrapbook*, vol. 6, microfilm roll 2 of LM 90; Correspondent, "From Kansas," *Boston Daily Advertiser*, January 1, 1856, with news clipping in *Webb Scrapbook*, vol. 8, microfilm roll 2 of LM 90; "Excerpt from letter, I. T. G. [Isaac Goodnow] to [unknown]," January/February 1856, *Territorial Kansas Online*; and J. M. W., "Sharpe's [sic] Rifles vs. Plows," *New York Times*, July 29, 1856.

17. The daughter-in-law of the man who opened the box told Axalla John Hoole the next day about the undiscovered cannon. Hoole reported it in a letter from Kansas City, Missouri, April 3, 1856, to his brother Thomas Hoole in South Carolina. See Hoole, "A Southerner's Viewpoint," 44–45; Oliver (Lawrence KS), March 24, 1856, correspondence, "From Kansas: Border Ruffians Searching a Young Lady's Piano—They Found No Rifles—Call for a Public Meeting," *New York Daily Times*, April 4, 1856; letter of Thomas H. Webb (secretary of Emigrant Aid Company), Boston, April 4, 1856, to J. S. Emery, Brandon, Vermont, in *James Stanley Emery Collection*, Kansas State Historical Society.

18. On Sharps's arms shipments, see Isely, "Sharps Rifle Episode," 546–66. On proslavery reaction to the shipments, see "From the *St. Joseph Cycle Extra*, Oct. 23. Startling Developments!!—Treason in Kansas!!," reprinted in *Keosauqua (IA) Democratic Union*, November 17, 1855.

19. Isely, "Sharps Rifle Episode," 551–52.

20. For the story of the incident with the Sharps rifles on the *Arabia*, see Rutherford, "The *Arabia* Incident," 39–47; Isely, "Sharps Rifle Episode," 546–66; and "Highway Robbery," *Lawrence (Kansas Territory) Herald of Freedom*, April 12, 1856.

21. Rutherford, "The *Arabia* Incident," 43. Immediately following the incident, the Free-State *St. Louis Daily Missouri Democrat* claimed that the arms seized at Lexington were only U.S. rifles accidentally detained on their way to Ft. Leavenworth. The incident was viewed as an intentional attempt to divert public opinion from "the incendiary and unholy designs of the abolitionists," according to the staff editor who wrote "Capture of Arms at Lexington, Mo.," *Leavenworth Kansas Weekly Herald*, March 22, 1856.

22. Rutherford, "The *Arabia* Incident," 41.

23. The Emigrant Aid Company subsequently collected 50 percent of his cargo's value from the *Arabia*'s owners. But by mid-August, Hoyt was dead, killed by two proslavery men and the *Arabia* sunk two weeks later. Four years later the Sharps rifles were returned, and the owners reinstalled the breechblocks before sending them off to James Montgomery, the antislavery guerrilla leader fighting in southeastern Kansas. Rutherford, "The *Arabia* Incident," 47.

24. Of anyone, Dr. Cutter should have known better than to chance traveling up the Missouri River. Only three months earlier he had helped carry overland the breechblocks removed from the Sharps rifles that David Hoyt had lost to the Missourians who boarded the *Arabia*. Now Cutter had returned to Worcester to move his family to Kansas at the head of an emigrant party, but upon his group's arrival in Chicago, friends convinced him that going by steamboat would be much easier than taking the arduous and poorly known Iowa route.

25. Lengthy accounts are T. W. Higginson, "Late Outrages on the Missouri," *New York Tribune*, reprinted in the *New York (NY) National Anti-slavery Standard*, July 12, 1856; T. W. Higginson's follow-up article from the *Worcester (MA) Spy* and *New York Tribune*, reprinted in the *New York (NY) National Anti-Slavery Standard*, July 19, 1856; and Mrs. E. P. Cutter, "The Missouri River Pirates," *Worcester (MA) Spy*, reprinted in the *New York (NY) National Anti-Slavery Standard*, July 19, 1856.

26. "The Chicago Company," *Albany (NY) Atlas*, July 7, 1856; "Kansas Emigrants," *Chicago Tribune*, reprinted in *Iowa City Republican*, June 30, 1856; "Particulars of the Lexington Affair," *Chicago Tribune*, reprinted in *Iowa City Republican*, July 1, 1856; and "Another Outrage," *Iowa City Republican*, July 1, 1856.

27. Higginson, "Late Outrages on the Missouri."

28. Cutter, "The Missouri River Pirates," and Higginson's follow-up article appeared in "The Missouri River Pirates," *Worcester (MA) Spy*, and were reprinted in the *New York (NY) National Anti-Slavery Standard*, July 19, 1856. Calvin Cutter, then a forty-nine-year-old physician, had become a noted educational lecturer on anatomy, physiology, and hygiene and had written a popular textbook *Cutter's Anatomy and Physiology* (1845), for which several editions were published. His thirty-six-year-old wife, Eunice Powers Cutter, had in her own

right become a lecturer throughout New England on matters of health. Later she wrote a history of Warren, Massachusetts, and two histories of Worcester County after 1880. Brown, *Cyclopaedia of American Biography*, 2:305.

29. Higginson, follow-up article in "Missouri River Pirates."

30. Quoted in Andreas, *History of the State of Kansas*, 138–39.

31. Andreas, *History of the State of Kansas*.

32. Andreas, *History of the State of Kansas*.

33. Higginson, follow-up article in "Missouri River Pirates."

34. "Kansas Emigrants," *Keokuk (IA) Daily Gate City*, July 7, 1856.

35. G. D. Woodin of the Kansas Central Committee, Iowa, made a complete tour of the participating counties and enlisted the following sympathetic and reliable men:

Wasonville—Isaac Farley, Myron Frisbee, N. G. Field

Sigourney—M. H. Keath, A. T. Page, T. S. Byers, A. C. Price

Oskaloosa—William H. Seevers, A. M. Cassiday, James A. Young, Louis Reinhart, S. A. Rice

Knoxville—J. M. Bayley, James Mathews, Hiram W. Curtis, William M. Stone, James Sample, Joseph Brobst

Indianola—B. S. Noble, Geo. W. Jones, Lewis Todhunter, J. T. Lacy, G. W. Clark, H. W. Maxwell

Osceola—J. D. Howard, G. W. Thompson, A. F. Sprague, John Butcher, J. G. Miller, G. L. Christie

Quincy—R. B. Lockwood, T. W. Stanley, H. B. Clark, E. G. Bengen, D. Richey

Winterset—H. J. B. Cummings, W. L. McPherson, D. F. Arnold, W. W. McKnight, J. J. Hutchings

Des Moines—A. J. Stevens, T. H. Sypherd, W. W. Williamson, R. S. Chrystal

Newton—H. Welker, W. Skiff, W. Springer, E. Hammer, H. J. Skiff

This list is from *The History of Washington County, Iowa*, 595–96.

36. Eldridge, "Recollections of Early Days," 2:72–73. The names of various companies that went overland across Iowa are noted in a July 30, 1856, memorandum of Samuel G. Howe that Thaddeus Hyatt printed in the *New York Tribune*, August 13, 1856, and is reprinted in Morrow, "Emigration to Kansas in 1856," 8:308–13. See also a listing by Noble, *John Brown*, 36–37.

37. Grimes doubtless knew arms from other states had come into the hands of both antislavery and proslavery partisans. S. N. Wood's emigrant company from Ohio had carried with them twenty boxes of muskets borrowed from the Ohio militia. Sixty proslavery men in November 27, 1855, had stolen guns, cutlasses, and munitions from the United States Arsenal at Liberty in western Missouri. The *St. Louis Daily Missouri Democrat* claimed in late June that

Missouri's governor, Sterling Price, had sent cannon and twenty-two boxes of muskets to arm proslavery operations in Kansas. On the number of federal arms provided to the state of Iowa, see the *Vinton (IA) Eagle*, July 16, 1856. Concerning reports and rumors of arms being made available by Iowa and other states to Free-State and proslavery forces, see Hinton, *John Brown and His Men*, 56; and staff editorial, "From Kansas," *Boston Daily Advertiser*, January 1, 1856, in clippings of *Webb Scrapbook*, vol. 8, microfilm roll 2 of LM 90. Rumors and reports of militia arms going to proslavery and antislavery forces are mentioned in Eldridge, "Recollections of Early Days," 77; Shalhope, *Sterling Price*, 129, which indicates the story of the governor's involvement was more rumor than fact; Butler, *Personal Recollections*, 86–87; Blackmar, *Kansas*, 2:618; and Paxton, *Annals of Platte County, Missouri*, 209.

38. Eldridge, "Recollections of Early Days," 75; and Noble, *John Brown*, 36.

39. "Kansas Emigrants—Dubuque," *Davenport (IA) Daily Gazette*, June 11, 1856; and "Dubuque, All Right," *Galena (WI) Gazette*, reprinted in *Davenport (IA) Daily Gazette*, June 19, 1856.

40. Letter, S. G. Howe to Charles Sumner, July 27, 1856, quoted in Richards, *Letters and Journals*, 2:423–24; Sanborn, "Early History of Kansas, 1854–1861," 345; and Sanborn, *Recollections of Seventy Years*, 1:54.

41. TYPO, "Letter from Nebraska, Nebraska City, Nebraska Territory, July 20, 1856," *Boston Daily Evening Traveller*, August 7, 1856, clipping in *Webb Scrapbook*, vol. 15, microfilm roll 4 of LM 92, 240–41.

42. Thomas Wentworth Higginson's story of his tour is in "A Ride through Kanzas," which comprised a series of his dispatches to the *New York Tribune* and was published in Meyer, *The Magnificent Activist*, 74–75. Samuel G. Howe witnessed similar emigrant struggles on the route. "What a scene! And what considerations does it involve, to find eastern and western emigrants, men from New England and from Indiana and Illinois, slowly and painfully drawing their families in carts with oxen across the whole State of Iowa because Missourians block up the highway of the river by which the emigration would naturally go to Kansas! How long will the North eat dirt and not turn sick?" Letter, S. G. Howe, Tabor, Iowa, to Charles Sumner, July 31, 1856, quoted in Richards, *Letters and Journals*, 2:427–28.

43. Eldridge, "Recollections of Early Days," 74.

44. Eldridge, "Recollections of Early Days," 73, 75.

45. From 1840 to 1844 George and Maria Gaston had lived in the West, where George worked as a government farmer among the Pawnee Indians in what later became Nebraska. Returning to Ohio to farm, by 1847 his thoughts turned to founding an institution of learning like Oberlin in the West. In the autumn of 1848 the Gastons and a small party of like-minded persons arrived at the rural hamlet of Civil Bend in southwestern Fremont County, where George's sister Elvira lived with her husband, Lester W. Platt. By 1852, the

Gaston group moved from this place to higher ground and established the town of Tabor. See Todd, *Early Settlement*, 22–29, 42–43.

46. L. E. Webb, "Tabor 45 Years Ago: Some Recollections," *Tabor (IA) Beacon*, May 11, 1900, and reprinted in *Tabor (IA) Beacon-Enterprise*, February 21, 1985.

47. Todd, *Early Settlement*, 53–54.

48. Eldridge, "Recollections of Early Days," 75, 110.

49. Higginson, in Meyer, *The Magnificent Activist*, 77–78.

50. Hinton, *John Brown and His Men*, 96–97; and "A Bulletin from Gen. Lane's Camp—Incidents of the March from Kansas to Iowa," *Democratic Press*, September 23, 1856, reprinted in *Janesville (WI) Free Press*, October 1, 1856.

51. Connelley, "Col. Richard J. Hinton," 7:489.

52. Connelley, "Col. Richard J. Hinton," 7:489.

53. Andreas, *History of the State of Kansas*, 141; Eldridge, "Recollections of Early Days," 82; and letter, Thomas Wentworth Higginson, Nebraska City, Nebraska Territory, to a friend, September 16, 1856, in Higginson, *Letters and Journals*, 140. On the establishment of settlements along the new route from Iowa, see three articles in the *Kansas Tribune* (Topeka, Kansas Territory): "Road to Nebraska City," July 9, 1856; "The Kansas Emigrant Trail," August 18, 1856; and "New Route to Iowa," September 5, 1856.

54. "The Kansas Emigrant Train," *Topeka (Kansas Territory) Tribune*, August 18, 1856.

5. Ho! For Kansas

1. Butler, *Personal Recollections*, 87.

2. Connelley, *James Henry Lane*, 46.

3. Thomas Hopkins in *Webb Scrapbook*, 5:49, and quoted in Martin, "First Two Years of Kansas," 7.

4. Stephenson, *Political Career of General James H. Lane*, vol. 3, chapters 5, 7, 15.

5. On the personal characteristics of Charles Robinson and as they compare to James Lane's, see the contemporary comments in Phillips, *Conquest of Kansas*, 139–40.

6. Richardson, *Beyond the Mississippi*, 45; and Hinton, *John Brown and His Men*, 117.

7. Stephenson, *Political Career of General James H. Lane*, 160.

8. Letter, Thomas Wentworth Higginson, Nebraska City, Nebraska Territory, to Frank B. Sanborn, September 18, 1856, with a copy at West Virginia Memory Project, John Brown/Boyd B. Stutler Collection Database.

9. Letter, Higginson to Sanborn, September 18, 1856.

10. Stephenson, *Political Career of General James H. Lane*, 160.

11. John L. Davies, "Republican Meeting," *Davenport (IA) Daily Gazette*, June 11, 1856; and "The Meeting," *Davenport (IA) Daily Gazette*, June 11, 1856.

12. "Col. Lane at Burlington," *Iowa City Republican*, June 23, 1856.

13. Stephenson, *Political Career of General James H. Lane*, 74, citing *Cincinnati Gazette*, January 10, 1857.

14. Excerpt of comments quoted from the *Iowa City Reporter* in "Disgraceful," *Iowa City Republican*, June 20, 1856.

15. On Lane's Oskaloosa teamster troubles, see *Davenport (IA) Daily Iowa State Democrat*, July 9, 1856; "Kansas Emigrants," *Iowa City Republican*, reprinted in *Davenport (IA) Daily Gazette*, July 10, 1856; and "It's a Long Lane that Has No Turning," *Iowa City Daily Evening Reporter*, July 19, 1856.

16. "Lane and His Armed Band," *Leavenworth Kansas Weekly Herald*, July 26, 1856.

17. "Kansas—the Exaggerated Reports," *Keokuk (IA) Daily Gate City*, August 30, 1856; and "Col. Lane's Foray into Kansas," *Iowa City Daily Evening Reporter*, September 4, 1856.

18. After leaving Tabor, the organized emigrations commonly crossed over into Nebraska on ferries located at Nebraska City, where they camped nearby before embarking on the final stage of their trek to Kansas.

19. Eldridge, "Recollections of Early Days in Kansas," 80–82, nn46, 47, related Col. Sam Walker's report about Lane's removal from command and his subsequent disguised reentry into Kansas Territory; letter, S. G. Howe to Charles Sumner, July 27, 1856, and Howe to P. T. Jackson, camp of the emigration, Weeping Water, Nebraska Territory, July 31, 1856, quoted in Richards, *Letters and Journals*, 2:424–25; and Gleed, "Samuel Walker," 267–68.

20. Letter, Mrs. E. G. Platt, Oberlin, Ohio, to William E. Connelley, Topeka, Kansas, September 24, 1900, in Platt Family Papers; and Gleed, "Samuel Walker," 6:267–68.

21. Lane agreed to the letter's decision on condition that if the proslavery forces should attack the expedition, he could join in its defense as a common soldier. See Eldridge, "Recollections of Early Days," 81–82n47; and letter, S. G. Howe to P. T. Jackson, camp of the emigration, Weeping Water, Nebraska Territory, July 31, 1856, quoted in Richards, *Letters and Journals*, 2:424–25. For excerpts on Lane contained in the report of S. G. Howe and Thaddeus Hyatt to the National Committee of Aid of Kansas on August 11, 1856, see Andreas, *History of the State of Kansas*, 141–42.

22. "Civil War on the Border: Latest News from Kansas," *Leavenworth (Kansas Territory) Journal*, August 24, 1856, reprinted in *Bloomfield Iowa Flag*, August 30, 1856.

23. "The War in Kansas," *New York Times*, August 25, 1856. For these months of Bleeding Kansas in 1856, see Andreas, *History of the State of Kansas*, 141–45; and Connelley, *Standard History of Kansas*, chapters 31 and 32. On Lane's situation, see Stephenson, *Political Career of General James H. Lane*, 74–79, 81; Eldridge, "Recollections of Early Days," 80–82; and letter, A. D. Searl to Thaddeus Hyatt, August 21, 1856, Territorial Kansas Online.

24. E[lvira] G[aston] P[latt], "Lane and His Men—Testimony of a Lady," *Burlington (IA) Daily Hawk-eye & Telegraph*, October 4, 1856; Villard, *John Brown*, 254–55; Reynolds, *John Brown, Abolitionist*, 202–4; and Todd, *Early Settlement*, 56.

25. Connelley, "The Lane Trail," 13:270–75; and Joseph C. Miller, receipt and memorandum concerning receipt listing weapons and ammunition received by Preston Plumb in Iowa City, September 27, 1856, in Franklin Loomis Crane Collection, 320, Box 2, vol. 2, Kansas State Historical Society, Topeka.

26. See Rev. John Todd, "Incidents in the History of Tabor during the Troubles in Kansas in 1856," in *History of Fremont County, Iowa*, 590.

27. John Todd, Tabor, Iowa, to William Salter, Burlington, Iowa, September 17, 1856, in Salter, *Papers*. From his letter one can tell he and others were dazzled by and proud of the notables coming through: "Messrs. [Samuel Gridley] Howe, [Thaddeus] Hyatt, [Thomas Wentworth] Higginson &c have been here, & anything which can be done here to forward the cause of Freedom will be done most cheerfully. Br. J.V. Parsons of Barnstable, Mass.—a man of excellent Spirit & conductor of a Mass. company has been with us much of the time for more than a fortnight but left on the 16th inst."

28. Speer, *Life of Gen. James H. Lane*, 128.

29. Todd, *Early Settlement*, 58; Todd's history of Kansas's troubles in *History of Fremont County*, 591–92; Noble, *John Brown*, 56–57; Eldridge, "Recollections of Early Days," 2:100–101; Morrow, "Emigration to Kansas in 1856," 8:304–6; and "Letter, J. M. Winchell to My Dear Sir [Thaddeus Hyatt]," Thaddeus Hyatt Collection, 401, Box 1, Folder 4, Kansas State Historical Society, with a copy at *Territorial Kansas Online, 1854–1861*.

30. Todd, *Early Settlement*, 57; and Todd's history of Kansas's troubles in *History of Fremont County*, 591.

31. Todd *Early Settlement*, 58; and Todd's history of Kansas's troubles in *History of Fremont County*, 591.

32. Villard, *John Brown*, 262.

33. Villard, *John Brown*, 262; and Reynolds, *John Brown*, 207.

34. Villard, *John Brown*, 268. The biographer wrote: "Here he stored arms he had brought with him, and this place he chose as the coming headquarters of the band of one hundred 'volunteer-regulars' for whom he now planned to raise funds in the East to the amount of twenty thousand dollars, and here actual training for war-service against forces of slavery was soon to begin."

35. Villard, *John Brown*, 268–70.

36. Letter, Watson Brown to Dear Mother, [Mary Brown] Brother and Sister, October 30, 1856, *John Brown Collection*, 299, Box 1, Folder 17, item number 102557, Kansas State Historical Society, with a copy at *Territorial Kansas Online*, http://www.territorialkansasonline.org/cgiwrap/imlskto/index.php?SCREEN=show_document&document_id=102557&PageTitle=Letter,

%20Watson%20Brown%20to%20Dear%20Mother,%20%5BMary%20Brown%5D%20Brother%20and%20Sister.

37. The story of the Sharps rifle carbines used by John Brown's men at Harpers Ferry is set forth by William F. M. Arny, January 17, 1860, in testimony he gave before the U.S. Congress, *Report [of] the Select Committee of the Senate*, 82–84. Also, page 51 of the report indicates the lids of Sharps rifle boxes captured at Harpers Ferry were marked "T. B. Eldridge, Mt. Pleasant, Iowa." T. B. was Shalor Eldridge's brother.

38. Villard, *John Brown*, 270.

39. Letter, M. C. Dickey, Mount Pleasant, Iowa, to Mr. [Thaddeus] Hyatt of the National Kansas Committee, October 23, 1856, in Thaddeus Hyatt Collection, 401, Box 1, Folder 4, Kansas State Historical Society, with a copy at *Territorial Kansas Online*, http://www.territorialkansasonline .org/~imlskto/cgi-bin/index.php?SCREEN=show_document&document _id=101450&PageTitle=Letter,%20M.%20C.%20Dickey%20to%20Mr.%20 %5BThaddeus%5D%20Hyatt.

40. Richman, *John Brown*, 16.

41. Todd, *Early Settlement*, 58; and Dykstra, *Bright Radical Star*, 143.

42. Todd's history of Kansas's troubles in *History of Fremont County*, 592.

43. *Kansas Tribune* (Topeka, Kansas Territory), December 1, 1856.

44. Grimes's letter was reprinted in Salter, *Life of James W. Grimes*, 84–86. For reaction to it, see the *Keokuk (IA) Daily Gate City*, October 4, 1856; *Muscatine (IA) Daily Journal*, September 18, 1856; *Lawrence (Kansas Territory) Herald of Freedom*, November 8, 1856; and "Sec'ry Marcy to Gov. Grimes," *Liberty (Clay County MO) Tribune*, November 14, 1856. The latter informed Grimes that the language of his letter "implies a right to enforce obedience and the power to compel it, neither of which is entrusted to your Excellency."

45. "The State Arms—Where Are They?," *Des Moines Iowa State Journal*, March 6, 1858; and "Those Muskets," *Davenport (IA) Daily Morning News*, June 29, 1858, and July 5, 1858. The best overall discussion of Grimes and the missing arsenal arms is found in Dykstra, *Bright Radical Star*, 139–43.

46. James W. Grimes to Samuel J. Kirkwood, December 24, 1859, Governor's Papers Correspondence, Military War Matters, Miscellaneous 1839–1908, State Historical Society of Iowa. On September 9 another body of arms, comprising "several boxes of muskets, ammunition, &c.," was stolen from the warehouse of Daniels & Co. in Iowa City and then destroyed. The Democratic editor of the *Reporter*, hinting at justification for the robbery, charged that "the weapons were unquestionably designed for bloody uses in the Territory of Kansas, and belonged to the same category of 'Agricultural Implements' which have been paraded through the State during the past season." It turned out, however, that the weapons were those of the Council Bluffs Guards ordered from the East and, upon arrival, had been temporarily stored in the

warehouse. "Border Ruffians in Iowa," *Davenport (IA) Daily Gazette*, September 17, 1856; "The Route to Kansas," *Davenport (IA) Daily Gazette*, September 26, 1856; and *Vinton (IA) Eagle*, October 22, 1856.

47. Letter, James W. Grimes to Samuel J. Kirkwood, December 24, 1859, in *Governor's Papers*.

48. John Stringfellow's partner, Robert Kelley, bitterly resented the fact that a Massachusetts Free-State man, Samuel C. Pomeroy, had bought their *Squatter Sovereign* paper and made it a Free-State paper. On June 21, 1857, he wrote Pomeroy: "I am authorized by all of the subscribers to the *Squatter Sovereign* in Charleston, S. C., to have their papers discontinued. When they subscribed to the journal, they done so to advance the pro-slavery interest in the territory. When traitors, for *gold*, sell themselves and their country, they do not consider themselves bound by the bargain. They are unwilling to support, either directly or indirectly, traitors, *abolitionists* and *negro stealers*. Do not further insult them by continuing the paper." In days to come, "may *sickness, disease*, and, finally, *death*, be the result of your connection with the *Squatter Sovereign*, is the sincere wish of Robert S. Kelley." This statement, in *Webb Scrapbook*, 12:153, is reprinted in Martin, "First Two Years of Kansas," 137n74.

49. "Important Inquiries," quotes excerpts of the *Squatter Sovereign* lament in *Lawrence (Kansas Territory) Herald of Freedom*, January 10, 1857; Cecil-Fronsman, "'Death to All Yankees,'" 33; Stephenson, *Political Career of General James H. Lane*, 85; and Parrish, *David Rice Atchison*, 208–9. On southern reluctance to send people to Kansas, see excerpts from the *Winnsborough (SC) Register* and the *Charleston (SC) Standard* in "Southern Emigration to Kansas," *New York Times*, April 23, 1856.

50. Quote from Tuchman, *Stilwell and the American Experience*, 132.

51. *History of Vernon County*, 221. A view along similar lines is presented in Lewis, "Propaganda and the Kansas-Missouri War," 135–48, which was a reprint of the article that first appeared in the *Missouri Historical Review*'s October 1939 issue. On the importance of individual correspondents writing to the large northern newspapers on the Kansas situation, see Weisberger, "Newspaper Reporter," 633–56.

52. As a writer of Vernon County's history observed: "The Missourians had been wont to consider it rare sport to invade Kansas and 'make it hot for the Free State men,' but it was not long until the Free State men raided Missouri at their will, carried off horses, mules, slaves and other property, and returned to their homes in safety, while, for his life, a Missourian dared not cross the line in pursuit, because it was probable that the pursuit would cost him that life." *History of Vernon County*, 218.

53. "Future Emigration," *Lawrence (Kansas Territory) Herald of Freedom*, December 6, 1856.

6. Scramble to Freedom

1. Connelley, "The Lane Trail," 269–70n2. Also, although he was not a physician, Blanchard was referred to as "Doctor Blanchard," perhaps because he was an ordained minister.

2. Civil Bend was but a spread of farm residences erected on the Missouri bottoms. The rural hamlet contained a mix of people from Ohio (the Blanchard and Platt families) and a few New Englanders, and not far away were others from slave states. Ira Blanchard worked closely with, and relied on the help of, a core of local antislavery families and those few willing to transport runaways directly to the next stop, Congregationalist Tabor in northern Fremont County.

3. "'U.G.R.R.' in Iowa," *New York (NY) National Anti-Slavery Standard*, November 21, 1857; and Morgans, *John Todd*, 180.

4. Gihon, *Geary and Kansas*, 66.

5. Todd, *Early Settlement*, 55. Titus was captured. Though John Brown and others wanted him punished for badly treating many settlers, Capt. Samuel Walker refused. He turned Titus over as a negotiated prisoner exchange.

6. For information about George Clarke and Judy Clarke, see Gihon, *Geary and Kansas*, 66; *Lawrence (Kansas Territory) Herald of Freedom*, January 3, 1857; and advertisement of reward for Judy Clarke's return in *Lecompton (KS) Union*, December 11, 1856.

7. Upon reaching Tabor, Iowa, in early March 1857, Judy Clarke told Mrs. S. R. Shepardson what had happened to her. This episode is described in a Shepardson attachment of "Reply of Mrs. E. G. Platt of Tabor, Iowa to the U.G.R.R. Circular," Tabor, Iowa, to W. H. Siebert, Columbus, Ohio, Siebert, *Collection*, Box 45.

8. John Armstrong, "Reminiscences of Slave Days in Kansas," collected by Miss Zu Adams in 1895, History Slaves collection, *Territorial Kansas Online*, http://www.kansasmemory.org/item/3475.

9. Armstrong, "Reminiscences of Slave Days."

10. On Reverend Burgess, see Denton, "Unitarian Church," 313–14.

11. Denton, "Unitarian Church."

12. Denton, "Unitarian Church."

13. At Civil Bend, Ira Blanchard headed up the Underground Railroad efforts and arranged among local residents for the shelter and transport of runaways. Among them were Lester and Elvira Platt, Sturgis Williams, J. B. Hall, H. B. Harton, Reuben Williams, Rev. M. F. Platt, and Joe Treat. See letter, Sturgis Williams, Percival, Iowa, reply to U.G.R.R. circular to Wilbur H. Siebert, Siebert, *Collection*, Box 45, MSS116AV; letter, J. E. Todd, Vermillion, South Dakota, to Wilbur H. Siebert, Siebert, *Collection*, Box 45, MSS116AV; and Ricketts and Ricketts, "The Underground Railroad of Southwestern Iowa."

Most controversial was Ira Blanchard. In 1848 Reverend Blanchard, along with his wife Mary Walton Blanchard and her sister Abbie Walton, came from the Delaware Baptist Mission in eastern Kansas, where they had served since 1839 but recently had been defrocked and dismissed. Blanchard's dismissal happened after Ira—an ordained Baptist preacher in 1844—was charged with having had "sexual relations with a woman who was not his wife," namely, his younger relative and mission teacher, Sylvia Case. See correspondence in "I. D. Blanchard (Delaware, 1837–1847)"; Mott, "Charles Wesley Tolles," 621–32; and Kinnan, *Who Was Ira D. Blanchard?*

14. At Tabor George B. Gaston was the main receiver of incoming runaways. He then found help to shelter and conduct the passengers to the next stop from several men, including S. H. Adams, Marcus Pearse, William L. Clark, L. B. Hill, E. S. Hill, Rev. John Todd, A. C. Gaston, James K. Gaston, John Hallam, Irish Henry, George Hunter, J. L. Smith, Edward Sheldon, Jonas Jones, Jesse West, Origin Cummings, H. S. Cummings, D. A. Woods, Newton Woodford, Cephas Case, D. E. Woods, Mason Pascal, Egbert Avery, and Jesse West. Todd, *Early Settlement*, 59–65; letter, J. E. Todd, Vermillion, South Dakota, to Wilbur H. Siebert, Siebert, *Collection*, Box 45 MSS116AV; and Mrs. Ellen Gaston Hurlbutt, Tabor, Iowa, "The Underground Railroad in Tabor and Vicinity," to Wilbur H. Siebert, Siebert, *Collection*, Box 45, MSS116AV.

15. "Negro Killed," *Independence (MO) Western Dispatch,* reprinted in *Davenport (IA) Daily Iowa State Democrat*, March 26, 1856.

16. "Negro Killed."

17. "Insurrectionary Movements among Slaves," *St. Louis Republican,* November 26, 1856, reprinted in the *Davenport (IA) Daily Iowa State Democrat*, December 3, 1856.

18. "Negro Hunting in Nebraska—a White Man Killed," *Burlington (IA) Weekly Hawk Eye*, September 23, 1857, and in the *Dubuque (IA) Daily Republican*, September 23, 1857; and Hubert Garrett, "A History of Brownville, Nebraska" (thesis, August 5, 1927), in Box 46, Folder 3, Siebert, *Collection.* Garrett cites as sources for this story the *Nebraska Advertiser*, September 10 and November 26, 1857, and March 21, 1872. For a different take on the event—it states that two men from Nemaha County and two from Atchison County, Missouri, went after the runaways—see William Cutler, "Nemaha County, Pioneer Incidents, Brownville," in Andreas, *History of the State of Nebraska*. The wounded runaway was released from pending trial after the man who shot Myers was found and killed in the Iowa bottoms.

19. "Fugitive Slaves," *St. Joseph (MO) Gazette,* reprinted in *New York Times,* December 7, 1857, and *New York (NY) National Anti-Slavery Standard*, December 12, 1857.

20. "Fugitive Slaves."

21. "Stock for the Fair and Negroes for the South," *St. Louis (MO) Democrat*, September 20, 1859, reprinted in *St. Joseph (MO) Weekly Free Democrat*, September 24, 1859. The name "Dorriss" refers to George P. Dorriss, an early

merchant in Platte City (Platte County), a Democratic representative to the Missouri legislature, and an active slave trader. See Paxton, *Annals of Platte County, Missouri*, 764–65.

22. "Slavery in Missouri," *St. Joseph (MO) Weekly West*, October 1859, with comments on a letter reprinted from a person in Missouri that was sent to the *Dubuque (IA) Herald*.

23. Reprinted from the *Independence (MO) Occidental Messenger* in the *New York (NY) National Anti-Slavery Standard*, August 6, 1859.

24. Lewis Bodwell, "A Home Missionary Journey Never before Reported," *Manhattan Kansas Telephone*, August 1893. The information concerning Reverend Bodwell's journey with the runaways is taken from his account.

25. Bodwell, "Home Missionary Journey"; and letter, Mrs. S. R. Shepardson, Glenwood (Fremont County), Iowa, to W. H. Siebert, Columbus, Ohio, November 6, 1894, Siebert, *Collection*, Box 45, Folder 11A.

26. Shepardson letter to Siebert, November 6, 1854.

27. Shepardson letter to Siebert, November 6, 1854.

28. On Stephen Nuckolls, see Dale, *Otoe County Pioneers*, 1926–27, in a copy of the manuscript at Nebraska City Public Library. For information on Nuckolls's search through Civil Bend and Tabor, see E[lvira] G[aston] P[latt], "Nebraska Negro Catchers in Iowa, Western Iowa, Jan. 7, 1859," *Burlington (IA) Daily Hawk-eye*, January 21, 1859. For events in Chicago, see "Great Fugitive Slave Excitement—a Colored Girl Rescued," *Chicago Daily Evening Journal*, November 13, 1860.

7. Raising the Stakes

1. Hinton, *John Brown and His Men*, 155; Oates, *To Purge This Land*, 243; and George B. Gill, Attica, Kansas, manuscript of interview with Katherine Mayo, November 12, 1908, *Villard Collection*. A daguerreotype of a "Free-State emigrants' battery," which shows George Gill (second from the left), dates to 1856 and is contained in the Kansas State Historical Society's collections and at its online Kansas Memory website, www.kansasmemory.org/item/90323.

2. Letter, Salmon Brown to William E. Connelley, November 6, 1913, reprinted in John Brown/Boyd D. Stutler Collection Database, West Virginia Memory Project, http://www.wvculture.org/history/wvmemory/jbdetail .aspx?Type=Text&Id=730.

3. Hinton, *John Brown and His Men*, 200–201, 536–37.

4. Villard, *John Brown*, 313–14.

5. Gill interview.

6. Gill interview. On what drew together young men behind the antislavery cause, see a discussion of how in modern times friendship and kinship have influenced youth to join radicalized groups in Sageman, *Leaderless Jihad*, 66–70.

7. Hinton, "John Brown and His Men," 695.

8. Hinton, *John Brown and His Men*, 157.

9. From John Edwin Cook's Harpers Ferry statement of his connection with Capt. John Brown, in Hinton, *John Brown and His Men*, 702.

10. Letter, L[uke]. F. Parsons, Osawatomie, Kansas Territory, to "Dear Friends Redpath & Hinton," December 1859, Hinton, *Collection*, 384, Box 1, Folder 10, item number 103063, copy at http://www.territorialkansas online.org/~imlskto/cgi-bin/index.php?screen=show_document&document _id=103063&PageTitle=Letter,%20l.%20f.%20parsons%20to%20%22dear %20friends%20redpath%20&%20ohinton%22. On the incarcerated black man, see "Negro Hunting in Nebraska"; and Garrett, "A History of Brownville, Nebraska."

11. Letter, Parsons, to "Dear Friends Redpath & Hinton"; letter, Luke F. Parsons, Salina, Kansas, to Charles Wesley Tolles, Ottumwa, Iowa, October 18, 1913, published in Mott, "Charles Wesley Tolles," 631; and Villard, *John Brown*, 311–12.

12. George B. Gill prepared "Biographical Notes on Coppoc, Edwin and Barclay, Taylor, Hazlett, Leeman, J. G. Anderson, Kagi, Stevens, Tidd, Cook and Brown," for R. J. Hinton about 1893. See Hinton, *Collection*, Box 8, Folder 1, M,2.

13. Gill, "Biographical Notes."

14. Gill, "Biographical Notes."

15. Gill, "Biographical Notes."

16. Gill, "Biographical Notes"; and letter from A[mos] Bixby, Grinnell, Poweshiek County, Iowa, to his brother Lewellyn (possibly in Maine), February 22, 1859, in Stephen B. Dudley's "Letters From Iowa," an unpublished report of six original letters by Amos Bixby that are transcribed with Dudley's comments and notes, Wilsonville OR, 1992, and a copy of which is in the Amos Bixby folder of the Underground Railroad project files, State Historical Society of Iowa, Des Moines IA.

17. Lloyd, "John Brown among the Pedee Quakers," 668.

18. Gill, "Biographical Notes."

19. Gill, "Biographical Notes"; and Gill interview.

20. Gill, "Biographical Notes."

21. Gill, "Biographical Notes."

22. Gill interview; Gill, "Biographical Notes"; and letter, George B. Gill, Milan, Kansas, to Robert J. Hinton, July 7, 1893, in Hinton, *Collection*, Box 8, Folder 1, and reprinted in Wilson, *John Brown Soldier of Fortune*, 130–31. In Hinton's *John Brown and His Men*, 191, the range of contradictions to Brown's "remarkable personality" was recalled by this admiring Kansas companion. Brown was, he wrote, "as ignorant of the power of actual facts as a hermit in the desert, and at the same time wonderfully fitted by nature and training to seize the best chance at first sight under the most difficult circumstances, and to accomplish the most with the smallest means; illogical as a child, and yet

following his own path as steadily as the sun; with a horror of fighting, and yet offering up himself and his family in an insane war against the whole nation; so tenderhearted that he stakes and loses his own life and the lives of his followers, of his sons-in-law and sons . . . ; so terribly stern that he unconditionally approves a horrible five-fold murder; never excited to revenge even by the worst injustice exercised toward himself and toward those dearest to him, but goaded on to such a rage by the wrong done to the negro slaves that he recklessly transgresses all positive law and only recognizes as binding what he considers to be God's command." These unpredictable aspects were not yet visible to Brown's followers, who were drawn by his single-minded hatred of slavery and shared much of that feeling.

23. Letter, L[uke]. F. Parsons, Osawatomie, Kansas Territory, to "Dear Friends Redpath & Hinton," December 1859, Hinton, *Collection*, 384, Box 1, Folder 10, item number 103063, http://www.territorialkansasonline .org/~imlskto/cgi-bin/index.php?screen=show_document&document _id=103063&PageTitle=Letter,%20l.%20f.%20parsons%20to%20%22dear %20friends%20redpath%20&%20hinton%22; Villard, *John Brown*, 311–12; letter, J. H. Kagi, Springdale, Iowa, to "My Dear Sister," December 27 or 29, 1857, Hinton, *Collection*, 384, Box 1, Folder 7, item number 103050, Kansas State Historical Society; letter, Luke F. Parsons, Salina, Kansas, to Charles Wesley Tolles, Ottumwa, Iowa, October 18, 1913, in Mott, "Charles Wesley Tolles," 631; Gill, "Biographical Notes"; and account of Luke F. Parsons in Aurner, *Topical History of Cedar County*, 1:444.

24. Kagi letter to "My Dear Sister."

25. Before moving into Maxson's house, the ten men had been staying at Quaker John H. Painter's place. Richard Realf joined them, having left Quaker James Townsend's Traveler's Rest tavern, where he and Brown had been staying near the eastern edge of West Branch. Cedar County Historical Society, *John Brown in Cedar County*, 11. Maxon's grout house was made of stone and covered in cement.

26. Correspondence of John Brown, Jr., to F. B. Sanborn, in Sanborn, *Life and Letters of John Brown*, 494; Villard, *John Brown*, 343; *History of Cedar County*, 2:16; and "Funeral of Owen Brown—the Last Survivor of John Brown's Historic Raid on Harpers Ferry, Va., in 1859," *Pasadena (CA) Standard*, January 12, 1889, reprinted online at http://tchester.org/sgm/msc/brown_funeral _notice.html.

27. Hinton, *John Brown and His Men*, 156; and Parsons, to "Dear Friends Redpath & Hinton."

28. Hinton, *John Brown and His Men*, 156; and Parsons to "Dear Friends Redpath & Hinton."

29. Villard, *John Brown*, 315; and "Reminiscences of George B. Gill," an appendix to Hinton, *John Brown and His Men*, 729.

30. The secretary's book of the mock legislature was in the possession of Narcissa Macy Smith at the time she wrote about the meetings in her "Reminiscences of John Brown," 231–33.

31. Hinton, *John Brown and His Men*, 728–29; and Parsons to "Dear Friends Redpath & Hinton."

32. Gill, "Biographical Notes;" and *History of Cedar County*, 2:20-21. West Liberty from 1856 through 1858 had grown considerably. According to the November 29, 1858, issue of the *Davenport (IA) Daily Gazette*, West Liberty was then shipping more stock and grain "than from any other point on the railroad between Davenport and Iowa City. The town contains a good steam flouring mill, 4 dry goods stores, 2 groceries, one drug store, 2 lumber yards, 3 blacksmith shops, one cooper shop and one real estate agency" plus "a good church and school privileges" through the West Liberty Academy with its seventy students.

33. Hinton, *John Brown and His Men*, 731.

34. Villard, *John Brown*, 336; and Oates, *To Purge This Land*, 246–47.

35. Hinton, *John Brown and His Men*, 733–34.

36. Villard, *John Brown*, 343–44; and Hinton, *John Brown and His Men*, 734.

8. Heaven Sent

1. See Neely, *Border between Them*.

2. Hougen, "Marais des Cygnes Massacre," 74–94.

3. Villard, *John Brown*, 351; and Sanborn, *Life and Letters of John Brown*, 475–76.

4. Hinton, *John Brown and His Men*, 212, 214; and Sanborn, *Life and Letters of John Brown*, 472–74.

5. Oates, *To Purge This Land*, 254; and Sanborn, *Life and Letters of John Brown*, 472–73. On James Montgomery's activities and character, see Dirck, "By the Hand of God," 100-115.

6. Villard, *John Brown*, 358; and Sanborn, *Life and Letters of John Brown*, 476–78, 480.

7. Hinton, *John Brown and His Men*, 216.

8. Villard, *John Brown*, 364–67.

9. *History of Vernon County*, 225.

10. George B. Gill, account of December 20, 1858, Missouri raid to free slaves in correspondence to Richard J. Hinton, July 4, 1895, in Hinton, *Collection*, MC384, Box 8. Nearly all of the manuscript is contained in Hinton, "Rescue of Missouri Slaves," *John Brown and His Men*, chapter 7.

11. The locations of the farms were identified as follows in *History of Vernon County*, 223: The estate of James Lawrence, where the Hicklins lived as tenants, was in the southern half of the southeast quarter of section 5, Township 37N, Range 33W; John Larue's place was in the northwest quarter of the

southeast quarter of section 8, Township 37N, Range 33W; and David Cruise lived in the northeast quarter of the southeast quarter of section 21, Township 37N, Range 33W.

12. *History of Vernon County*, 223; and biographical sketch of Jeremiah G. Anderson in Villard, *John Brown*, 681. Mention of "Pickles" as Wright in "From Kansas, Renewal of the Border Troubles—Missourians in Conflict with Kansas Men," *New York Times*, August 30, 1859; and Villard, *John Brown*, 368.

13. *History of Vernon County*, 222.

14. "Statement of Harvey G. Hicklin," letter dated August 9, 1886, from Hume, Bates County, Missouri, sent to the compilers of *History of Vernon County*, 226.

15. Gill account of December 1858 raid.

16. "Hicklin statement," 226–27; and Gill account of December 1858 raid.

17. "Hicklin statement," 227; and Gill account of December 1858 raid.

18. "Hicklin statement," 227; and Gill account of December 1858 raid.

19. *History of Vernon County*, 228, 230.

20. Letter of Rufus M. Cruise, Halesbory, Texas, February 6, 1887, to compilers of *History of Vernon County*, 411–12.

21. *History of Vernon County*, 411; and Gill account of December 1858 raid.

22. *History of Vernon County*, 412; and Gill account of December 1858 raid.

23. Gill account of December 1958 raid; and *History of Vernon County, Missouri*, 229.

24. Affidavit of Isaac B. Larue filed with Justice of Peace N. R. Marchbank, December 20, 1858, in *History of Vernon County*, 237; and Gill account of December 1858 raid.

25. Gill account of December 1858 raid.

26. Villard, *John Brown*, 369.

27. Villard, *John Brown*, 371–72.

28. Villard, *John Brown*, 371–72.

29. "Reward Offered for Brown and Montgomery," *Lawrence (Kansas Territory) Republican*, reprinted in the *White Cloud (Kansas Territory) Kansas Chief*, January 20, 1859.

30. *History of Vernon County*, 236.

31. *History of Vernon County*, 221–22.

32. For a glimpse into George W. Brown's views toward what he regarded as the more extreme Free-State elements during this time, see his articles in *Lawrence (Kansas Territory) Herald of Freedom*: "The Excitement of the Past Week," February 6, 1859; "The Robin Hood of Kansas" and "Keep Quiet," February 26, 1859; and "Revolution and Disunion," March 26, 1859. In the last article he identifies the radical northern correspondents as "Redpath, Phillips, Thacher, Walden, Ralph, Cook, Hinton, Conway, and others," and the fire-eater Kansas papers included the *Lawrence Republican*, *Leavenworth Times*, and *Doniphan Kansas Crusader of Freedom*.

33. Brown's attitudes toward George W. Brown and his paper are noted in Villard, *John Brown*, 354; and Hinton, *John Brown and His Men*, 565. For other impressions of George W. Brown, see William Elsey Connelley, *John Brown* (Topeka: Crane, 1900), 243–44, 246; and Connelley, *An Appeal to the Record*.

34. "Troubles in Kansas," *The Weekly Highlander* (Highland KS), January 6, 1859.

35. Letter, Rev. Samuel L. Adair to James Hanway, Osawatomie, Kansas, February 2, 1878, Hanway Papers, Kansas State Historical Society, quoted in Villard, *John Brown*, 372.

36. Gill account of December 1858 raid; Hinton, *John Brown and His Men*, 221; and Villard, *John Brown*, 372, 379.

37. Villard, *John Brown*, 375–78.

38. Villard, *John Brown*, 379–80; and Phillips, "Three Interviews with Old John Brown," 738–44. On James Abbott and Joel Grover, see Nancy Smith, "The 'Liberty Line' in Lawrence, Kansas Territory," in Sheridan, *Freedom's Crucible*, 2–6.

39. Doy, *Narrative of John Doy*, 123. For additional acknowledgement of organized slave-stealing at this time, see "Kidnappers Rampant in Kansas," *Lawrence (Kansas Territory) Republican*, February 20, 1859; and "Kidnapping a Felony," *Lawrence (Kansas Territory) Republican*, January 20, 1859.

40. Doy, *Narrative of John Doy*.

41. Doy, *Narrative of John Doy*.

42. John Doy, "From Our Kidnapped Friends in Missouri: Letter from Dr. Doy and Son—Barbarous Inhumanity of the Missourians," February 7, 1859, Platte City Prison, in *Lawrence (Kansas Territory) Republican*, February 17, 1859; Doy, *Narrative of John Doy*, chapters 3 and 4; James B. Abbott, "The Rescue of Dr. John Doy," *Transactions of the Kansas State Historical Society, 1886–1888* (Topeka: Kansas Publishing House, State Printer, 1890), 4:312–23; and letter, Ephraim Nute, Lawrence (Kansas Territory), to unidentified recipient, February 14, 1859, in *John Brown Collection*, Box 2, Folder 1. A list of the captives, reprinted from the *Weston Argus, Extra*, January 26, 1859, is in "Thirteen Negroes Captured in Kansas," *Lawrence (Kansas Territory) Republican*, February 3, 1859.

43. Kiene, "Battle of the Spurs," 8:443–49; and Jacob Willits, Topeka, correspondence to F. B. Sanborn, in Sanborn, *Life and Letters of John Brown*, 487.

44. Kiene, "Battle of the Spurs"; and Gill account of December 1858 raid in Hinton, *John Brown and His Men*, 223.

45. Villard, *John Brown*, 381.

46. "River Open," *White Cloud Kansas Chief*, December 30, 1858; and Kiene, "The Battle of the Spurs."

47. George Gill, it turned out, had noticed this group's movements earlier when Brown's party approached Topeka late one night on the first day of its

journey. "A comrade" [George Gill], correspondence to F. B. Sanborn, in Sanborn, *Life and Letters of John Brown*, 485–86; Gill account of December 1858 raid; and Hinton, *John Brown and His Men*, 224.

48. Kiene, "The Battle of the Spurs"; and Gill correspondence, Sanborn, *Life and Letters of John Brown*, 485–86.

49. Special correspondent, Holton, Kansas, February 9, 1859, "How Old Brown Wasn't Captured," *Leavenworth (Kansas Territory) Weekly Times*, February 19, 1859; Nathan, "Another Dream—How It Was Done—Old John Brown Again," Lawrence, February 5, in *Leavenworth (Kansas Territory) Weekly Times*, February 12, 1859; and "How Old John Brown Wasn't Captured," *Leavenworth (Kansas Territory) Times*, reprinted in *Lawrence (Kansas Territory) Republican*, February 10, 1859; and Sanborn, *Life and Letters of John Brown*, 484–85.

50. Gill correspondence in Sanborn, *Life and Letters of John Brown*, 485–86; and Villard, *John Brown*, 381–82. Another account states that by the time Brown's men moved toward the stream to engage the proslavery forces, John Woods had already abandoned command to a notorious Atchison man named Davis who also lost his nerve, and "a sudden panic seized his men, and all fled precipitously down a steep hill, to the Spring Creek crossing." This account is according to the special correspondent, "How Old Brown Wasn't Captured."

51. Kiene, "The Battle of the Spurs"; and Gill correspondence in Sanborn, *Life and Letters of John Brown*, 486.

52. Hamilton, "John Brown in Canada," 5.

53. Gill correspondence in Sanborn, *Life and Letters of John Brown*, 486; Gill account of December 1858 raid; Hinton, *John Brown and His Men*, 224; Nathan, "Another Dream" *Leavenworth (Kansas Territory) Weekly Times*; and "Late from Kansas: Four Men Taken Prisoners by Ossawatamie Brown," *St. Joseph (MO) Gazette*, February 4, 1859, reprinted in the *Topeka (Kansas Territory) Tribune*, February 10, 1859.

54. Kiene, "The Battle of the Spurs."

55. Villard, *John Brown*, 383; Morris W. Werner, "Lane's Trail and the Underground Railway," *Kansas Heritage Group* (1988–89), http://www.kansasheritage.org/werner/lane.html (accessed August 4, 2009); and "History of Albany, Kansas" (reprinted letter of William B. Slosson to George W. Martin of the Kansas State Historical Society), http://www.cityofsabetha.com/Albany.html (accessed July 28, 2013).

56. Statement of William Graham of Sabetha, Kansas, to W. E. Connelley of the Kansas State Historical Society, January 1901, quoted in Villard, *John Brown*, 383; and Tennal, *History of Nemaha County, Kansas*, 144–45.

57. Gill account of December 1858 raid; Hinton, *John Brown and His Men*, 225; and Dale, *Otoe County Pioneers*, 1749–50, 1394–95.

58. Gill account of December 1858 raid; Hinton, *John Brown and His Men*, 225; and "Old John Brown, of Osawatomie, Passes through Nebraska City with

His Troop of Niggers and a Gang of Horse Thieves," *Nebraska City (Nebraska Territory) News*, February 12, 1859.

59. E[lvira] G[aston] Platt, Oberlin, Ohio, to William E. Connelley, Topeka, Kansas, May 28, 1900, in which she states that John Brown "slept at my home when he made his last trip from Missouri, but greatly to my regret, I was with Tabor friends at that time."

60. Villard, *John Brown*, 384-85; and Todd, *Early Settlement*, 70.

61. "The Under Ground Railroad in Iowa: A Story of Deacon Adams and John Brown," *Des Moines (IA) Register and Leader*, June 28, 1908, section 3, 8.

62. George Gill mentions various stopovers made on the trek from the territories through Iowa. Between the Tolles family's cabin and Des Moines, Brown's group stopped at Calvin Bradway's farm in southeast Pottawattamie County; the farm of Oliver Mills, a cousin of John Brown's, just north of Lewis in Cass County on February 13; David A. Barnett's Grove City House in Cass County; John Porter's tavern at Dalmanutha; and John Murray's farm just east of today's town of Redfield. See Gill account of December 1858 raid; Hinton, *John Brown and His Men*, 217-27; and "Pioneer Days: Some Personal Reminiscences by M. C. McGoehon," *Atlantic (IA) Telegraph*, October 16, 1889.

63. John Teasdale, "Old John Brown: Mr. Teesdale Supplements Our Last Sunday Story of the Old Hero's Visit to Des Moines—Smuggling a Load of Slaves through This City," *Des Moines Iowa State Register*, April 2, 1882.

64. Between Des Moines and Grinnell, Brown's wagon group stopped southeast of Des Moines at Brian Hawley's home and then at Cornwall Dickinson's farm a few miles west of Grinnell.

65. Grinnell, *Men and Events*, 207, 210-13.

66. "Ossawatomie Brown," *Iowa City Weekly State Reporter*, March 2, 1859; and remarks of Colonel Cooper (Grinnell's first newspaper editor) at memorial services, "Hon. J. B. Grinnell," *Grinnell (IA) Herald*, April 7, 1891.

67. See Bixby letter to Lewellyn, Underground Railroad project files, State Historical Society of Iowa. On antagonistic Democratic press reaction, see "Captain Brown at Grinnell," *Des Moines Iowa Weekly Citizen*, March 2, 1859; "Captain Brown at Grinnell: 'Hell Let Loose'," *Des Moines Iowa Weekly Citizen*, March 2, 1859; and a defense of Grinnell at "Hon. J. B. Grinnell and the Des Moines *Statesman*," *Montezuma (IA) Weekly Republican*, March 31, 1859.

68. In a stopover on February 23, they stayed at the Draper B. Reynold's farm just south of Marengo. See "Mrs. Cornelius Devore [daughter of Draper B. Reynolds] Tells Thrilling Story," *Cedar Rapids (IA) Republican*, April 20, 1917; United States Census, 1860 schedules for Marengo Township, Iowa County; Gill account of December 1858 raid; and Hinton, *John Brown and His Men*, 226-27.

69. Villard, *John Brown*, 387; and Hinton, *John Brown and His Men*, 226-27.

70. On William Penn Clarke, see Eriksson, "William Penn Clarke," 3-11; Stiles, *Recollections and Sketches*, 767-68; and Clarke, "William Penn Clarke," 35.

71. Grinnell, *Men and Events*, 216; and Villard, *John Brown*, 390. For a slightly different take on the arrangements, see Lloyd, "John Brown among the Pedee Quakers," 716-19; and Eriksson, "William Penn Clarke," 43-44.

72. Villard, *John Brown*, 389-90; and letter, George Gill, Springdale, Iowa, to Richard J. Hinton, June 15, 1860, in MC 384, Box 2, correspondence, June 1860, Hinton, *Collection*.

73. Gill account of December 1858 raid; and Hinton, *John Brown and His Men*, 227.

74. Excerpts from William Penn Clarke's letter to the *Des Moines Register* in Downer, *History of Davenport*, 1:622.

75. J. C. Burns, Iowa City, Iowa, to Laurel Summers, March 3, 1859, *Summers Papers*; Downer, *History of Davenport*, 1:622; and *History of Cedar County*, 16.

76. Reed, "African American Life," 371.

77. Villard, *John Brown*, 389-90. Pinkerton's involvement in slave and runaway matters is noted in "Slave Hunt in Chicago! Arrest of an Alleged Fugitive by the United States Marshal," *Chicago Western Citizen*, June 10, 1851; and "Great Excitement in Chicago—Supposed Fugitive Slave Case," *Dubuque (IA) Daily Republican*, September 3, 1857.

78. Correspondence, "Brown's Rescued Negroes Landed in Canada," *New York Tribune*, reprinted in *Linn County (IA) Register*, March 26, 1859.

79. "Arrival of Old Brown's Negroes in Canada," *Detroit Tribune*, March 15, 1859, reprinted in the *Davenport (IA) Daily Gazette*, March 23, 1859.

80. The status of the twelve runaways at their new home came to the *New York Tribune*, November 6, 1859, with a clipping in the *Webb Scrapbooks*, vol. 17, microfilm roll 4 of LM 92, 126, and is reprinted in Redpath, *Public Life of Capt. John Brown*, 228.

81. Villard, *John Brown*, 391-97.

82. Jeremiah Anderson, at age eighteen, joined his brother and sister attending Knox Academy (across the Mississippi River in Galesburg, Illinois) in 1851-52. In 1854 he attended the local Yellow Springs Collegiate Institute "but got along poorly because of his heterodoxy." This issue is noted in Muelder, *Fighters for Freedom*, 303, including footnote 5. In Hinton, *Collection*, Box 2, are three letters from those who knew Jerry Anderson: J. D. Anderson, Eddyville, Iowa, to R. J. Hinton, April 4, 1860; Daniel G. Cartwright, Kossuth, Des Moines County, Iowa, to R. J. Hinton, April 26, 1860; and W. W. King, to R. J. Hinton, May 17, 1860. On Jeremiah Anderson's thoughts about these events, see letter, J. G. Anderson to "Dear brother," J. Q. Anderson, January 14, 1859, in Hinton, *Collection*, Box 1, Folder 9; and letter, J. G. Anderson to "Dear Brother," February 18, 1858, in Hinton, *Collection*, Box 1, Folder 8, For a biographical sketch, see Villard, *John Brown*, 681-82.

83. Acton, "An Iowan's Death at Harpers Ferry," 186-97; and Hinton, *John Brown and His Men*, 533-34.

84. On Richardson, see Hinton, *John Brown and His Men*, 153, 262. On Richard Realf's situation, see Richard J. Hinton, "Facts about Richard Realf," *Chicago Current*, June 19, 1886; and Hinton, *John Brown and His Men*, 197–98. Leonhardt's involvement with Brown's Harpers Ferry plans is described in Mildfelt, *The Secret Danites*, 77–82; and Hinton, *John Brown and His Men*, 253–56.

85. Villard, *John Brown*, 344; and Hinton, *John Brown and His Men*, 734.

86. Account of Luke F. Parsons to C. Ray Aurner in Aurner, *Topical History of Cedar County*, 1:438.

87. Aurner, *Topical History of Cedar County*, 1:438. Among the letters of Brown's men captured at Harpers Ferry—selected and published as Document No. 1, appendix to "Governor Wise's Message" (December 1859), West Virginia Archives and History—are a few related to Kagi's recruitment efforts and the responses received. One from Luke F. Parsons (item 15) to Kagi is dated May 16, 1859; another from C. W. Moffett (item 22) is dated June 26, 1859. See also Villard, *John Brown*, 344.

88. Villard, *John Brown*, 344; John Brown letter, Washington County, Missouri, August 6, 1859, to "Dear friends all," published as item 70 in Document No. 1, appendix to "Governor Wise's Message"; and Gill interview. Ultimately, after his term ended teaching school, Gill decided to join his comrades at the Kennedy farm in Maryland, but he had just started on his way when he learned news of the raid at Harpers Ferry.

89. George Gill's admiration for Edwin Coppoc extended to naming his first child after Coppoc. However, whereas outside observers saw Barclay as a "restless" and "adventurous" spirit, Gill thought him "treacherous and unprincipled and lacking in manhood and true courage." Such traits made Gill "unable to eulogize him or his memory in any way." Gill, "Biographical Notes."

90. Some of the men had known Brown for quite some time. For instance, Jeremiah Anderson had been with James Montgomery and joined Brown for the Missouri Raid in 1858, while Albert Hazlett had also been part of Montgomery's fighters and knew Brown from the Kansas operations. Barclay Coppoc and Edwin Coppoc came to know Brown's fellows while they were training in Springdale during the winter of 1857–58 and from Brown's stay in March 1859 with the twelve liberated slaves. Stewart Taylor had joined George Gill at the end of winter training in Springdale. Of the five black men, Osborne Anderson, John Copeland Jr., Lewis Leary, and Dangerfield Newby were freedmen, and Shields Green was an escaped slave. For biographical sketches of the raid's participants, see Villard, *John Brown*, 412, 678–87.

91. See two articles on the letters written to the secretary of war by Gue, "Iowans in John Brown's Raid," *American Historical Magazine* 1 (1906), 164–69; and "John Brown and His Iowa Friends," 110–11.

92. Aurner, *Topical History of Cedar County*, 1:418.

93. George Gill stated that Barclay Coppoc, one of John Brown's Iowa men who successfully escaped after Harpers Ferry, told Gill that upon learning

of the sheriff's imminent arrival, "the boys begged" Brown to abandon the scheme and insisted that it would mean "certain death." Brown told them he could not do so, given that "his friends had furnished him all the means he could ask for" and he "could ask no more." Gill interview.

94. George Gill commented that John Brown "was awful cautious for a very brave man. He would turn aside where [Aaron] Stevens would go straight through" (Gill interview). On the internal dispute over capturing and holding Harpers Ferry, see Villard, *John Brown*, 423–24; Hinton, *John Brown and His Men*, 258–60; Hinton, "John Brown and His Men," 698–99; Keeler, "Owen Brown's Escape," 343; and Oates, *To Purge This Land*, 279–80.

95. For detailed examinations of the raid, see Villard, John Brown, 426–66; and Tony Horwitz, *Midnight Rising: John Brown and the Raid that Sparked the Civil War* (New York: Henry Holt, 2011).

96. Hinton, *John Brown and His Men*, 517; and Keeler, "Owen Brown's Escape," 342–66. According to Luke Parsons, Cook "wore two large Colt's revolvers, one on either side, with John E. Cook engraved on the handles," and when captured Parsons thought that "the engraving on his arms gave him away." See Aurner, *Topical History of Cedar County*, 1:442–43.

97. Keeler, "Owen Brown's Escape."

98. Keeler, "Owen Brown's Escape."

99. Keeler, "Owen Brown's Escape," 362–66.

100. Keeler, "Owen Brown's Escape."

101. Keeler, "Owen Brown's Escape."

102. Peterson, *John Brown*, 24.

103. "From Kansas: Sympathy for John Brown—Anti-Slavery Mass Meeting at Lawrence," *New York Times*, December 12, 1859.

104. Phillips, "Lecture by William A. Phillips," in Redpath, *Echoes of Harper's Ferry*, 377–83.

105. On rumors of plots to rescue Brown, see McMaster, *History of the People*, 8:422–24.

106. Hinton, "John Brown and His Men," 702; and Villard, *John Brown*, 571–72.

107. Higginson, *Thomas Wentworth Higginson*, 196–200; Villard, *John Brown*, 471, 570–80; and Morse, "Attempted Rescue of John Brown," 8:213–26. Though Morse's account confuses the contemplated attempt to rescue Brown with the actual attempted get-together of men seeking to rescue Stevens and Hazlett, the editor's notes contain informative contemporary letters exchanged between participants on their plans to free the two men. The antislavery men who gathered at Harrisburg included James Montgomery, Silas Soule, J. A. Pike, Joseph Gardner, Henry Carpenter, Augustus Wattles, S. J. Willis, and from Linn County, Iowa, the brothers Henry Seaman and Benjamin Seaman.

108. Villard, *John Brown*, 573-78.

109. Villard, *John Brown*, 573-78.

110. Thoreau followed up his lectures with two other essays on Brown—"Martyrdom of John Brown," and "The Last Days of John Brown." On the Transcendentalists' influence in shaping the legend of John Brown, see Woodward, *Burden of Southern History*, 52-56.

111. On the entry of Brown into song, see "John Brown in Song," *Chicago Tribune*, August 9, 1861; "John Brown, Dead yet Speaketh," *New York (NY) National Anti-Slavery Standard*, September 7, 1861; and Plers, "The New John Brown Song: War Songs for the Army and the People—No. 2," *Chicago Tribune*, December 16, 1861.

112. Phillips, *Speeches, Lectures, and Letters*, 290.

113. Letter, E. James, Burlington, Iowa, to "My dear niece," December 14, 1859, and published in Pammel, "Dr. Edwin James," 288-89.

114. On Jo Shelby's regard for Brown's importance, see Connelley, *Quantrill and the Border Wars*, 288-89. On the issue of John Brown's importance in Kansas developments, James C. Malin argues it has been vastly inflated in his *John Brown and the Legend of Fifty-Six*.

115. Editorial view in *Davenport (IA) Gazette*, October 19, 1859.

116. Gill's comment quoted in Acton, "An Iowan's Death at Harpers Ferry," 186.

9. North and Back

1. "A Kidnapping Case," *Pacific City (IA) Herald*, February 9, 1860, identifies the four blacks as having lived in the Choctaw Nation. Connelley, in *Quantrill and the Border Wars*, reports that they ran away from the Cherokees (146-47). One Glenwood, Iowa-based proslavery correspondent incorrectly claimed in the *St. Joseph (MO) Gazette*, February 29, 1860—reprinted in the *Pacific City (IA) Herald*, March 8, 1860—that three runaways came to Tabor, where they joined a fourth one; and the *St. Joseph Gazette* reported the three as having escaped from Mt. Vernon, Missouri. The ages and look of the four fugitives is noted in Lucas, "Men Were Too Fiery," 16.

2. Connelley, *Quantrill and the Border Wars*, 146-47.

3. "A Kidnapping Case"; and Jonathan Spikes, "Kidnapping and Rescue," *Des Moines Daily Iowa State Register*, February 14, 1860.

4. "A Kidnapping Case"; and Spikes, "Kidnapping and Rescue."

5. Joe Foster recruited Jim Gardner of Glenwood to drive the wagon, and four others named Castle of Glenwood, W. K. Follett, Wyatt, and George Linville, whose barn had been used to initially house the captives. Todd, *Early Settlement*, 64; and "A Kidnapping Case."

6. In "Tabor," *Pacific City (IA) Herald*, March 8, 1860, the editor reprints comments of another writer followed by his own as to what actually happened.

7. "A Kidnapping Case"; and Todd, *Early Settlement*, 63–64. Whereas Dr. E. S. Hill—one of the two Tabor fellows directly involved—attributes the tip about the slaves being at Foster's to William B. Wilson, John Todd states the discovery of the black men at Foster's house came when a man attending the proceedings at Cramer's, "McMillen by name (others say Wing), inquired of one of the Tabor boys if he could keep a secret. On being assured that he would, he handed him a paper" stating they were two miles away at Foster's. It may well be that the two Tabor men verified rather than discovered the activity going on at Joe Foster's house.

8. Letter, E. S. Hill, Atlantic, Iowa, to Prof. W. H. Siebert, Columbus, Ohio, October 30, 1894, in Siebert, *Collection*, Box 45, Folder 11A; and Todd, *Early Settlement*, 64.

9. Hill letter to Siebert; Todd, *Early Settlement*, 64; and letter to editor from "One Who Knows" to "Friend Shoemaker," *Clarinda (IA) Page County Herald*, February 24, 1860. The reference to the black men shooting two shots in the air is from Spikes, "Kidnapping and Rescue."

10. Todd, *Early Settlement*, 64.

11. The three escorts on the final trip to Lewis were identified by Rev. E. S. Hill in his letter to Siebert; however, Rev. John Todd, in *Early Settlement*, states there were more escorts on the trip, including "O. Cummings, D. E. Woods, L. B. Hill, Pascal Mason, and others on horseback" (65).

12. The Grinnell portion of the story of the four black men relies on two principal sources: Lucas, "Men Were Too Fiery," 12–21; and Parker, "Notes for *History of Poweshiek County*."

13. Lucas, "Men Were Too Fiery," 17.

14. Lucas, "Men Were Too Fiery," 17.

15. Parker, "Notes"; and Parker, *History of Poweshiek County*, 1:222–23.

16. Parker, "Notes."

17. Parker, "Notes."

18. Parker, "Notes."

19. That Parker arranged for Frances Overton to relocate to a Quaker settlement is noted in a letter by Amos Bixby, Boulder, Colorado, to Leonard Parker, Grinnell, Iowa, May 23, 1887, in Leonard Parker Papers, Box 1, Folder A1, Grinnell College Libraries, Department of Special Collections, Grinnell, Iowa.

20. For Dr. R[ansom] L. Harris's story of his living with the Pardee Quakers during the time of the Morgan Walker raid, see his article, "Kansas to Honor John Brown," 4. For an account of the three blacks from Indian Territory joining the Quaker men in Pardee, Kansas, see Connelley, *Quantrill and the Border Wars*, 146–49.

21. Harris, "Kansas to Honor John Brown"; Lutz, "Quantrell, the Guerilla Chief," 509–20; and chapters 9 and 10 of Connelley's *Quantrill and the Border Wars* cover the Morgan Walker events. Connelley's study contains the most

detailed research, including letters of contemporaries on the Morgan Walker raid, and modern biographical treatments of this event in Quantrill's life being derivative of his work, including Leslie, *The Devil Knows How to Ride*, chapter 4; and Schultz, *Quantrill's War*, chapter 4.

22. Connelley, *Quantrill*, 148–49.

23. Information is unclear both about John Dean's participation in the raid, whether he was there and helped cooperate in events at the Morgan Walker farm, and about Albert Southwick, whether he was taking care of the horses or came in a team with Dean at the moment of the raid. The account given here takes the lead from accounts provided by Ransom L. Harris, the Pardee Quaker cabin mate, and the research results of William Elsey Connelley.

24. On Morgan Walker and his farm, see Wilcox, *Jackson County Pioneers*, 313–14; *The History of Jackson County, Missouri* (Kansas City MO: Union Historical Company, 1881), 317; and Connelley, *Quantrill and the Border Wars*, 154–57.

25. Harris, "Kansas to Honor John Brown"; Connelley, *Quantrill and the Border Wars*, 156, 160; and Lutz, "Quantrill and the Morgan Walker Tragedy," 324–31.

26. Connelley, *Quantrill and the Border Wars*, 154–59.

27. Connelley, *Quantrill and the Border Wars*, 159–60, especially footnote 6.

28. Additionally, the coroner found on Morrison "one silver watch and one butcher knife and one Allen's pattern Revolver pistol, one small flask of powder, and some pistol balls and some molds, one box of gun caps, one purse with nothing in it, and one pocket knife and one belt." The coroner's verdict is contained in Wilcox, *Jackson County Pioneers*, 314–15; and the burial of Morrison is noted in Connelley, *Quantrill and the Border Wars*, 174.

29. Connelley, *Quantrill and the Border Wars*, 174–77.

30. Connelley, *Quantrill and the Border Wars*, 174–77.

31. Parker, "Notes"; and OPPOSITION, "More Trouble at Grinnell," *Des Moines Iowa State Journal*, October 27, 1860. The sojourn of the three back to Kansas is described in Connelley, *Quantrill and the Border Wars*, 132–33, 146–49.

32. For details of Charles Leonhardt's activity in Kansas and later in Iowa, see Mildfelt, *Secret Danites*.

33. John E. Stewart, Wakarusa, Kansas, letter to Thaddeus Hyatt, December 20, 1859, in Thaddeus Hyatt Collection 401, Box 1, Folder 7, Kansas State Historical Society. A copy of the full letter is also published in Sheridan, *Freedom's Crucible*, 45–47.

34. "Kidnapping in Kansas," *Lawrence (Kansas Territory) Republican*, August 16, 1860, reprinted in the *New York (NY) National Anti-Slavery Standard*, September 1, 1860; and Doy, *Narrative of John Doy*, 23.

35. Letter from Silas S. Soule to Messrs. Thayer, Eldridge, Hinton, etc., dated Coal Creek, May 9, 1860, and quoted in Sheridan, *Freedom's Crucible*, 131–32. Soule's letter states there were five captors, but in his *Quantrill*

and the Border Wars, 119–20, Connelley identifies seven: Jake Herd [Hurd], Jake McGee, Tom McGee, "Cuckold Tom" McGee, Henry McLaughlin, Esau Sager, and Quantrill.

36. Morton and Watkins, *History of Nebraska*, 462.

37. Leonhardt, unpublished manuscript on "The Last Train," in the Leonhardt Papers.

38. Leonhardt, "The Last Train."

39. Leonhardt, "The Last Train."

40. Leonhardt, "The Last Train."

41. Leonhardt, "The Last Train."

42. "U.G.R.R.—Full Cargo in Charge of Coppic [*sic*], Doyle and Ball," *Newton (IA) Jasper Free Press*, August 16, 1860. Some newspapers that reprinted the story included the *Davenport (IA) Daily Gazette*, August 22, 1860; *Des Moines Weekly Iowa State Register*, August 22, 1860; and *Burlington (IA) Weekly Hawk-Eye*, August 25, 1860.

43. "For the North Star," *Des Moines Weekly Iowa State Register*, August 22, 1860; and "Republican Leaders Running off Negroes," *Des Moines Weekly Iowa State Register*, August 25, 1860.

44. Leonhardt, "The Last Train"; "From the Home of J. B. Grinnell—Testimony from a Neighbor," *Des Moines Iowa State Journal*, August 25, 1860; and "Runaway Niggers," *Cedar Rapids (IA) The Cedar Democrat*, August 30, 1860.

45. Grinnell's note to Clarke, quoted in Eriksson, "William Penn Clarke," 44, citing correspondence of William Penn Clarke, Charles Aldrich Collection, State Historical Society of Iowa, Des Moines.

46. "Republican Leaders Running off Negroes"; and "Runaway Niggers."

47. "Republican Leaders Running off Negroes"; and "Runaway Niggers."

48. "Running off Negroes!," *Des Moines Iowa State Register*, September 5, 1860.

49. Leonhardt, "The Last Train." On Gilman Folsom, see Stiles, *Recollections and Sketches*, 571, 763–64; *History of Johnson County, Iowa*, 822; and Clarence Ray Aurner, *Leading Events in Johnson County Iowa History* (Cedar Rapids IA: Western Historical Press, 1912), 626–27.

50. Leonhardt, "The Last Train."

51. Leonhardt, "The Last Train."

52. Leonhardt, "The Last Train."

53. "Kidnapping in Kansas."

54. Connelley, *Quantrill and the Border Wars*, 106–9.

55. Doy, *Narrative of John Doy*, 25–28, 51.

56. Letter to editor from Council Bluffs citizen dated September 26, 1860, "Three Negroes Kidnaped near Council Bluffs and Run into Missouri—Great Excitement," *Burlington (IA) Daily Hawk-eye*, October 3, 1860; and "Kidnapping," *Page County (IA) Herald*, October 12, 1860. An article in the *Des Moines*

Iowa State Register, October 10, 1860, states that Council Bluff citizens raised $75 to secure Williamson's release. One possible associate of the Missourian kidnappers was locally notorious Philip McGuire. This connection is made by Black, "Lynchings in Iowa," 209. The author incorrectly states that "Philip McGuire kidnapped John Williamson and a woman in Pottawattamie County and attempted to sell them into slavery." Afterward McGuire was captured on the Missouri River, having in his possession plenty of stolen goods, horses, and mules, and brought to the Cottonwood Jail in Council Bluffs. Then on October 16 a mob hanged him from a tree on Mount Lincoln with a sign attached: "Hanged for all kinds of rascality." While the author may be correct, given that it happened at the same time as the Williamson and Garner seizures, the reference source cited does not directly connect the two; instead, it treats them as separate events. See *History of Pottawattamie County, Iowa*, 168.

57. Manuscript schedules of the Iowa Census, 1856, Benton Township; manuscript schedules for the 1860 United States Census for Pottawattamie County, Iowa; Bloomer, "History of Pottawattamie County," 281; Fremont County, Iowa Marriage Records, http://www.cofremontia.us/fremcorecdbirth .htm; and settlement of assault case by Henry Garner vs. Stephen Nuckolls for $6,000 noted in the *Clarinda (IA) Page County Herald*, June 22, 1860, and reprinted in *Burlington (IA) Daily Hawk-Eye*, June 30, 1860.

58. "Kidnapping," *New York (NY) National Anti-Slavery Standard*, October 20, 1860; and "Kidnapping in Iowa," *Des Moines Iowa State Register*, October 17, 1860.

59. Todd, *Early Settlement*, 66.

60. Todd, *Early Settlement*, 66; and "The Police Trip to Iowa with Three Alleged Kidnappers," *St. Louis Daily Missouri Democrat*, October 16, 1860. The chapter's subsequent information concerning Hurd's reckoning with the law is taken from this newspaper account.

61. "The Police Trip to Iowa."

62. "The Police Trip to Iowa." On J. A. Harvey, see "Twenty Years Ago," *Sidney (IA) Argus-Herald*, January 25, 1934.

63. "Imprisoned," *Davenport (IA) Daily Democrat & News*, November 19, 1860; "Jail Delivery," *Clarinda (IA) Page County Herald*, December 7, 1860; "Jacob Hurd," *St. Louis Daily Missouri Democrat*, December 7, 1860; *History of Pottawattamie County*, 168; and Todd, *Early Settlement*, 67.

64. "Kidnapping in Iowa."

65. Editor, commentary, *Muscatine (IA) Weekly Journal*, October 12, 1860.

Epilogue

1. See two articles by Christopher Phillips—"'The Crime against Missouri,'" 60–81; and "The Southernization of Missouri," 89–117—in Moore, Sinisi, and White, *Warm Ashes*.

2. Phillips, "'The Crime against Missouri,'" 62–64. On the westerners as a force to which both antislavery and proslavery foes appealed, see Cecil-Fronsman, "'Advocate the Freedom of White Men,'" 102–15.

3. William Walker to David R. Atchison, July 6, 1854, David Rice Atchison Papers, Mss. 71, Folder 4, State Historical Society of Missouri/University of Missouri at Columbia, as quoted in Phillips, "'The Crime against Missouri,'" 73.

4. "Col. Lane's Foray into Kansas," *Iowa City Daily Evening Reporter*, September 4, 1856; and "Civil War on the Border: Latest News From Kansas," *Leavenworth (Kansas Territory) Journal*, reprinted in *Bloomfield Iowa Flag*, August 30, 1856.

5. Americus Democraticus, "The Democratic Party," *Dubuque (IA) Herald*, October 6, 1854, reprinted in *Muscatine Iowa Democratic Enquirer*, October 12, 1854.

6. See Dykstra, *Bright Radical Star*, chapters 10–12.

7. Drehle, "The Way We Weren't," 42.

8. Phillips, *Conquest of Kansas*, 147.

9. Gleed, "Samuel Walker," 254.

10. Special correspondent, "Kansas Lies Prostrate," *New York Weekly Tribune*, July 26, 1856, with clipping in *Webb Scrapbooks*, vol. 6, microfilm roll 2 of LM 90, 4; and "Citizens of Jackson County Arrested, Robbed and Turned back from Kansas by 300 Armed Missourians," *Davenport (IA) Gazette*, reprinted in the *Grand Rapids (MI) Eagle*, July 22, 1856, with a copy in *Webb Scrapbooks*, vol. 15, microfilm roll 4 of LM 92, 70.

11. "Citizens of Jackson County Arrested, Robbed and Turned back from Kansas by 300 Armed Missourians."

12. A stanza of John Greenleaf Whittier's poem, "The Kansas Emigrants," from his *Anti-Slavery Poems*, 173.

SELECTED BIBLIOGRAPHY

Archival Sources

Allamakee County IA Archives Military Records. "Some Military Land Grants in Allamakee County Iowa for Soldiers of the War of 1812." Compiled by Linda S. Ayres. USGenWeb Archives, December 16, 2010. http://files.usgwarchives.net/ia/allamakee/military/warof1812/other /somemili107nmt.txt.

"Blanchard, I. D. (Delaware, 1837–1847)." FM 98. *American Baptist Foreign Mission Societies, Records, 1817–1859.* American Baptist Historical Society, Atlanta GA.

Brown, John, Collection. Kansas State Historical Society, Topeka.

Emery, James Stanley, Collection. Number 339, box 2, Folder Correspondence 1855–1859. Kansas State Historical Society, Topeka. http://www .territorialkansasonline.org/~imlskto/cgi-bin/index.php?screen=show _document&document_id=100500&screen_from=keyword&selected _keyword=Emery,%20james%20stanley&startsearchat=0.

Governor's Papers: Correspondence, Military War Matters, Miscellaneous, 1839–1908. State Historical Society of Iowa, Des Moines.

"Governor Wise's Message, Appended Documents Relative to the Harpers Ferry Invasion." West Virginia Archives and History, Charleston WV. http://www.wvculture.org/history/jbexhibit/virginiadocuments.html.

Hinton, Richard J. *Collection.* Kansas State Historical Society, Topeka.

Leonhardt, Charles W. *Leonhardt Papers.* Kansas State Historical Society, Topeka.

Platt Family Papers. Series 2 in RG0907.AM. Nebraska State Historical Society, Lincoln.

Salter, William. *Papers.* Box 1, Folder 4. State Historical Society of Iowa, Des Moines.

Siebert, Wilbur H. *Collection.* Ohio Historical Society, Columbus.

Summers Papers. Putnam Museum, Davenport IA.

Territorial Kansas Online, 1854–1861. Kansas State Historical Society, Topeka. http://www.territorialkansasonline.org/~imlskto/cgi-bin /index.php.

Villard Collection. Columbia University Rare Book and Manuscript Library, New York.

Wakarusa River Valley Heritage Museum, Bloomington Park KS. http:// wakarusamuseum.org/.

Webb Scrapbooks. Vols. 6–9, 12–17, 1854–60. Topeka: Kansas State Historical Society.

West Virginia Memory Project. John Brown/Boyd B. Stutler Collection Database. West Virginia Archives and History, Charleston WV. http:// www.wvculture.org/history/wvmemory/jbdetail.aspx?Type=Text&Id =915.

Writers' Program of the Work Projects Administration (WPA) in the State of Iowa. "WPA Iowa Federal Writers' Project 'The Negro in Iowa' Collection (Unpublished), 1935–1942." State Historical Society of Iowa, Des Moines.

Published Sources

Acton, Richard. "An Iowan's Death at Harpers Ferry." *The Palimpsest* 70, no. 4 (Winter 1989): 186–97.

Alexander, W. E. *History of Winneshiek and Allamakee Counties, Iowa, 1882.* Sioux City IA: Western Publishing, 1882.

Andreas, A. T. *History of the State of Kansas.* Chicago: A. T. Andreas, 1883.

———. "Nemaha County." *History of the State of Nebraska.* Chicago: A. T. Andreas, 1882. http://www.kancoll.org/books/andreas_ne/nemaha /nemaha-p1.html.

Aurner, C. Ray. *A Topical History of Cedar County, Iowa.* Vol. 1. Chicago: S. J. Clarke Publishing, 1910.

Baltimore, Lester B. "Benjamin Stringfellow: Fight for Slavery on the Missouri Border." *Missouri Historical Review* 62, no. 1 (October 1967): 14–29.

Black, Paul Walton. "Lynchings in Iowa." *Iowa Journal of History and Politics* 10 (April 1912): 151–254.

Blackmar, Frank W. *Kansas.* Vol. 2. Chicago: Standard Publishing, 1912.

Bloomer, D. C. "Notes on the History of Pottawattamie County." *Annals of Iowa*, 1st series, 10, no. 4 (October 1872): 270–86.

Brown, G. W. *Reminiscences of Old John Brown: Thrilling Incidents of Border Life in Kansas.* Rockford IL: Abraham E. Smith, Printer, 1880.

Brown, John Howard. *Cyclopaedia of American Biography: Comprising the Men and Women of the United States Who Have Been Identified with the Growth of the Nation.* Vol. 2. Boston: James H. Lamb, 1899.

Butler, Pardee. *Personal Recollections of Pardee Butler with Reminiscences, by His Daughter, Mrs. Rosetta B. Hastings*. . . . Cincinnati: Standard Publishing, 1889.

Cecil-Fronsman, Bill. "'Advocate the Freedom of White Men, as Well as That of Negroes': The *Kansas Free State* and Antislavery Westerners in Territorial Kansas." *Kansas History* 20, no. 2 (Summer 1997): 102–15.

——. "'Death to All Yankees and Traitors in Kansas': The *Squatter Sovereign* and the Defense of Slavery in Kansas." *Kansas History* 16, no. 1 (Spring 1993): 22–33.

Cedar County Historical Society. *John Brown in Cedar County*. Tipton IA: Cedar County Historical Society, undated.

Clarke, William Penn. "William Penn Clarke." In *Proceedings of the Ninth Annual Meeting of the Iowa State Bar Association Held at Des Moines, Iowa, July 16–17, 1903*. Tipton IA: Conservative, 1903, 35.

A Clergyman of the Episcopal Church. *In Perils by Mine Own Countrymen: Three Years on the Kansas Border*. New York: Miller, Orton & Mulligan, 1856.

Connelley, William Elsey. *An Appeal to the Record*. Topeka KS: William Connelley, 1903.

——. "Col. Richard J. Hinton." *Transactions of the Kansas State Historical Society*. Vol. 7. Topeka KS: State Printer, 1902, 486–93.

——. *James Henry Lane: The "Grim Chieftain" of Kansas*. Topeka KS: Crane & Company, 1899.

——. "The Lane Trail." *Collections of the Kansas State Historical Society, 1913–1914*. Vol. 13. Topeka: Kansas State Printing Plant, 1915, 268–79.

——. *Quantrill and the Border Wars*. New York: Pageant Book Company 1956. First published 1909 by Torch Press.

——. *A Standard History of Kansas and Kansans*. Vol. 1. Chicago: Lewis Publishing, 1918. http://skyways.lib.ks.us/genweb/archives/1918ks/.

——. Statement, Topeka, June 7, 1907, about a conversation with John Anderson in 1906 concerning old times in Kansas. In John Brown/ Boyd B. Stutler Collection Database. http://www.wvculture.org /history/wvmemory/jbdetail.aspx?Type=Text&Id=1266.

Cordley, Richard. *A History of Lawrence, Kansas*. Lawrence KS: Lawrence Journal Press, 1893.

Craik, Elmer LeRoy. "Southern Interest in Territorial Kansas, 1854–1858." *Collections of the Kansas State Historical Society, 1919–1922*. Vol. 15. Topeka KS: State Printer, 1923, 334–450.

Dale, Raymond E. *Otoe County Pioneers: A Biographical Dictionary*. Part 7, Me–Q. Lincoln NE, 1964.

Denton, Charles Richard. "The Unitarian Church and 'Kanzas Territory,' 1854–1861." Part 1, "1854–1855." *Kansas Historical Quarterly* 30, no. 3 (Autumn 1964): 307–38.

Dirck, Brian R. "By the Hand of God: James Montgomery and Redemptive Violence." *Kansas History: A Journal of the Central Plains* 27 (Spring–Summer 2004): 100–115.

Downer, Harry E. *History of Davenport and Scott County Iowa*. Vol. 1. Chicago: S. J. Clarke, 1910.

Doy, John. *The Narrative of John Doy, of Lawrence, Kansas*. New York: Thomas Holman, 1860.

Drehle, David Von. "The Way We Weren't: The Civil War, 1861–2011." *Time* 177, no. 15 (April 18, 2011): 42.

Dykstra, Robert R. *Bright Radical Star: Black Freedom and White Supremacy on the Hawkeye Frontier*. Cambridge MA: Harvard University Press, 1993.

Eldridge, Shalor Winchell. "Recollections of Early Days in Kansas." *Publications of the Kansas State Historical Society*. Vol. 2. Topeka: Kansas State Printing Plant, 1920.

Eriksson, Eric McKinley. "William Penn Clarke." *Iowa Journal of History and Politics* 25, no. 1 (January 1927): 3–11.

Etcheson, Nicole. *Bleeding Kansas: Contested Liberty in the Civil War Era*. Lawrence: University Press of Kansas, 2004.

———. "The Great Principle of Self-Government: Popular Sovereignty and Bleeding Kansas." *Kansas History* 27, no. 1–2 (Spring–Summer 2004): 14–29.

———. "Where Popular Sovereignty Worked: Nebraska Territory and the Kansas-Nebraska Act." In Wunder and Ross, *Nebraska-Kansas Act of 1854*, 159–82.

Fehrenbacher, Don E. *The Dred Scott Case: Its Significance in American Law and Politics*. New York: Oxford University Press, 1978.

Freehling, William W. *The Road to Disunion*. Vol. 1, *Secessionists at Bay, 1776–1854*. New York: Oxford University Press, 1990.

Gienapp, William E. *The Origins of the Republican Party, 1852–1856*. New York: Oxford University Press, 1987.

Gihon, John H. *Geary and Kansas: Governor Geary's Administration in Kansas*. Philadelphia: Chas. C. Rhodes, 1857.

Gleed, Charles S. "Samuel Walker," *Transactions of the Kansas State Historical Society*. Vol. 6. Topeka KS: W. Y. Morgan, State Printer, 1900, 249–74.

Gray, P. L. *Gray's Doniphan County History: A Record of the Happenings of Half a Hundred Years*. Bendena KS: Roycroft Press, 1905. http://skyways.lib.ks.us/genweb/archives/doniphan/history/1905/.

Grinnell, Josiah Bushnell. *Men and Events of Forty Years*. Boston: D. Lothrop, 1891.

Gue, Benjamin F. "Iowans in John Brown's Raid, and the Author of the Mysterious 'Floyd Letter.'" *American Historical Magazine* 1 (1906): 164–69.

———. "John Brown and His Iowa Friends." *Midland Monthly* 7, no. 2–3 (February 1897): 103–13; (March 1897): 267–77.

Hale, William Harlan. *Horace Greeley: Voice of the People.* New York: Harper & Brothers, 1950.

Hamilton, James Cleland. "John Brown in Canada: A Monograph." *Canadian Magazine*, December 1894, 1–21.

Harlow, Ralph Volney. "The Rise and Fall of the Kansas Aid Movement." *American Historical Review* 41, no. 1 (October 1935): 1–26.

Harris, Dr. R. L. "Kansas to Honor John Brown: Will Celebrate 50th Anniversary of Battle of Osawatomie." *San Francisco (CA) Call*, August 12, 1906, 4.

Harrold, Stanley. *Border War: Fighting over Slavery before the Civil War.* Chapel Hill: University of North Carolina Press, 2010.

Hawes, Alex G. "In Kansas with John Brown." *The Californian* 4 (July–December 1881): 68–75.

Higginson, Mary Thacher. ed. *Letters and Journals of Thomas Wentworth Higginson, 1846–1906.* Boston: Houghton Mifflin, 1921.

———. *Thomas Wentworth Higginson: The Story of His Life.* Boston: Houghton Mifflin, 1914. Reprint, Freeport NY: Books for Libraries Press, 1972.

Hinton, Richard J. *John Brown and His Men.* Rev. ed. New York: Funk & Wagnalls, 1894.

———. "John Brown and His Men, before and after the Raid on Harper's Ferry, October 16th, 17th, 18th, 1859." *Frank Leslie's Popular Monthly* 27, no. 6 (June 1889): 691–703.

The History of Cedar County with a History of Iowa. 2 vols. Chicago: Historical Publishing, 1901.

History of Johnson County, Iowa . . . from 1836 to 1882. Iowa City, 1883.

History of Pottawattamie County, Iowa. Chicago: O. L. Baskin, 1883.

History of Vernon County, Missouri. St. Louis: Brown, 1887.

The History of Washington County, Iowa, Containing a History of the County, Its Cities, Towns, &c. (Des Moines IA: Union Historical, 1880.

Hoole, William Stanley. "A Southerner's Viewpoint of the Kansas Situation, 1856–1857: The Letters of Lieut. Col. A. J. Hoole, CSA," *Kansas Historical Quarterly* 3, no. 1 (February 1934): 43–56.

Hougen, Harvey R. "The Marais des Cygnes Massacre and the Execution of William Griffith." *Kansas History* 8 (Summer 2003): 74–94.

Howe, Daniel Walker. "The Evangelical Movement and Political Culture in the North during the Second Party System." *Journal of American History* 77, no. 4 (March 1991): 1216–39.

———. *The Political Culture of the American Whigs.* Chicago: University of Chicago Press, 1979.

Iowa Census, 1856. Manuscript schedules for Benton Township, Fremont County.

Isely, W. H. "The Sharps Rifle Episode in Kansas History." *American Historical Review* 12, no. 3 (April 1907): 546–66.

Johannsen, Robert W. *Stephen A. Douglas*. New York: Oxford University Press, 1973.

Johnson, Samuel A. "The Emigrant Aid Company in the Kansas Conflict." *Kansas Historical Quarterly* 6, no. 1 (February 1937): 21–33.

Kansas: A Cyclopedia of State History, Embracing Events, Institutions, Industries, Counties, Cities, Towns, Prominent Persons, etc. Vol. 2. Chicago: Standard Publishing, 1912.

Kansas Territorial Legislature. "An Act to Punish Offences against Slave Property, August 14, 1855." *Kansas Memory* (website), Kansas Historical Society. http://www.kansasmemory.org/item/6835.

Keeler, Ralph. "Owen Brown's Escape from Harper's Ferry." *Atlantic Monthly* 33, no. 197 (March 1874): 342–66.

Kiene, L. L. "The Battle of the Spurs and John Brown's Exit from Kansas." *Kansas Historical Collections* 8 (1903–1904): 443–49.

Kinnan, Kay McAlexander. *Who Was Ira D. Blanchard?* Dallas: Legacy Printing, 2009.

Lekwa, Verl L., and Bennett Community Club. *Bennett, Iowa, and Inland Township: A History*. Privately printed, 1983.

Leonhardt, Charles W. "The Last Train." Unpublished manuscript. *Leonhardt Papers*. Kansas State Historical Society, Topeka.

Leslie, Edward E. *The Devil Knows How to Ride: The True Story of William Clarke Quantrill and His Confederate Raiders*. New York: Da Capo Press, 1998.

Lewis, Lloyd. "Propaganda and the Kansas-Missouri War." *Missouri Historical Review* 92, no. 2 (January 1998): 135–48.

Lloyd, Frederick. "John Brown among the Pedee Quakers." *Annals of Iowa*. Series 1, 4 (April 1866): 665–70; (July 1866): 712–19; (October 1866): 759–764.

Lucas, Thomas A. "Men Were Too Fiery for Much Talk: The Grinnell Anti-Abolitionist Riot of 1860." *Palimpsest* 68, no. 1 (Spring 1987): 12–21.

Lutz, Reverend John J. "Quantrell, the Guerilla Chief: Quantrell and His Base Betrayal of the Iowa Slave Liberators." *Midland Monthly* 7, no. 6 (June 1897): 509–20.

———. "Quantrill and the Morgan Walker Tragedy." *Transactions of the Kansas State Historical Society*. Vol. 6. Topeka: W. Y. Morgan, State Printer, 1904, 324–31.

Lynch, William O. "Popular Sovereignty and the Colonization of Kansas from 1854 to 1860." In *Proceedings of Historical Association, the*

Mississippi Valley. Vol. 9, part 3, *Year 1917-1918*. Cedar Rapids IA: Torch Press, 1919, 380-92.

———. "Population Movements in Relation to the Struggle for Kansas." *Indiana University Studies* 12 (1925): 383-404.

Malin, James C. "Housing Experiments in the Lawrence Community, 1855." *Kansas Historical Quarterly* 21, no. 2 (Summer 1954): 95-121.

———. *John Brown and the Legend of Fifty-Six*. Philadelphia: American Philosophical Society, 1942. Reprint, New York: Haskell House, 1971.

———. "Judge Lecompte and the 'Sack of Lawrence,' May 21, 1856." *Kansas Historical Quarterly* 20, no. 7 (August 1953): 465-94.

———. *The Nebraska Question, 1852-1854*. Lawrence KS: Author, 1953.

Martin, George W. "The First Two Years of Kansas." *Transactions of the Kansas State Historical Society, 1907-1908*. Vol. 10. Topeka: State Printing Office, 1908, 120-48.

McKivigan, John R. *Roving Editor*. University Park: Penn State University Press, 2004.

———. *The War against Proslavery Religion: Abolitionism and the Northern Churches, 1830-1865*. Ithaca: Cornell University Press, 1984.

McKivigan, John R., and Mitchell Snay, eds. *Religion and the Antebellum Debate over Slavery*. Athens: University of Georgia Press, 1998.

McMaster, John Bach. *A History of the People of the United States: From the Revolution to the Civil War, 1850-1861*. Vol. 8. New York: D. Appleton, 1913.

Meyer, Howard N., ed. *The Magnificent Activist: The Writings of Thomas Wentworth Higginson*. Cambridge MA: Da Capo Press, 2000.

Mildfelt, Todd. *The Secret Danites: Kansas' First Jayhawkers*. Winfield KS: Central Plains Book Manufacturing, 2003.

Morgans, James Patrick. *John Todd and the Underground Railroad*. Jefferson NC: McFarland, 2006.

Morrow, Robert. "Emigration to Kansas in 1856." *Transactions of the Kansas State Historical Society, 1903-1904*, Vol. 8. Topeka: Geo. A. Clark, State Printer, 1904, 302-15.

Morse, O. E. "An Attempted Rescue of John Brown from Charlestown, Va., Jail." *Kansas Historical Collections* 8 (1904): 213-26.

Morton, J. Sterling, ed. *Illustrated History of Nebraska: A History of Nebraska from the Earliest Explorations of the Trans-Mississippi Region*. Vol. 1. Lincoln NE: Jacob North, 1907.

Morton, J. Sterling, and Albert Watkins. *History of Nebraska*. Rev. ed. Lincoln NE: Western Publishing and Engraving, 1918.

Mott, David C. "Charles Wesley Tolles." *Annals of Iowa*. Series 3, 14, no. 8 (April 1925): 621-32.

Muelder, Hermann R. *Fighters for Freedom*. Galesburg IL: Knox College, 1959.

Neely, Jeremy. *The Border between Them: Violence and Reconciliation on the Kansas-Missouri Line*. Columbia: University of Missouri Press, 2007.

Neely Jr., Mark E. "The Kansas-Nebraska Act in American Political Culture." In Wunder and Ross, *Nebraska-Kansas Act of 1854*, 13–46.

Nichols, Roy F. "The Kansas-Nebraska Act: A Century of Historiography." *Mississippi Valley Historical Review* 43, no. 2 (September 1956): 187–212.

Noble, Glenn. *John Brown and the Jim Lane Trail*. Broken Bow NE: Purcells, 1977.

"Notes on the Proslavery March against Lawrence." *Kansas Historical Quarterly* 11, no. 1 (February 1942): 45–64.

Oates, Stephen B. *To Purge This Land with Blood: A Biography of John Brown*. 2nd ed. Amherst: University of Massachusetts Press, 1984.

Pammel, L. H. "Dr. Edwin James," *Annals of Iowa*. Series 3, 8, no. 3–4 (October 1907): 161–85; (January 1908): 277–95.

Parker, Leonard F. *History of Poweshiek County, Iowa*. Vol. 1. Chicago: S. J. Clarke, 1911.

——. "Notes for *History of Poweshiek County*." In Manuscript Collection Ms.01.51: "1856–1860, the Grinnell Public School and the Superintendent." Grinnell College Libraries, Department of Special Collections, Grinnell IA.

Parrish, William E. *David Rice Atchison of Missouri: Border Politician*. Columbia: University of Missouri Press, 1961.

Paxton, W. M. *Annals of Platte County, Missouri*. Kansas City MO: Hudson Kimberly, 1897.

Peterson, Merrill D. *John Brown: The Legend Revisited*. Charlottesville: University of Virginia Press, 2002.

Phillips, Christopher. "'The Crime against Missouri': Slavery, Kansas, and the Cant of Southernness in the Border West." *Civil War History* 48, no. 1 (2002): 60–81.

——. "The Southernization of Missouri: Kansas, the Civil War, and the Politics of Identity on the Western Border." In *Warm Ashes: Issues in Southern History at the Dawn of the Twenty-First Century*, edited by Winfred B. Moore Jr., Kyle S. Sinisi, and David H. White Jr., 2000 Citadel Conference on the South, 89–117. Columbia: University of South Carolina Press, 2003.

Phillips, Wendell. *Speeches, Lectures, and Letters*. Boston: James Redpath, 1863.

Phillips, William A. *The Conquest of Kansas, by Missouri and Her Allies*. Boston: Phillips, Sampson, 1856.

——. "Lecture by William A. Phillips." In *Echoes of Harper's Ferry*, edited by James Redpath, 377–83. Boston: Thayer and Eldridge, 1860.

——. "Three Interviews with Old John Brown." *Atlantic Monthly* 44, no. 266 (December 1879): 738–44.

Pierce, Franklin. "Special Message," January 24, 1856. Online by Gerhard Peters and John T. Woolley, *The American Presidency Project*, http://www.presidency.ucsb.edu/ws/?pid=67636.

Pierson, Michael D. "'A War of Extermination': A Newly Uncovered Letter by Julia Louisa Lovejoy, 1856." *Kansas History* 16, no. 2 (Summer 1993): 120–23.

Potter, David M. *The Impending Crisis: America before the Civil War, 1848–1861*. New York: Harper Perennial, 1976.

Rawley, James A. "Stephen A. Douglas and the Kansas-Nebraska Act." In Wunder and Ross, *Nebraska-Kansas Act of 1854*, 67–92.

Ray, P. Orman. *The Repeal of the Missouri Compromise: Its Origin and Authorship*. Cleveland OH: Arthur H. Clark, 1909.

Redpath, James. *The Public Life of Capt. John Brown*. Boston: Thayer and Eldridge, 1860.

Reed, Christopher R. "African American Life in Antebellum Chicago, 1833–1860." *Journal of the Illinois State Historical Society* 94, no. 1 (Winter 2001/2002): 356–82.

Reynolds, David S. *John Brown, Abolitionist*. New York: Alfred A. Knopf, 2005.

Richards, Laura E., ed. *Letters and Journals of Samuel Gridley Howe*. Vol. 2. Boston: Dana Estes, 1909.

Richardson, Albert D. *Beyond the Mississippi: From the Great River to the Great Ocean; Life and Adventure on the Prairies, Mountains, and Pacific Coast . . . 1857–1867*. Hartford CT: American Publishing Company, 1867.

Richman, Irving B. *John Brown among the Quakers, and Other Sketches*. Chicago: R. R. Donnelley & Sons, 1894. Reprint, Des Moines: Historical Department of Iowa, 1904.

Ricketts, S. P., and Grace L. Ricketts. "The Underground Railroad of Southwestern Iowa." Manuscript. *Iowa Women's Archives*. University of Iowa Libraries, Iowa City, n.d.

Root, George A., ed. "The First Day's Battle at Hickory Point: From the Diary and Reminiscenses [*sic*] of Samuel James Reader." *Kansas Historical Quarterly* 1, no. 1 (November 1931): 28–49.

Rosenberg, Morton M. *Iowa on the Eve of the Civil War: A Decade of Frontier Politics*. Norman: University of Oklahoma Press, 1972.

Russel, Robert R. "The Issues in the Congressional Struggle over the Kansas-Nebraska Bill, 1854." *Journal of Southern History* 29, no. 2 (May 1963): 187–210.

Rutherford, Phillip R. "The *Arabia* Incident." *Kansas History* 1, no. 1 (Spring 1978): 39–47.

Ryan, Leo V. "Brother Leo V. Ryan Discusses Allamakee County DPOs," *Waukon (IA) Allamakee County Standard*, August 25, 2004, http://

www.waukonstandard.com/main.asp?Search=1&ArticleID=28024
&SectionID=37&SubSectionID=167&S=1.

Sageman, Marc. *Leaderless Jihad*. Philadelphia: University of Pennsylvania
Press, 2008.

Salter, William. *The Life of James W. Grimes*. New York: D. Appleton, 1876.

Sanborn, F. B. "The Early History of Kansas, 1854–1861." In *Proceedings of
the Massachusetts Historical Society*. Series 3, vol. 1, *1907, 1908*. Boston:
Massachusetts Historical Society, 1908, 331–59.

——, ed. *The Life and Letters of John Brown*. Boston: Roberts Brothers, 1891.

——. *Recollections of Seventy Years*. Vol. 1. Boston: Richard G. Badger, the
Gorham Press, 1909.

Schultz, Duane. *Quantrill's War: The Life & Times of William Clarke
Quantrill, 1837–1865*. New York: St. Martin's, 1997.

SenGupta, Gunja. *For God and Mammon: Evangelicals and Entrepreneurs,
Masters and Slaves in Territorial Kansas, 1854–1860*. Athens: University
of Georgia Press, 1996.

——. "Review Essay Series: Bleeding Kansas." *Kansas History: A Journal of
the Central Plains* 24, no. 4 (Winter 2002–2002): 318–41.

——. "Servants for Freedom: Christian Abolitionists in Territorial Kansas,
1854–1858." *Kansas History* 16, no. 3 (Autumn 1993): 200–213.

Shalhope, Robert E. *Sterling Price: Portrait of a Southerner*. Columbia:
University of Missouri Press, 1971.

Sheridan, Richard B., ed. and comp. *Freedom's Crucible: The Underground
Railroad in Lawrence and Douglas County, Kansas, 1854–1865: A Reader*.
Lawrence: Division of Continuing Education, University of Kansas, 1998.

Silbey, Joel H., and Samuel T. McSeveney. *Voters, Parties, and Elections:
Quantitative Essays in the History of American Popular Voting Behavior*.
Lexington MA: Xerox College Publishing, 1972.

Smith, Narcissa Macy. "Reminiscences of John Brown." *Midland Monthly* 4
(September 1895): 231–36.

Speer, John. *Life of Gen. James H. Lane*. Garden City KS: John Speer, 1897.

Stephenson, Wendell Holmes. *Publications of the Kansas State Historical
Society Embracing the Political Career of General James H. Lane*. Vol. 3.
Topeka: Kansas State Printing Plant, 1930.

Stevens, Frank Everett. "Introduction." In John A. Wakefield, *Wakefield's
History of the Blackhawk War*, 7–13. Jacksonville IL: Press of Calvin
Goudy, 1834. Reprint, Chicago: Caxton Club, 1907. http://www.archive
.org/stream/wakefieldshistoroowakerich#page/n9/mode/2up.

Stiles, Edward H. *Recollections and Sketches of Notable Lawyers and Public
Men of Early Iowa*. Des Moines IA: Homestead, 1916.

Strickler, Hiram Jackson. "Report of H. J. Strickler, Commissioner to Audit
Claims of Citizens of the Territory of Kansas." 1859. Call number

328.7304/Un3/serial number 1017. Kansas State Historical Society, Topeka, last modified July 25, 2012. http://www.territorialkansasonline .org/~imlskto/cgi-bin/index.php?SCREEN=show_document &SCREEN_FROM=pol_govt&document_id=101154&FROM _PAGE=&topic_id=46.

Sumner, Charles. "Speech of Hon. C. Sumner of Massachusetts, in the Senate, May 19, 1856." *Appendix to the Congressional Globe*, 34th Cong., 1st sess., 1856, 535. Library of Congress.

Sweet, William Warren. *The Story of Religion in America*. New York: Harper & Brothers, 1950.

Tappan, Lewis. *The Fugitive Slave Bill: Its History and Unconstitutionality, with an Account of the Seizure and Enslavement of James Hamlet, and His Subsequent Restoration to Liberty*. 3rd ed. New York: William Harned, 1850. http://medicolegal.tripod.com/tappan1850.htm.

Tennal, Ralph. *History of Nemaha County, Kansas*. Lawrence KS: Standard Publishing, 1916.

Todd, Rev. John. *Early Settlement and Growth of Western Iowa, or Reminiscences*. Des Moines: Historical Department of Iowa, 1906.

Tuchman, Barbara W. *Stilwell and the American Experience in China, 1922–1945*. New York: Grove Press, 2001.

United States Census, 1860. Manuscript schedules for Marengo Township, Iowa County, Iowa, and Pottawattamie County, Iowa.

U.S. Congress. *Report [of] the Select Committee of the Senate Appointed to Inquire into the Late Invasion and Seizure of the Public Property at Harper's Ferry*. Washington DC: 1860.

U.S. House of Representatives. *Report of the Special Committee Appointed to Investigate the Troubles in Kansas, with the Views of the Minority of Said Committee*. 34th Cong. Washington DC: Cornelius Wendell, Printer, 1856.

Villard, Oswald Garrison. *John Brown, 1800–1859, A Biography Fifty Years After*. Boston: Houghton Mifflin, 1910.

Wakefield, Homer, comp. *Wakefield Memorial Comprising in Historical, Genealogical and Biographical Register of the Name and Family of Wakefield*. Bloomington IL: Privately printed for the compiler, 1897.

Weisberger, Bernard A. "The Newspaper Reporter and the Kansas Imbroglio." *Mississippi Valley Historical Review* 36, no. 4 (March 1950): 633–56.

Whittier, John Greenleaf. *Anti-Slavery Poems: Songs of Labor and Reform*. Cambridge MA: Riverside Press, 1888. Available at Univ. of Michigan Humanities Text Initiative, Ann Arbor, http://quod.lib.umich.edu/a /amverse/bae0044.0001.001?rgn=main;view=fulltext.

Wilcox, Pearl. *Jackson County Pioneers*. Independence MO: Jackson County Historical Society, 1975.

Wilder, Daniel W. *The Annals of Kansas*. Topeka: Geo. W. Martin, Kansas Publishing House, 1875.

——. "The Story of Kansas." *Kansas Historical Collections, 1897-1900, 6* (1900): 336-42.

Wilson, Hill Peebles. *John Brown Soldier of Fortune: A Critique*. Boston: Cornhill, 1913.

Wilson, Nathan. "Congregationalist Richard Cordley and the Impact of New England Cultural Imperialism in Kansas, 1857-1904." *Great Plains Quarterly* 24 (Summer 2004): 185-200.

Woodward, C. Vann. *The Burden of Southern History*. 3rd ed. Baton Rouge: Louisiana State University Press, 1993.

Woodworth, Steven E. *Manifest Destinies: America's Westward Expansion and the Road to the Civil War*. New York: Alfred A. Knopf, 2010.

Wulfkuhle, Margaret. "Kanwaka." *Bald Eagle* (Lecompton KS) 19, no. 2 (Summer 1993): 3. http://www.lecomptonkansas.com/pdfs/Bald .Eagle.Vol19.No2.Summer.1993.pdf.

Wunder, John R., and Joann M. Ross. "'An Eclipse of the Sun': The Nebraska-Kansas Act in Historical Perspective." In *The Nebraska-Kansas Act of 1854*. edited by John R. Wunder and Joann M. Ross, 1-12. Lincoln: University of Nebraska Press, 2008.

INDEX

companies, 108–19, 120–24, 125, 126–28. *See also* emigrant aid societies; recruits

Compromise of 1820. *See* Missouri Compromise

Compromise of 1850, 3–5, 6, 219n3

Congregationalists: as abolitionists, xii, 2, 4, 13, *151*; Ira Blanchard as, 77–78, 91–92, *92*, 96, 202–6, 226n7, 240nn1–2, 240n13; John Todd as, 80–82, 96, 148, 179, 202–3; Josiah Grinnell as, 149–51, *151*, 196–97; Lewis Bodwell as, 100–102, 144; Maria Gaston as, 66–67, *67*, 103, 226n7, 234n45; Mary Blanchard as, 96, 240n13; settlements of, 146, 149–51, 180–82, 196–97. *See also* Civil Bend IA; Gaston, George; Tabor IA

conventions, 47, 55, 71, 123, 227n10

Cook, John E.: capture of, 166, 252n96; Charles E. Lenhart and, 36, 38, 110; with company of John Brown, 110, 111–12, 113, 120, 121, 124, *217*; Harpers Ferry WV raid and, 156, 163, 164, 165, 166, *217*

Coppoc, Barclay, 160, 162, *162*, 165–68, *217*, 251nn89–90, 251n93

Coppoc, Edwin, 160–61, *161*, 167, 170, *217*, 251nn89–90

Coppoc, Joseph, 194, 197, 199

correspondents: regarding guerrillas, 35–37; and John Brown, 95, 111, 113–14, 115, 140, 168–69, 171; northerners and southerners as, 89–90, 246n32. See also *New York Tribune*

Council Bluffs IA, 201, 202, 207, 256n56

Cramer, John, 176–77, 178

crowds, 31–32, 55–56, 180–82, 195, 204–7. *See also* mobs

Cruise, David, 132–34, 246n11

Cruise, Rufus, 132–34

Cutter, Calvin, 56, 58, 59, 60, 63, 232n28

Cutter, Eunice, 58, 59, 65, 232n28

dangers, 97, 140–42, 191, 192–93. *See also* struggles

Daniels, Jim, 128, 130, 131, 134, 139

Davenport IA: Charles E. Lenhart in, 34, 37; editors and newspapers in, 21, 63–64, 74, 175, 229n46, 245n32; John Brown and, 154, 175; meetings in, 13, 27

Dean, John, 183, 185, 186, 188, 255n23

deaths: of David Cruise, 133, 136; of David Starr Hoyt, 232n23; of Edwin Morrison, 187–88, 255n28; by hangings, 168, 170, 207, 257n56; by shootings, 187–88, 191; by sicknesses, 38

debates, 2–3, 14

Democratic Party: Augustus Caesar Dodge in, 4, 5–6, 8, 14; David Rice Atchison in, 6, 13–15, 16–17, 18–19, 20–21, 88; editors in, 4, 8, 9, 13, 75–77, 197, 211–12, 238n46; in Iowa, 3–4, 8, 10–14, 197, 207–8, 210–12; James W. Grimes and, 10–13, *11*, 63, 81, 86–87, 233n37, 238nn44–45; in Missouri, 210; slavery and, 3–4, 5–6, 8, 10–15, 70–71, 207–8, 220n17, 241n21; Stephen Douglas in, 5–6, 8. *See also* politics

Denver, James, 126–27

Des Moines IA, 9, 86–87, 149, 207–8, 256n56

Dickey, Milton C., 68, 77, 83, 85

Dodge, Augustus Caesar, 4, 5–6, 8, 14

Doliphan KS, 37, 44

Donaldson, I. B., 47–48, 225n1

Douglas, Stephen, 5–6, 8

Douglas Bill. *See* Kansas-Nebraska Act
Douglas County KS Territory. *See* Lawrence KS Territory; Wakefield, John A.
Douglass, Frederick, 155
Doy, John, 140-42, 192-93, 200-201
Dubuque IA, 13, 63, 211-12, 242n22

the East, 26, 82, 108, 120, 138, 237n34
easterners, 15-17, 21-22, 23, 222n18, 224n44. *See also* northerners
East Nishnabotna River. *See* Nishnabotna River
editors: in Bloomfield IA, 211; Burlington IA and, 4, 25, 75, 221n22; in Clinton IA, 27, 227n16; in Davenport IA, 21, 63-64, 74, 175; in Democratic Party, 4, 8, 9, 13, 75-77, 197, 211-12, 221n22, 238n46; in Des Moines IA, 86-87, 149; in Dubuque IA, 13; George W. Brown as, 34, 137-38, 246n32; Horace Greeley as, 6-7, 8; in Iowa City IA, 75-76, 76-77; John H. Stringfellow as, 19, 44, 52, 58, 59; John Teasdale as, 149; in Keokuk IA, 21, 46, 60; in Keosauqua IA, 9, 13; in Lawrence KS Territory, 34, 86, 90, 137-38, 193; in Leavenworth KS Territory, 59, 232n21; in Missouri, 18, 19, 20, 97, 100; in Nebraska City NE Territory, 147; in Republican Party, 25, 89; Robert S. Kelley as, 19, 40, 44, 58, 59, 88, 239n48. *See also* newspapers
education. *See* schools
Eldridge, Shalor W., 62, 63, 65, 67, 68, 81, 105
Eldridge, Thomas, 83, 85, 87, 238n73
elections: campaigns for, 10-13, 14-15, 18-19, 207-8; in territories,

18-19, 20, 30-32, 54, 55, 88; votes and voters in, 12, 18-19, 20-21, 30-32, 227n16
Emerson, Ralph Waldo, 172
emigrant aid companies. *See* emigrant aid societies
emigrant aid societies: as abolitionists, 17, 19; Calvin Cutter and, 56, 58, 59, 60, 63, 232n28; caravans and wagon trains for, 62-64, 65-69, 83, 85, 233n36; Charles Robinson and, 34-35, 54; Kansas Aid Committee as, 56, 64; in Kansas Territory, 15-17, 19, 42-43, 52, 222n16; Massachusetts Emigrant Aid Company as, 15-17, 34-35, 54, 55, 232n23; Milton C. Dickey and, 68, 77, 83, 85; National Kansas Committee as, 60, 62, 64, 76, 77, 83, 85; Shalor W. Eldridge and, 62, 63, 65, 67, 68, 81, 105; from South Carolina, 42-43; in Tabor IA, 62, 65-67; Thomas Eldridge and, 83, 85; from Worcester MA, 56-60, 63, 64-65, 67-68
emigrants: acts of plundering toward, 28, 37, 56; arms for, 63, 75, 80, 81-82, 233n37; and border ruffians, 27, 58; from Chicago IL, 57-58, 60, 62, 63; expeditions of, 45-46, 76-68, 230n3, 236n21; Free Staters as, 26-33; in Iowa, 22, 27-28, 224n44; in Kansas Territory, 18, 19, 21-24; meetings about, 27, 60; in Missouri, 21; Missouri River as route for, 28, 57-58, 59-60, 62, 65, 68, 88; from New England, 15-17, 21-22; northerners as, 17, 21, 22-23, 24, 56-60; provisions for, 62-63, 65, 80-81; settlements by, 68, 69; southerners as, 18, 21, 22, 23-25, 45-46;

emigrants (*cont.*)
    struggles regarding, 64–65,
    234n42; in Tabor IA, 62, 65–67,
    80–82; travel routes for, 27–28,
    56, 59–69, *61*, 86, 234n42. *See
    also* settlers
emigration: Calvin Cutter as leader
    for, 56, 58, 59, 60, 63, 232n28;
    Charles Robinson as agent for,
    34–35, 54; James Lane as leader
    for, 75, 76–77; to Kansas Terri-
    tory, 21–24, 60, *61*, 62–69, 236n18;
    Martin Stowell as leader for, 56,
    58, 60, 63, 68; Shalor W. Eldridge
    as agent for, 62, 63, 65, 67, 68, 81,
    105; speeches about, 75; Thomas
    Eldridge as agent for, 83, 85
escapees. *See* runaways
escapes: from jails and prisons, 38,
    93, 142, 169–71, 177–78, 192, 207;
    and rescues concerning raids,
    165–68, 169–71, 188, 252n107; of
    runaway slaves, 93–96, 97–104,
    142, 192, 201. *See also* liberation
escorts, 145, 156, 182, 195, 198, 199,
    254n11
evangelicals. *See* Congregational-
    ists; Quakers
exaggerations: about James Lane,
    76, 79; about John Brown and
    raids, 138, 175; about Kansas Ter-
    ritory, 89, 212; in newspapers,
    79, 89, 138, 196, 211; regard-
    ing troops, 76, 225n1. *See also*
    propaganda
executions. *See* deaths
expeditions, 45–46, 76–78, 191, 194–
    99, 230n3, 236n21

fanatics, 2, 17, 223n21
farms: near Harpers Ferry WV, 163,
    164; raids of, 129–35, 184, 185–91,

255n23; of William Maxon, 117–
    19, *119*, 120–22, 198
ferries, 29, 68, 194, 236n18
firearms. *See* arms; Sharps rifles
fires, 33, 49, 213
Forbes, Hugh, 108–9, 120, 123
forts: Bain's Fort, 130, 136, 137; Fort
    Scott, 125, 128, 138; Fort Titus,
    93, 225n1, 240n5
Foster, Joe, 177–79, 253n5, 254n7
Franklin County KS Territory. *See*
    Pottawatomie Creek KS Territory
freedmen, 191, 192–203, *218*, 251n90
Free-Soil Party: and James W.
    Grimes, 10–11, *11*; John A. Wake-
    field in, 30, 31; Pardee Butler in,
    39, 40, 41; regarding slavery, 4,
    10–11, 89, 220n9, 220n17
Free State Hotel, 47, 49, 62
Free Staters: arrests of, 32–33; at bor-
    ders, 129; Charles Robinson as,
    34–35, 47, 49, 71; emigrants and
    settlers as, 15–17, *18*, 26–33, 52–
    54, 90, 93; George B. Gill as, 105,
    106, 107, 109, 242n1; as guer-
    rillas, 33–37, 107–8, 109, 174–75;
    Iowa and, 28–33, 211–12; James
    Lane as, 37, 71, 74, 76–77; con-
    cerning legislatures, 19–20, 31; in
    militias, 33, 37, 50, 77–80, 95, 105–
    7, *106*, 225n1; from New England,
    15–17, 21–22; newspaper articles
    about, 26, 27, 35–36, 36–37, 90,
    211–12; Pardee Butler as, 38–44,
    39; as radicals, 107–8, 125, 138,
    174–75; Samuel Walker as, 18–
    19, 33, 77–78, 213, 225n1, 240n5;
    Sharps rifles for, *53*, 54–56; shoot-
    ings of, 126; and troops, 26, 46–
    47, 76, 225n1; violence toward,
    28–29, 31–32, 33–34, 49, 93; Wil-
    liam Henry Leeman as, 108

Fremont County IA. *See* Sidney IA; Tabor IA
fugitives. *See* runaways
Fugitive Slave Act, 3-4, 219n3
funds, 82, 108, 120, 150, 154, 156, 163, 237n34

Garner family, 201, 202-3, 207, 257n56
Gaston, George: searches for freedmen and, 202; as settler, 226n7, 234n45; in Tabor IA, 66, 67, 96, 102-3, 177, 235n45, 241n14; Underground Railroad for runaways and, 96, 102-3, 226n7, 241n14
Gaston, Maria, 66-67, 67, 103, 226n7, 234n45
Geary, John W., 79
Georgia, 24, 45-46, 230n1
Gill, George B.: regarding company and recruits of John Brown, 113-16, 121, 122-23, 124, 175, 217, 251n89, 251-52nn93-94; as Free Stater, 105, 106, 107, 109, 242n1; health and sicknesses of, 140, 146-47, 154, 159-60; regarding Jim Daniels, 128, 134; concerning raids, 130-31, 133-34, 159-60, 251n88, 251-52nn93-94; travel with slaves and, 139, 140, 142-43, 144, 145, 146-47, 150, 247n47
governors: arms from, 63, 81, 87, 136-37, 233n37, 238n45; regarding Barclay Coppoc, 167-68; Charles Robinson as, 47, 49; Daniel Woodson as, 20, 79; James Denver as, 126-27; James W. Grimes as, 11, 12, 13, 63, 81, 86-87, 233n37, 238nn44-45; James Lane as, 70; John W. Geary as, 79; Robert M. Stewart as, 136-37, 207; Samuel Kirkwood as, 87, 167-68, 207; Sterling Price as,

79, 234n37; Wilson Shannon as, 34, 47, 48, 56, 79
Greeley, Horace, 6-7, 8
Grimes, James W., 10-13, 11, 63, 81, 86-87, 233n37, 238nn44-45
Grinnell IA, 149-51, 180-82, 196-97
Grinnell, Josiah, 149-51, 151, 196-97
groups. *See* companies; recruits
Grover, Joel, 140, 141, 168
guerrillas: Free Staters as, 33-37, 107-8, 109, 174-75; leaders of, 34-37, 93, 107, 110, 125-26, 127-28, 232n23. *See also* Brown, John; militias
gunfights. *See* shootings

handbills, 18-19, 168, 169, 169
hangings, 42, 168, 170, 207, 229n45, 257n56
Harper, Jane, 132, 133-35, 135
Harper, Sam, 131, 135, 135
Harpers Ferry WV: farms near, 163, 164; newspaper articles about, 167, 171; Quakers on, 160-63, 161, 162; raid of, 155-57, 160-65, 217-18; recruits for raid of, 156-63, 157, 161, 162, 175, 217-18, 251nn87-90, 251-52nn93-94; Sharps rifles at, 238n37
Harris, Ransom L., 183, 255n23
Hart, Charley. *See* Quantrill, William Clarke
Hazlett, Albert, 128, 129, 158, 165, 170-71, 218, 251n90, 252n107
Herald of Freedom, 34, 46, 49, 90, 137-38
Herd, Jacob. *See* Hurd, Jacob
Hicklin, Harvey G., 129-31, 132, 245n11
Higginson, Thomas Wentworth, 56-57, 59-60, 64-65, 72, 74, 170, 234n42

Holton KS Territory, 69, 101, 140–41, 143
hostages. *See* prisoners
hotels. *See* Free State Hotel
Howe, Samuel Gridley, 64, 77, 78, 233n36, 234n42
Hoyt, David Starr, 55–56, 232n23
hunters. *See* slave catchers
Hurd, Jacob, 141, 193, 200–201, 202, 203–4, 205–7
Hyatt, Thaddeus, 77, 192, 233n36

illnesses. *See* sicknesses
Indiana, 70
Indians: agents for, 93; missionaries and, 226n7; slaves of, 176, 180, 183, 184, 185, 191, 253n1
Iowa: arsenals in, 43, 63, 81, 209; black people as runaways in, 176–82, 191, 194–99, 214; Bloomfield, 211; Burlington, 4, 25, 75, 221n22, 229n46; Clinton, 27, 227n16; Council Bluffs, 201, 202, 207, 256n56; Democratic Party in, 3–4, 8, 10–14, 197, 207–8, 210–12, 221n22; Des Moines, 9, 86–87, 149, 207–8, 256n56; Dubuque, 13, 63, 211–12, 242n22; emigrants and settlers on, 22, 27–33, 52, 60, 214, 224n44, 226n7, 226n9; Free Staters and, 28–33, 211–12; and the Fugitive Slave Act, 4; James W. Grimes as governor of, *11*, 12, 13, 63, 81, 86–87, 233n37, 238n45; Grinnell, 149–51, 180–82, 196–97; Iowa City, 60–63, *61*, 75–76, 76–77, 83, 87, 105, 211, 238n46; John Brown and, 147–52, 175, 249n62, 249n64, 249n68; John A. Wakefield and, 29–33, 226–27nn9–10; Kansas Central Committee in, 60–63,

61, 233n35; and Kansas Territory, xi–xiii, 4–13, *7*, 22, 25, 27, 209–12, 213–14, 221n22; Keokuk, 21, 46, 60, 230n1; Keosauqua, 9, 13; meetings and rallies in, 13, 27, *51*; Muscatine, 8, 12, 208; and Nebraska Territory, 5, 6, 7, 8–13, 27, 221n22, 221n5 (chap. 2); Newton, 195–96; populations in, 210; railroads in, 5, 60, 62, 81; Republican Party in, 211, 212; Samuel Kirkwood as governor of, 87, 167–68, 207; senators for, 4, 5–6, 8, 10–12, *11*, 14, 49, 87; Sidney, 5, 62, 206; Springdale, 117–22, 160–62, 163, 182, 189, 198, *217–18*; travel routes through, 27–28, 56, 59–69, *61*, 73–74, 86, 214, 233n36, 234n42; westerners in, 210; West Liberty, 122, 159–60, 245n32; Whig Party in, 9. *See also* Civil Bend IA; Davenport IA; Nishnabotna River
Iowa City IA, 60–63, *61*, 75–76, 76–77, 83, 87, 105, 211, 238n46

Jackson, Clairborne F., 31, 227n16
Jackson County MO, 100, 185–91
jails: black people and runaways in, 93, 98, 112, 177–79, 200–202; escapes and rescues from, 38, 93, 142, 169–71, 192, 207; John Doy in, 141–42, 192, 200–201; kidnappers in, 207, 257n56
Jayhawkers. *See* Free Staters
Jones, George Wallace, 4, 8, 49
Jones, John, 227n28
Jones, Samuel, 48–49, 225n1
journeys. *See* travel
judges, 30, 31–33, 46–47
justices of the peace, 176–77, 178, 226–27nn9–10

Kagi, John: with James Montgomery, 125–26, 127–28; John Brown and, 111, 113, 117, 127, 149, 150, 155–56, *217*; letters by, 156, 158, 159, 160, 164; as newspaper correspondent, 95, 111, 113, 115
Kansas Aid Committee, 56, 64
Kansas Central Committee, 60–63, *61*, 233n35
Kansas Free State, 46, 49
Kansas-Nebraska Act, 5–12, 13–14, 15, 70, 71, 220n17
Kansas Territory: acts of plundering in, 46, 49, 88; Atchison, 38, 40–44; Bain's Fort, 130, 136, 137; borders of, 125–28; Doliphan, 37, 44; emigrant aid societies in, 15–17, 19, 42–43, 52, 222n16; emigrants and settlers in, 18, 19, 21–24, 28–33, 45–46, 212–14, 226n7; emigration to, 21–24, 60, *61*, 62–69, 236n8; exaggerations about, 89, 212; fires in, 33, 49, 213; Fort Scott, 125, 128, 138; Fort Titus, 93, 225n1, 240n5; governors of, 20, 34, 47, 48, 49, 56, 79, 126–27; Holton, 69, 101, 140–41, 143; Iowa and, xi–xiii, 4–13, *7*, 22, 25, 27, 209–12, 213–14; James Lane and, 71, 73–74, 76–78; John Brown and, 105, 123, 125–28, 136, 139–41, 142–46, 173, 248n50; Leavenworth, 45, 59, 79, 232n21; Lecompton, 46–47, 93–95, 199, 200, 225n1; Massachusetts Emigrant Aid Company in, 15–17, 34–35, 54; missionaries in, 96, 226n7; Missouri and, 6–9, *7*, 13–17, 22–25, 89, 209–11, 213–14, 239n52; Mound City, 125–26, 136; Osawatomie, 105, 127, 139, 184–85, 191; Pardee, 182–83, 255n23; Platte City, 100, 241n21; Pottawatomie Creek, 50, 107, 173, 174; propaganda about, 23, 90; settlements in, 21–24, 68, 69, 224n43; the South regarding, 22, 23–25, 88, 230n1; Spring Creek, 145, 248n50; Straight Creek, 143–44; Wakarusa, 191; Weston, 17, 223n23. *See also* Lawrence ks Territory; *Squatter Sovereign*; Topeka ks
Kansas Weekly Herald, 45, 59, 232n21
Kelley, Robert S.: as editor, 19, 40, 44, 58, 59, 88, 239n48; in Lawrence ks Territory, 47; and Pardee Butler, 40–41, 42–43
Keokuk Daily Gate City, 21, 46, 60, 230n1
Keosauqua ia, 9, 13
kidnappers: as danger, 140–42, 192–93; Jacob Hurd as, 141, 193, 200–201, 202, 203–4, 205–7; Joe Foster as, 177–79, 253n5, 254n7; from Lecompton ks Territory, 199, 200; as prisoners, 203–4, 205–7, 257n56; of runaway slaves, 177–79, 199–200, 253n5, 254n7; William Clarke Quantrill as, 184
kidnappings: newspaper articles about, 193, 200, 207–8, 256n56, 257n60; of runaway slaves, 177–79, 192–93, 253n5, 254n7, 255n35
Kirkwood, Samuel, 87, 167–68, 207

landings: in Canada, 154–55; on Missouri River, 38, 40–44, 52, 54, 55–56, 68, 99–100; *Squatter Sovereign* on, 52, 58, 59. *See also* stops
Lane, James, 37, 60, 70–71, 72–80, *73*, 81–82, 236n21
Lane Trail, 60

79; John Brown and, 110–12, 148,
150, 155–56, 168–69, *169*; about
Kansas-Nebraska Act, 12, 221n5;
and rallies regarding militias,
50, *51*; about slavery, 12, 13, 17,
148, 223n21
merchants, 21, 89. *See also* trade
Meriam, Francis J., 163, 165, 166, *218*
military troops. *See* troops
militias: arms from, 233n37; autho-
rizations and calls for, 48, 50,
76, 79; Free Staters in, 33, 50, 77–
80, 95, 105–7, *106*, 109, 225n1;
at Harpers Ferry wv, 165; of
James Lane, 37, 78–80; meetings
and rallies for, 50, *51*; of Samuel Walker, 33, 77–78, 225n1; supporters of slavery in, 33, 88. *See
also* guerrillas; troops
ministers: and acts of tar and feathering, 43, 229nn45–46; Ira
Blanchard as, 240n1, 240n13;
John Stewart as, 184, 191–94,
199; John Todd as, 80–82, 96,
148, 179, 202–3; Josiah Grinnell
as, 149–51, *151*, 196–97; Lewis
Bodwell as, 100–102, 144; meetings for, 13; Pardee Butler as, 38–
44, *39*; Samuel L. Adair as, 107,
127, 139; Thomas Wentworth
Higginson as, 56–57, 59–60, 64–
65, 72, 74, 170, 234n42
missionaries, 96, 226n7
Missouri: acts and bills regarding, 6–10, 12, 13–14, 220n17; border ruffians in, 26–27, 52, 55–56;
borders of, 17, 18–19, 21, 125–35,
136–37, 174, 224n38; David Rice
Atchison as senator for, 6, 13–
15, 16–17, 20–21, 88; Democratic
Party in, 210; editors and newspapers in, 18, 19, 20–21, 97, 100,
182, 228n29, 253n1; election voters from, 18–19, 20–21, 31–32,
227n16; governors of, 79, 136–
37, 207, 234n37; Jackson County,
100, 185–91; John Brown and,
129–37, 173–74; and Kansas Territory, 6–9, *7*, 13–17, 22–25, 89, 209–
11, 213–14, 239n52; Lexington,
55–56; Liberty, 19; and Nebraska
Territory, 6–9, *7*, 13–17; populations in, 21, 210; proslavery attitudes toward eastern emigrants
in, 16–17, 21–22; raids in, 129–36,
136–37, 184, 185–91, 255n23; runaways from, 91, 97, 98, 99, 112,
241n18; slaveholders and slavery
in, 16, 97–100, 173–74; St. Joseph,
18, 99, 100, 141–42, 207, 253n1;
Vernon County, 89, 129–36, 136–
37, 239n52, 245n11. *See also* Missouri River; Nishnabotna River;
St. Louis MO
Missouri Compromise, 6, 8–10, 12,
14, 220n17
Missouri River: ferry landings on,
29, 68, 194, 236n18; merchants
and trade on, 59–60, 89; as route
for emigrants, 28, 57–58, 59–60,
62, 65, 68, 88, 234n42; steamboat stops and landings on, 38,
40–44, 52, 54, 55–58, 59–60, 99–
100, 202
mobs: acts of tar and feathering by,
43, 229nn45–46; kidnappers and,
257n56; and Pardee Butler, 40–
41, 42–43; runaway slaves and,
98, 104; shootings by, 33; steamboat searches by, 55–56, 57. *See
also* crowds
Moffett, Charles, 110, 111, 114, 124,
158, *217*
money. *See* funds

Montgomery, James, 107–8, 125–26, 127–28, 137, 170–71, 232n23
Morgan Walker raid. *See* Walker, Morgan
Morrison, Edwin, 182–83, 185, 187–88, 194, 199, 255n28
Mound City KS Territory, 125–26, 136
Muscatine IA, 8, 12, 208
muskets. *See* arms; Sharps rifles

National Kansas Committee, 60, 62, 64, 76, 77, 83, 85
Native Americans. *See* Indians
Nebraska City NE Territory, 29, 68, 72, 74, 98, 112, 147, 236n18
Nebraska Territory: Brownville, 98–99, 112; and Iowa, 5, 6, 7, 8–13, 221n22, 221n5 (chap. 2); John Brown in, 146–47; and Kansas-Nebraska Act, 5–9, 7, 220nn11–12; missionaries for Indians in, 96, 226n7; Missouri and, 6–9, 7, 13–17; Nebraska City, 29, 68, 72, 74, 98, 112, 147, 236n18; Nemaha River, 101–2, 146; settlers in, 28, 226n7; southerners in, 22, 224n41. *See also* Nebraska City NE Territory; Nishnabotna River
Negroes. *See* black people; runaways; slaves
Nemaha River, 101–2, 146
New England, 15–17, 21–22
New England Emigrant Aid Company. *See* Massachusetts Emigrant Aid Company
newspapers: attacks regarding, 49, 150; in Burlington IA, 4, 25, 229n46; in Chicago IL, 36–37; in Davenport IA, 74, 229n46, 245n32; in Des Moines IA, 9, 86–87, 149, 207–8, 256n56; in

Doliphan KS Territory, 37; in Dubuque IA, 211–12, 242n22; in the East, 26, 138; exaggerations in, 79, 89, 138, 196, 211; in Iowa City IA, 75, 211; and Kansas-Nebraska Act, 220n17, 221n22; in Keokuk IA, 21, 46, 60, 230n1; in Lawrence KS Territory, 34, 46, 49, 193; in Leavenworth KS Territory, 45, 59, 79; in Liberty MO, 19; in the North, 89; propaganda in, 58–59, 90; in the South, 24, 89–90; in St. Joseph MO, 18, 100, 253n1; in St. Louis MO, 20–21, 23–24, 230n1, 232n21, 233n37. *See also* articles; editors; *New York Tribune*; *Squatter Sovereign*
Newton IA, 195–96
New York Tribune: correspondents and writers for, 7, 35–36, 113, 139–40, 168–69, 171; Horace Greeley and, 6–7, 8; regarding runaways, 250n80; Thaddeus Hyatt and, 233n36; Thomas Wentworth Higginson and, 56, 57, 67, 234n42
Nishnabotna River, 103, 176, 178, 179
northerners: emigrants and settlers as, 17, 18, 21, 22–23, 24, 56–60; on John Brown, 172; as newspaper correspondents, 89–90, 246n32. *See also* easterners
notes. *See* letters
Nuckolls, Stephen F., 68, 104, 194, 201–2, 204–5

Ohio: arms and, 119, 167, 233n37; John Brown and, 112, 117, 155; senators for, 13; settlers from, 22–23, 66, 96, 234n45, 240n2
orations. *See* speeches

raids (*cont.*)
escapes and rescues concerning, 165–68, 169–71, 188, 252n107; of farms, 129–35, 184, 185–91, 255n23; John Brown and, 129–37, 155–65, 167, *217–18*, 251n87, 251n90, 251–52nn93–94; prisoners from, 132, 133, 134; Quakers and, 160–63, *161, 162,* 183, 185–89, *189,* 191; shootings during, 133, 136, 187–88, 191; slaves and, 131–32, 134–36, *135,* 139, 140, 142–43, 145–55, 185–91; William Clarke Quantrill and, 184, 185–91
railroads, 5–6, 9, 45, 60, 62, 81, 152–54
rallies. *See* meetings
Realf, Richard, 110, 111, 112, 113–14, 121, 123, 158, *217*
recruits: for Harpers Ferry wv raid, 156–63, *157, 161, 162,* 175, *217–18,* 251nn87–90, 251–52nn93–94; with Jefferson Buford expedition, 45–46, 230n3, 230n5; letters about, 46, 156, 158–59, 160, 251n87. *See also* companies
Redpath, James, 171, 246n32
reporters. *See* correspondents
Republican Party: Amos Bixby in, 180, 197, 243n16, 254n19; correspondents and editors in, 25, 89; creation of, 13; in Iowa, 211, 212; Josiah Grinnell in, 196–97
rescues. *See* escapes
rewards, 137, 166, 184–85
Richardson, Richard, 114, 122–23, 158, *217*
rifles. *See* Sharps rifles
Ritchie, John, 38, 100, 144, 146
roads. *See* routes
Robinson, Charles, 34–35, 47, 49, 54, 71
Ross, Edmund G., 63, 143

routes: through Iowa, 27–28, 59–69, *61,* 73–74, 86, 214, 233n36, 234n42; Missouri River as, 28, 57–58, 59–60, 62, 65, 68, 88, 234n42. *See also* travel
runaways: captures of, 141, 142, 176–77, 192–93; escapes of, 93–96, 97–104, 142, 192, 201; Frances Overton as, 180, 181, 182, 254n19; Fugitive Slave Act and, 3–4; Gaston family and, 102–3, 226n7; Ira Blanchard regarding, 91–92, *92,* 96, 240n2, 240n13; kidnappers and kidnappings concerning, 177–79, 192–93, 199–200, 253n5, 254n7, 255n35; from Missouri, 91, 97, 98, 99, 112, 241n18; *New York Tribune* regarding, 250n80; Platt family and, 91, 96, 226n7, 240n2, 240n13; shootings and, 36, 97, 98, 99; in Tabor IA, 176–79, 253n1, 254n7; in Topeka KS, 99, 100–101, 142–43; Underground Railroad for, 91–96, *92,* 100–103, 147–49, 226n7, 240n2, 240n13, 241n14. *See also* black people; slaves

sackings, 42, 48–49, 50, 62
schools, 180–82
searches, 52, 54, 55–56, 57, 58–59, 164, 202–3
Self-Defensive Association, 17, 223n23
senators: Augustus Caesar Dodge as, 4, 5–6, 8, 14; Charles Sumner as, 20, 49, 77; Daniel Sturgeon as, 4; David Rice Atchison as, 6, 13–15, 16–17, 20–21, 88; George Wallace Jones as, 4, 8, 49; Henry Clay as, 3; James W. Grimes as, 10–12, *11,* 87; regarding Kansas-

Underground Railroad (*cont.*)
Platt family and, 91, 96, 147,
226n7, 240n2, 240n13; for runaways, 91–96, 100–103, 147–49,
226n7, 240n2, 240n13, 241n14
United States troops. *See* troops

Vernon County MO, 89, 129–36,
136–37, 239n52, 245n11
violence, acts of: by crowds and
mobs, 31–32, 33, 40–41, 42–43,
229nn45–46; fires, 33, 49, 213;
toward Free Staters, 28–29, 31–32,
33–34, 49, 93; massacres, 50, 107,
126; sackings, 42, 48–49, 50, 62;
toward supporters of slavery, 33–
37, 50, 90; tar and featherings,
43, 229nn45–46. *See also* attacks;
plundering, acts of; shootings
Virginia. *See* Harpers Ferry WV
votes: for Fugitive Slave Act, 4; for
Kansas-Nebraska Act, 8, 70, 71;
and voters in elections, 12, 18–19,
20–21, 30–32, 227n16

wagon trains: arms on, 63, 83, 85,
195; for emigrant aid societies,
83, 85; escorts for, 145, 156, 182,
195, 198, 199, 254n11; from Iowa
City IA, 60, 62–63, 105; The Last
Train as, 191, 194–99; letters
about, 195; newspaper articles
about, 85, 196, 197, 213; Preston B. Plumb as leader of, 80; for

slaves from raids, 134, 136, 139,
140, 142–43, 145–55; in Topeka
KS Territory, 69, 85. *See also*
caravans
Wakarusa KS Territory, 191
Wakefield, John A., 29–33,
226–27nn9–10
Walker, Andrew J., 186–87, 191
Walker, Morgan, 184–91, 255n23
Walker, Samuel, 18–19, 33, 77–78,
213, 225n1, 240n5
warrants, 47–49, 164, 176–77, 205–6
Wattles, Augustus, 136, 139
westerners, 16, 23, 210, 222n18
West Liberty IA, 122, 159–60, 245n32
West Nishnabotna River. *See*
Nishnabotna River
Weston KS Territory, 17, 223n23
West Virginia. *See* Harpers Ferry WV
wharves. *See* landings; stops
Whig Party, 3, 9, 10–13
Whipple, Charles. *See* Stevens,
Aaron Dwight
Whitfield, John W., 30–31
Williamson, John, 201–2, 257n56
Wilmot, David, 2–3, 8
Woodford, Newton, 176–78
Woodson, Daniel, 20, 79
Worcester MA, 56–60, 63, 64–65,
67–68
writers. *See* correspondents
writs, 32–33

Yellow Springs IA, 13, 250n82